Religious Pluralism and Values in the Public Sphere

How can we, as people and communities with different religions and cultures, live together with integrity? Does tolerance require us to deny our deep differences or give up all claims to truth, to trade our received traditions for skepticism or relativism? Cultural philosopher Lenn E. Goodman argues that we can respect one another and learn from one another's ways without literally sharing them or relinquishing our own insights and heritage. Commitment to our own ideals and norms, he argues, need not mean dogmatism or intolerance. In this study, Goodman offers a trenchant critique of John Rawls's troubling claim that religious and metaphysical voices must be silenced in the core political deliberations of a democracy. Inquiry, dialogue, and open debate remain the safeguards of public and personal sanity. Any of us, Goodman shows, can learn from one another's traditions and explorations without abandoning our own.

Lenn E. Goodman is Professor of Philosophy and Andrew W. Mellon Professor in the Humanities at Vanderbilt University. A summa cum laude graduate of Harvard University, he received his D.Phil. as a Marshall Scholar at Corpus Christi College, Oxford University. His many books include *Creation and Evolution* (2010); *Love Thy Neighbor as Thyself* (2008); *In Defense of Truth: A Pluralistic Approach* (2001); and *God of Abraham* (1996), winner of the 1997 Gratz Centennial Prize. Goodman serves on the editorial boards of *History of Philosophy Quarterly*, *Political Theology*, and *Medieval Philosophy and Theology*. A past president of the Metaphysical Society of America, he is an associate editor of *Asian Philosophy* and has served as Vice President and Program Chair of the Institute for Islamic/Judaic Studies, as well as program chair for the APA panels of the Academy for Jewish Philosophy.

Religious Pluralism and Values in the Public Sphere

LENN E. GOODMAN
Vanderbilt University

CAMBRIDGE
UNIVERSITY PRESS

CAMBRIDGE
UNIVERSITY PRESS

32 Avenue of the Americas, New York, NY 10013-2473, USA

Cambridge University Press is part of the University of Cambridge.

It furthers the University's mission by disseminating knowledge in the pursuit of education, learning, and research at the highest international levels of excellence.

www.cambridge.org
Information on this title: www.cambridge.org/9781107658059

First published 2014

Printed in the United States of America

A catalog record for this publication is available from the British Library.

Library of Congress Cataloging in Publication data
Goodman, Lenn Evan, 1944–
Religious pluralism and values in the public sphere / Lenn E. Goodman, Vanderbilt University.
   pages cm.
Includes bibliographical references and index.
ISBN 978-1-107-05213-0 (hardback) – ISBN 978-1-107-65805-9 (paperback)
1. Cultural pluralism. 2. Multiculturalism. 3. Toleration. I. Title.
HM1271.G665 2013
201'.723–dc23   2013030084

ISBN 978-1-107-05213-0 Hardback
ISBN 978-1-107-65805-9 Paperback

Contents

Acknowledgments

Profound thanks are due to many for the warmth, candor, skill, and insight they expended in behalf of this project over a period of years. Each of the chapters began its life as a paper and received thoughtful comments from committed scholars and learned philosophers before it took its present form. Chapter 1, "Religious Pluralism," began as a paper for a conference on Varieties of Pluralism that my colleague Rob Talisse and I organized at Vanderbilt ten years ago. It profited from the probing comments of Nick Rescher, Joe Margolis, Bill Galston, John Lachs, Susan Haack, and others who took part in that conference. The paper grew and morphed over time. An abbreviated version appeared in *Political Theology* in 2012. Chapter 2, "Naked in the Public Square," was tried out in embryonic form at a conference on The Place of Theology in the Liberal State, held at the University of Wisconsin. Len Kaplan, David Novak, Jean Elshtain, and Arnie Eisen were among the participants whose valuable conversation enriched my understanding. Again the paper morphed and grew. A version appeared in *Philosophia* in 2012. Parts of Chapter 3 appeared in 2010 under the title "Some Moral Minima," published in *The Good Society*, a PEGS journal; in addition, I tried out some of my thoughts about the Decalogue, now developed in the same chapter, at a 2006 conference on the Ten Commandments held at the University of Wisconsin. Chapter 4,

"The Road to Kazanistan," grew from an article of the same title published in 2008 in *American Philosophical Quarterly*. Warm thanks are due to Julie Clague, the editor of *Political Theology*; Tom Bailey, the special editor, and Asa Kasher, the general editor of *Philosophia* (and to Springer Verlag, the publisher); to Stephen Simon, special editor of *The Good Society* (and Penn State University Press, the publisher); and finally to Nick Rescher, the founding executive editor of *American Philosophical Quarterly*. I owe a debt of gratitude to all of them, not just for their willingness and that of the journal publishers to see in new and expanded form the materials they first published but also for the warm welcome they gave to thoughts that sometimes ran against prevailing currents and fashions in academe.

As I worked to integrate the original essays into the present book, I was aided immensely by my student and research assistant Nick Oschman and by the careful readings of the full manuscript by Alan Mittleman at the Jewish Theological Seminary and David Novak at the University of Toronto. My colleagues, Rob Talisse and Larry May, made sure that the evolving manuscript knew the rough and tumble of any discussion addressed to political and social philosophy in general and to the contributions of John Rawls in particular. Neal Kozodoy gave me sage advice about the book, and Lewis Bateman at Cambridge University Press welcomed it there, conveying the heartening enthusiasm of his fellow editors and the Syndics of the Press, where this project found its proper home. As always I owe profound appreciation to Roberta, my loyal partner and fellow adventurer, for her insight, wisdom, and love of truth.

Introduction

Love and war have mingled human populations for eons.
Even seeming isolates are hardly homogeneous. No population remains untouched by the genetic markers of panmixia. So
with all our ethnic diversity, we humans remain one race. The
branches of our language tree attest to eons of migration, com-
merce, and congress that antedate our written records. We seem
fated to live together, and the rapid pace and broad franchise in
our travels and interactions today, complemented by the human
penchant for settling down in new surroundings, only raise to
new intensity the salient question of this book: how we can live
together with integrity.

Cultural and intellectual diversity have long prompted claims
in behalf of skepticism and relativism. But the claims are specious:
The fact of differences does not steal the warrant from all commitments or confirm the equal soundness of just any. Still less
does it make differences unreal – as to derive not-p from p. Yet
powerful pragmatic worries urge us to deny deep differences with
one another, or give up all claims to truth, or concede that no
way of thinking or living is better or worse than the rest. Otherwise, we are told, we are doomed to endless conflict, to bootless
bloodshed, and ultimate self-destruction.

What I want to argue in this book is a simple thesis: that we
humans, with all our differences in outlook and tradition, can

respect one another and learn from one another's ways, without sharing them or relinquishing the commitments we make our own. This is what I take to be pluralism. Pluralism is not relativism or skepticism. It is not lack of interest. It does not demand moral abdication or spiritual silence. Nor is the pluralism defended here the rather extreme claim that fundamental values are incompatible. In a way my pluralist thesis says just the opposite: There is room in a society for divergent values, practices, and beliefs, even in many central areas of human concern. The price of pluralism in this sense is the recognition that it need not be the case that everyone is right. The profit of pluralism is the space it allows for individuals and groups to retain their identity and commitments, not blurring the differences that make all the difference or blunting the seriousness that distinguishes high seriousness from mere entertainment.

I start from the matter of religious differences, the salient cultural differences among us. For it is in religions that the values we hold most precious are most elaborately articulated, verbally and intellectually, morally and symbolically: The language of ritual – spiritual or secular – projects a catena of values that structures most human lives and frames communities that reach out, often from the remote past and perhaps far into the future. Religious diversity does not mean that one who takes religion seriously and holds fast to personal or shared beliefs and practices somehow faces a forced choice between dogmatism or parochialism on the one hand and relativism or skepticism on the other. Tolerance, respect, and openness are not the inevitable fruits of skepticism – although a penchant for tolerance and a desire to show respect may prompt pleas for skepticism or tempt surrender to the doubts and restiveness that naturally accompany any claim to higher truths and any moral demands that press beyond the more immediate claims of appetite and passion. Relativism, at its best, is patronizing. It too may begin by urging openness. But once it places all claims to truth and virtue on a par, it vitiates the impulse it began from and ends up taking nothing seriously. There is more respect in arguing with others, treating them as equals, than in merely stroking them. Seriousness about others' views and practices means willingness to learn through dialogue and serious study. But fruitful dialogue demands our knowing something about who we are ourselves, what we believe and care about, and how what is other *actually is other*. Without the discipline of self-knowledge to complement our curiosity, interest collapses into mere projection and conjecture.

Some seek to iron out religious differences by dismissing their practical impact, reducing religion notionally to a matter of faith – as if beliefs about what matters most had no bearing on how we lead our lives. Some deny religious differences, imagining all religions alike at bottom and oblivious to the way that religious ideas may address quite different questions and concerns – or the way that religious practices and norms may challenge blanket toleration. Failing to spin familiarity from the unfamiliar, some inquirers into religious diversity indulge themselves by romanticizing what looks foreign. They essentialize the exotic and typify the extreme. None of these tactics opens a high road to pluralism for individuals or societies.

The self-knowledge that pluralism demands is hard won. It means coming to peace with oneself, reconciling one's heritage with one's personal outlook and existential insights, and integrating oneself in a community even as one differentiates oneself from it. But this kind of attachment and separation – always a work in progress – is part of what it takes to establish oneself as a moral and spiritual adult. Societies face a higher order task of integration. Their members do not need to think and live in lockstep, but they do need to find ways of living together. Tolerance is the minimum demand of pluralism in any healthy society. Religious tolerance does not mean homogenizing. Pluralism preserves differences. What it asks for is respect. That means openness, interest, and recognition of the room the universe affords for those who differ intellectually, morally, and spiritually. But tolerance has limits, implicit in the very idea and the values that sustain it: Religions that thwart human flourishing must themselves be thwarted. So a pluralistic society needs its own, rather open-ended, broad-minded vision of the human person, the boundaries of human dignity, and the dimensions of human fulfillment. Liberal ideology, with its secular heritage and secularizing rhetoric, may fight shy of such a vision or of enunciating the standards that would mark its parameters. But without such standards the liberal commitment to pluralism becomes self-defeating. Fortunately, the world's religions themselves, from which many a liberal ideal is abstracted, provide a congeries of useful models of respect. But not every ideal works smoothly and amicably alongside the rest. So today's societies, pluralistic de facto, have their work cut out for them.

If our public space were somehow cleared of discourse that smacks of spirituality, it is sometimes urged, the most troublesome excrescences of religious diversity would dissolve – or at least keep to the private sphere. Secularism is the cure for sectarianism. With such thoughts in mind, John Rawls argued that since government is inherently coercive, and since political discourse in a democracy is constitutive to the work of governance, public deliberations about core norms – those that raise constitutional issues – should, by rights, take place in a religion-free zone. Since the publication in 1971 of *A Theory of Justice*, Rawls's political philosophy has been widely taken as the touchstone of liberal thinking. But a deep ambivalence compromises the approach: Is liberal theory a clarion call for openness to diversity, or is it the manifesto of a secular age? Having left behind the religious sensibility of his youth, Rawls responded to the culture wars of our times by drawing away from the openness that *A Theory of Justice* was meant to champion, turning in a secularist direction. Lest his concerns seem unfairly to single out religions, he extended his warning against sectarianism to any proposal grounded in a "comprehensive doctrine," metaphysical or religious. That leaves those who stand outside the Rawlsian circle to wonder whether core values that anchor the liberal dispensation, such as the inestimable worth of the individual human life and the paramount worth of human flourishing, are among those to be muffled in deliberations about the basic rules that govern a society.

With an Orwellian twist, Rawls titled his guidelines and the book that proposed them *Political Liberalism*. Excluded from public debate about core matters of public principle were any arguments not deemed anchored in reason by those Rawls felt safe in accrediting as arbiters of the reasonable. Where the veil of ignorance had shaped core Rawlsian norms, a new nocturnal council is at work, at least within good Rawlsian conscience, and probably (as a natural consequence) in the sphere of social interactions as well. Mill would not be alone in blenching at hearing such demands called liberal. So, having sketched a basis for personal and societal pluralism as regards religion in my first chapter, I turn in the second to Rawls's argument that religious and metaphysical discourse has no proper place at the deliberative table in a democracy.

Central to the thoughts that motivated Rawls's proposal were the continuing objections of pro-life advocates to the widespread practice of abortion. But Rawls couches his case in universal terms. The sweeping generality that results slights the religious underpinnings of many a classic argument against slavery. In search of "reasonable" rather than religious or metaphysical warrant for environmental protections, Rawls seeks to ground environmental protections in the premise that it is irrational to foul one's bed: Religious or metaphysical appeals, say, to human stewardship or to the intrinsic worth of biodiversity or ecological preservation are apparently too dependent on a comprehensive doctrine. Property rights or national sovereignty are more suitably secular.

Rawls labors to delimit the scope of his restraints, but he is not very successful in framing a consistent screen. That aim itself is deeply flawed. Any real-world effort to implement what Rawls proposes would provoke widespread indignation at the chilling of free expression, *especially* in public deliberations. Should fashion, however, succeed in barring from public fora overt appeals to religious precepts or metaphysical concepts, the net effect would be a rising wave of hypocrisy, of motives cloaked, camouflaged, and dissociated from the traditions that inspired them. The Soviet experience presages what would happen next: Advocates of any suspect thought would couch in double meaning the arguments they hoped would win credit to their cause.

Concrete issues often drive seemingly universal claims. So Rawls's discomfort with (specific) religious postures is sublimated in universalism and legalism. Hoping to focus the issues more concretely, in Chapter 3 I address some moral minima and maxima: Are there some practices that we all should condemn and hope to see abolished? I cannot claim that the practices I name here – genocide, engineered famine, and germ warfare; terrorism, hostage taking, and the suborning of child warriors; slavery, polygamy, and incest; rape and cliterodectomy – are damned universally. There are cultures and subcultures, individual inclinations, and even some states that have sustained some of these practices historically and continue to sustain them. But I argue that they are wrong nonetheless. Unanimity is not the criterion of universality. There are good grounds for our revulsion, and it matters little whether objections are couched in religious or metaphysical (including humanistic) terms.

Turning from the minimal to the maximal, I consider the Decalogue, a classic code rooted in a distinctive cultural context, which gives thick, concrete articulation to the universal themes that underwrite such minimal norms as I have calendared, thereby transforming broad if abstract principles into the makings of an ethos and thus a way of life. In addressing the Decalogue, I do not argue from the premise that these commands are the words of God, the demands of the Transcendent made actionable. That kind of claim bears weight only for those who already embrace the twin tablets. Rather, as in all my work at the interface of religion and ethics, I think we must judge the source by the content before we can begin to understand the content by reference to its highest source.

In its original recension and in its living context at the heart of Mosaic law and practice, the Decalogue *is* predicated on the idea that its norms are God's commands. Clearly it would be wrong to try and legislate its precepts in a pluralistic society. Enough history clings to these rules to make such imposition of their norms oppressive and, for some of the commandments, impractical. Besides, the adjustments necessary in wrenching these norms from their context would deracinate them tellingly. The Decalogue is not a pre-Socratic fragment or a stand-alone canon. It is constitutive in an integrated system of law, organic enough that its components risk their integrity and lose the full richness of their meaning when isolated from the way of life they project. Yet these norms have been adapted in new contexts and have guided and steadied the moral lives of many who live beyond the tradition in which their imperatives took root.

The ethos informed by the Decalogue is perfectionist and aspirational. God's words here address the individual. That makes this tiny code potentially transformative. Interweaving moral and legal standards, it opens avenues of growth whose full reach is unbounded. The scattered examples of moral minima that I have sampled, by contrast, make no overt reference to transcendence. Yet they too allude, implicitly, to the divine, not as a source of authority but as a floor and backstop to the minimal claims of human dignity: If there is transcendent value in humanity, as our horror, say, at torture and mutilation may attest, then the human image itself bespeaks a higher canon of value – much as the beauty of a sunrise or the sublimity of the mountains or the sea elevates us from a world in which all values seem merely instrumental.

What do we learn about pluralism when we set the Decalogue's overt intentionality toward the transcendent alongside the erasure of divinity in self-consciously secular norms? Part of what we learn is the power of organic systems. The sweeping ideas and broad norms that Rawls called comprehensive can be dangerous or reassuring. So, the tone and tenor of an ethos are just as critical as the formal properties of an argument in determining what should count as reasonable. Like Alasdair MacIntyre, I think we need to keep alive our awareness that moral ideals function actively in living practice, but grow stale and sterile when abstracted from their systemic context. So do metaphysical ideals. That fact parallels what Kuhn saw (inspired, as Quine was, by the holism of Pierre Duhem) in scientific and cosmological constructs.

But holism is not the same as relativism. It does not make truth claims or moral norms arbitrary. If systems – of language or ritual, law, morals or propriety, theory or theology – are *constructed*, that does not make them somehow impertinent. Neo-Darwinism is no less true for being a construct, and the British and American Constitutions are no less just because they differ. There are many ways of weaving together a life or a vision, whether for an individual or for a society. One strength of pluralism as I understand it is that it does not iron diversity into pleats of secularity. It preserves the robust variety of norms, ideas, and ideals that give life and energy to human thought and practice. Many a would-be liberal finds particularity threatening, as if it meant particularism. But that bias may overlook the way values get their liveliness from their engagement in the thick of life and how thoughts get their concreteness by connecting not just with other thoughts but also with practices, persons, and peoples in their particularity.

The opposition of the particular to the universal balks at a false dichotomy. It ignores the constitution of authentic universals by the particulars that body them forth. Correspondingly, the universality of the secular is a high-priced illusion. Often it means giving up a hearty concreteness for pale abstractions. Secularism too often fails to keep its promises of universality. What grows very clear when Rawls lays his cards on the table is that a secularism that promised to embrace (and replace) what was precious in particularity has willfully suppressed vital strands of tradition, even the ones from which its own ideals are abstracted. Natan Sharansky recalls an image of Cynthia Ozick's that heartened him as he struggled with the false dichotomy that cast its shadow over his years of imprisonment and torment in the Soviet Union. Communism had summoned everyone to give up loyalty to a heritage – religious, ethnic, linguistic, or historical – to become a new Soviet man. A thinner particularity was to replace old identities and values. What Sharansky found, in making common cause with dissidents of every stripe, was that the particularities that moved his allies gave sinew to a more genuine universality. The image from Ozick was that of a shofar: "Nothing happens,"

Sharansky wrote, "if you blow into the wide end. But if you blow into the narrow end, the call of the shofar rings loud and true."[1]

In *The Law of Peoples*, Rawls asks how a liberal society should relate to societies that are not liberal, but "hierarchical." Rawls's intentions are irenic, but his means prove inefficacious. To demonstrate his pluralist good faith, he models a "society of liberal peoples" and the standards he imagines they would choose in relating to nonliberal but "decent" peoples. As in his work on justice, he invokes the veil of ignorance to augur what liberal peoples would (and therefore should) find tolerable. As the acid test, he pictures a "people" that he calls Kazanistan. The name is invented, like that of Pakistan, a word made up of the initials of that country's notional regions – Punjab, Afghania, Kashmir, Iran, Sindh, Tukharistan, Afghanistan, and in the end, Baluchistan. That naming was lightened by a play on "Paki," a word implying spiritual purity. But Rawls's invention exceeds his coinage of a name: Purity here becomes a postulate. To show that liberal societies can welcome "decent" peoples who do not share their own high standards of social and political legitimacy, he reverts to a habit of thought that is ultimately mathematical: Just as he defined rationality in *A Theory of Justice* so as to yield the very foundations he thought should undergird a just society, he now posits the conditions a "decent," if hierarchical, people would have to meet and *then* posits a people that meets them. The imagined society does meet the standard he sets. But it does so *ex hypothesi*. Here, as in *A Theory of Justice*, the reasoning is a slipknot: It holds so long as its conditions are met. But it meets them by stipulation.

A Theory of Justice is often thought to argue normatively. But its core claims are descriptive: They rest on an affirmation about what *we* would call justice, complemented by the claim that rational choosers behind a veil of ignorance would alight on just those standards. In extending this idea cross-culturally, Rawls posits liberal *peoples* who would accept in fellowship peoples who are not liberal but still decent. Of course, they would, if

[1] Sharansky, *Fear no Evil*, xxii.

those exotics met just the standards Rawls postulates that the representatives of liberal peoples would find both necessary and sufficient for acceptance. *The Law of Peoples*, then, contrary to Rawls's hopes, contributes little to global understanding or the prospects of world peace.

Pluralism, in my view, is neither quite as hard as finding a lowest common denominator among incommensurables nor as easy as positing the solution to a problem that *ex hypothesi* has exactly that solution. It is a real-world problem, not a mathematical puzzle. It demands real, ongoing work – good will, intelligence, open-mindedness, yes – but also work, domestically and internationally. It means making allowances, seeking understanding, knowing a bit about oneself and a bit about the others too. It does not demand the sacrifice of logic or common sense, declaring differences unreal or bracketing as inconsequent what matters most to others. It does not mean chucking our values or giving up what we think or know or hope to accomplish. It does not demand squaring the circle to make everything and everyone fit together neatly and nicely. The kind of acceptance pluralism asks for when it commends acceptance of others is a lot like the kind of acceptance that we hope we can give ourselves when we look in the mirror honestly enough to see our weaknesses and charitably enough not to minimize our strengths. That, after all, to see others as we best see ourselves is a fine corollary of the golden rule.

I

Religious Pluralism

There are plenty of reasons for pursuing some form of pluralism as to religion, and even more ways in which pluralism is sought, each with its own advantages and costs. Governments and irenic individuals might seek an end to sectarian strife or hope to build alliances in the interest of some common cause. The spiritually inclined might seek a higher unity, backgrounding their differences for the sake of inner growth. Some see relativism as the high road to tolerance, the surest antidote to dogmatism and bigotry. Others assign that work to skepticism. The baldest response to religious diversity is to reject it – I'm right; the rest are wrong. But exclusion can cause trouble because many place what matters most to them in the shiny coffer reserved for their religious beliefs. Intercultural understanding gets little help from the notion that those who fail to share one's own beliefs and practices will roast forever in hellfire. Nor does it help when atheists say, "Safety demands that religions should be put in cages."[1]

---

[1] Daniel Dennett, *Darwin's Dangerous Idea*, 515. For Dennett, Darwinian dangers are charming, puckish, worth grappling with; non-Darwinian ideas, by contrast, are irresponsible, even criminal: "Save the Baptists! Yes, of course, but not *by all means*. Not if it means tolerating the deliberate misinforming of children about the natural world.... Misinforming a child is a terrible offense. A faith, like a species, must evolve or go extinct.... It is not a gentle process in either case" (516).

Alvin Plantinga argues that it is neither arrogant nor arbitrary to hold onto one's own beliefs and reject others. He excuses himself from talk of practices and keeps to beliefs that have been considered carefully and prayerfully, in full awareness that others may dissent just as thoughtfully and with equal conviction. One's beliefs, he reasons, might rest on argument, as in Aquinas's case, or on religious experience, such as Calvin's Sensus Divinitatis.[2] If there's good warrant and one has duly considered alternative views,[3] Plantinga argues, it is not arbitrary to hold fast to the beliefs one has and to exclude others.

Plantinga assumes that at least one religious view is true. His eye is on *religious* critics of exclusivism, so he glosses over the possibility of religious incoherence, despite the long history of doubts about the triune God, the dying God, the God who begets a son, or even thoughts of a necessary being. The irritants here are charges that exclusivism amounts to arrogance, dogmatism, egotism, elitism, even a license for imperialism and sectarian oppression.[4] Disclaiming all such nastiness and dissociating his credo from any sins of pride to which he may be heir, Plantinga argues – modestly and soundly – that knowing that others hold views different from one's own may prompt some reexamination but is not sufficient ground for diminishing one's commitments. Sticking to one's guns is not arrogant per se. Others too prefer their own beliefs. Suspending judgment gains no ground here. For many will disagree even about suspending judgment in a case like this!

Plantinga favors faith in an all-good, all-knowing, personal Creator and in humankind's salvation by the sacrificial death and resurrection of that God's divine son. But he tests his ideal

---

[2] See Alston, *Perceiving God*; cf. Goodman, *God of Abraham*, 39.

[3] Plantinga, in Senor, ed., *The Rationality of Belief and the Plurality of Faith*, exempts his mother from the rigors of inquiry, along with others seen as simple believers. But even the most learned, conscientious, and au courant cannot track every religious option and possibility, and even "simple believers" (if there are any) have a duty to avoid dogmatism and epistemic bias.

[4] Ibid., 194, citing Gary Gutting, Wilfred Cantwell Smith, Joseph Runzo, John Hick, and John Cobb.

of steadfastness against moral claims: (1) "it is wrong to discriminate against people simply on grounds of race," and (2) it
is "deeply wrong for a counselor to use his position of trust to
seduce a client." Further, (3) "I am dead sure it is wrong to try
to advance my career by telling lies about my colleagues."[5] He
cites a biblical narrative to situate a fourth belief: (4) The prophet
Nathan told King David of a rich man who had seized a poor
man's only lamb. David did not see at first that the story pointed
to his own crime – sending the Hittite officer Uriah to the front
and taking Bathsheba, his wife (2 Samuel 12). Once Nathan has
explained his parable, "David sees what he has done. . . . I agree
with David: such injustice is utterly and despicably wrong."[6]

Some might think racial discrimination acceptable, even desirable. But, as Plantinga argues rightly, that should cut no ice.
There are those who can convince themselves that it is fine, even
helpful, for counselors to seduce their clients. We may know
people who find it perfectly acceptable to lie about their colleagues to boost their own careers. Examining such views does
not make them more attractive. But Plantinga's appeals to moral
knowledge are far less problematic than the sampling he offers of
his religious convictions. Even so, consider David's response to
Nathan. The king speaks with characteristic bluff machismo on
hearing Nathan's tale of the rich man and the poor man's lamb:
"The man who did this deserves to die," as Plantinga quotes the
text. Or, with the full force of the Hebrew: *David was incensed
at the man and said to Nathan, "God's life! He's a dead man to
do that! He'll pay fourfold for the lamb for what he did, and did
so ruthlessly!"* (2 Samuel 12:5–6).

So which royal judgment does Plantinga endorse? David did
not just call the malefactor a dead man, he swore it. But he
softened the oath even as he spoke: Fourfold restitution was
the law (Exodus 22:37), and there is no capital penalty in the
Torah for property crimes.[7] Plantinga knows that David did far

---

5 Ibid., 199, 201, 214.
6 Ibid., 204.
7 Greenberg, "Some Postulates of Biblical Criminal Law," 27.

worse than steal a poor man's lamb: He stole Uriah's wife and procured a loyal officer's death. Plantinga admits he may not know how to show those who differ with him about David's case just where they have gone wrong – he is no Nathan. But he remains convinced: "As a matter of fact, there isn't a lot I believe more strongly."[8] That is how it is with core beliefs: They often present as epistemic primitives.

Biblically, God commutes the death sentence David passed unwittingly on himself, taking the king's newborn son instead (2 Samuel 12:13–14). Is Plantinga as sure about the punishment as he is about the crime? David does not directly bear the onus, despite our moral intuitions and the Law's demand that no child die for a parent's wrongdoing (Deuteronomy 24:16). So, is there room at times for more than one opinion *in matters of religion*? Are there variant legitimate ideas about what God demands? Or is the biblical story a back projection, tracking not moral standards but the fortunes of David's line? For Bathsheba was Solomon's mother, coached by Nathan in holding David to his promise that her son would reign (2 Samuel 12:20, 1 Kings 1:11–31). If Plantinga can quote Calvin alongside Nathan and David, one might also recall Cromwell's earthy wisdom: "I beseech you in the bowels of Christ, think it possible that you may be mistaken."[9]

Pluralists take others' views seriously, yet they need not affirm multiple truths. A mild skepticism, the pennant of tolerance among Renaissance humanists, may be displaced today by a somewhat less reflective relativism. But neither tack is necessary.

---

[8] Plantinga, in Senor, 204. Susan Stebbing, by contrast, made Nathan's reproof a paradigm of moral instruction, as John Wisdom notes. Wisdom finds probative force in Nathan's allegory: "the merits of an argument may be brought out, proved, by setting beside it other arguments, in which striking but irrelevant features of the original are changed and relevant features emphasized.... This is the kind of thing we do when someone is 'inconsistent' or 'unreasonable.' This is what we do in referring to other cases in law." Indeed, reasoning is *called* analogy (*qiyas*) in Islamic law, a calque on the Latin *ratio*. What is critical in an analogy is its aptness. See Wisdom, "Gods," in *Philosophy and Psychoanalysis*, 160.

[9] Oliver Cromwell, Letter to the Church of Scotland, August 3, 1650.

As Nicholas Rescher remarks, "There is nothing rationally mandatory about the quest for consensus."[10] We need not assume that knowledge is impossible if we are to respect the views of others and keep our hands (and pillories) off those who hold or teach or publish divergent views. But an admission of fallibility, especially about ultimates, is never out of place. That is not relativism or skepticism but just an acknowledgment of our human limitations. We do not have to set all practices on a par to recognize that what looks odd to one person may be sacred to another. Recognition of integrity in others' thinking and of wholesome values in their ways need not diminish our commitment to our own.

Communities have always been diverse. But the speed and range of transportation, communication, and migration – free or forced – make religious diversity an ever more salient fact of life, and the project of building an open society raises insistent questions at the delicate joint between de facto and de jure diversity. We owe it to each other to take seriously one another's thoughts and practices. But our obligations to learn and respect entrain no duty to adopt each other's beliefs and ways or to slacken in our own. Krister Stendahl struck the right note in speaking of "holy envy." It was precious, in his view, to find the beauty to which the spiritual values of others point. But we vitiate that beauty if the romance of the exotic leads us to forget just who we are. To learn from others does not demand the uncritical, ultimately trivializing treatment of all beliefs and practices as equally sound or admirable. Indeed, widespread emulation of the exotic tends to homogenize and decorticate what was at first admired. It does not honor the distinctive ways and thoughts long rooted in a community's sense of history and destiny. It just extrudes a gray mash, if not a farrago of misprisions, as ideas and practices plucked from their familiar contexts are cooked down to uniformity.

There is plenty of room in an open society for diverse views and practices. Their interactions can cause friction, but can also

---

[10] Rescher, *Pluralism: Against the Demand for Consensus*, 121, 126.

promote understanding. Some of the richest historical epochs have been times of intercultural conversation. Bone deep, structural differences among religions are real – but they are also a resource to those who take religion seriously. Relativism sidesteps such seriousness – and global skepticism is no more a mark of respect than a stand-up comic's protestations of equal ridicule for all ethnicities. When a critical impulse dismisses all thoughts about the ultimate, its critical edge is not sharpened but dulled. When a spirit of generosity, no matter how sincerely, imputes equal truth and value to all outlooks and lifeways, it does not respect them, but only devalues the currency.[11]

Poetics, Problematics, and Perspectives

Everyone knows the story of the blind men and the elephant. Stumbling into the great beast, one swore it was a wall. Another, feeling its tail, thought it was a rope. A third, who got hold of its trunk, took it for a snake. A fourth, who felt a tusk, thought it was a spear. Partial truths have their uses, but they can be terribly misleading. The worst pretension is to set them up as the whole truth.[12] The elephant story does not deny that elephants exist: It mocks only our limited capacity to take in the full nature of the beast.

Some might say that pluralism proclaims multiple truths and denies that one reality underlies them all. That view is not pluralism but relativism. And the view that there are multiple,

[11] See Goodman, *In Defense of Truth*, 15, 91.
[12] The old parable, perhaps best known in the West through the verses of John Godfrey Saxe (1816–87), is found in the Buddhist Sutras and said to be of Jain origin; it stresses the doctrine of *anekanta*, the multifacetedness of things. See Vidyananda (fl. 775–840), *Tattvarthaslokavartika* 116, p. 806; cf. Mihir Yast 10.2; *Analects* 15.5, p. 1020. "The story of course is told from the point of view of the sighted person among the blind. But . . . the claim to be sighted in the world of the religiously blind cannot be rationally confirmed; there is no perspective 'above' the faiths and the unfaiths in that sense." Heim, *Salvations*, 211. Yet we are not all stone-blind. Triangulation among traditions can help us tack between traditions and experience; cf. Goodman, *In Defense of Truth*, 97, 170–71.

irreconcilable goods is not pluralism either, but a claim as to the inevitability of tragedy. Pluralism can see more than one good life for an individual or a society, and it acknowledges that there are diverse, even incompatible perspectives on the truth. The faith of pluralism is that values can be reconciled and that diverse perspectives do not reflect an underlying incoherence in reality itself. So pluralism takes issue not only with skepticism and relativism but also with the tragic view of life and the human condition.[13]

Theories, like novels, paintings, and other works of art, get their scope not just from what they cover but also from what they omit. Abstraction allows Newton or Einstein to survey a universe. But wherever there is abstraction, something is abstracted from. Can we really call a theory that ignores the human condition a theory of everything? By the same token, religions should not claim comprehensiveness if they know nothing of DNA and evolution, cannibal galaxies, black holes, neutrinos, and the red shift – or make false use of them, punting downfield to quantum indeterminacy in behalf of human volition or divine agency, or pretending that ancient texts knew all along about the expanding universe. Religions can hardly claim comprehensiveness if each grasps a different organ of the same beast – or some other animal altogether. Maimonides argues that we come ever closer to God's perfection as we shed the feeble notions we have used to suggest it. All our common terms name general types and signify particulars by relating them to a class. So familiar language is of little help in addressing the unique.[14] Even poetry adds little unless we heed the limits of our imagery. Part of the power of a metaphor, as art, lies in its hinting that it is a metaphor – and in our recognizing its limitations.

Are ultimates, then, always beyond thought and expression? It is all very well to talk about ineffability, but punting in that direction is hardly edifying or helpful to mutual understanding

---

[13] See Goodman, *In Defense of Truth*; for the roots of the tragic view in pagan piety and sophist practice, see Goodman, *God of Abraham*, chapter 1.

[14] Maimonides, *Guide* I 52–53, 56–60, 73; "Eight Chapters," 5.

and conversation across boundaries. Even ineffability, after all, has its flavors and colors. There might be ineffable horror or love, unspeakable beauty or wonder, anguish or elation. Not all that is ineffable is spiritual. Our trouble in speaking of our intimate or elevated experiences clearly does not leave us with nothing to say about them. Nor does it give us license to make a virtue of necessity and simply give up a search for meaning in experiences that may point beyond their own immediacy. Yet any meanings we find will be shaped by what we take to be "beyond" – what we think is ultimate and where we expect to find it.

The fleeting and fragmentary experiences that seem to point upward are hardly self-certifying. But it is tempting to call them that, even at the price of self-caricature, thereby striking attitudes that ape rather than emulate the objects of our quest. Humility seems more fitting, and wiser, than pyrrhonian skepsis or protagorean relativism. Humility, lightly worn, projects no aura of invincible ignorance, but rather a sense of fellow feeling, recognizing that religious notions are at best approximations. Religious myth and poetry, humbly handled, can guide us, even as they reveal how feebly we grasp ultimates and how gingerly we must touch them. Humility renounces literalism, which, like dogmatism, is less a sign of innocence than a response to conflict, cognitive dissonance, and doubt.

If religions, generically, are defined by the ultimacy they seek and differentiated by the values they canonize, the differences can be enlightening: Perhaps others see what we do not. One seeker's stepping-stone is another's summit. Recognizing that our vision is partial – both fragmentary and prone to bias – does not dissolve all differences. But that is not the aim of pluralism. Humility is part of what we can learn from skeptics: The weaknesses we need to know best are our own.

The personal question for religious pluralism is ethical and epistemic: What should it mean to us that others cherish beliefs and norms unlike our own? The social question is different: How much diversity can a society tolerate, and what must it never tolerate? The two questions are readily confused. Hence the presumption Plantinga faced – that serious commitments sin inevitably against difference, liberty, and progress. It is a little too easy to brand as a bigot anyone whose beliefs exclude their alternatives. So it is helpful to distinguish the social from the personal question – but they do intertwine.

Yet pluralism has limits and sets limits: Indiscriminate acceptance of just any view or practice yields only confusion for the individual and loss of the candor that gives the sacred its appeal. As for societies, we do not all need to share, let alone enforce, a single outlook or way of life. Attempts to prescribe such unity are delusory – as procrustean as descriptions that try to jimmy diversity into a single matrix. But in this context it is not just readings but human lives that are crushed into pigeonholes. Pigeonholes have rigid walls and fixed positions, but pigeons fly around.

Societies do not need the kind of coherence and self-definition that individuals seek. Anyone's values will blend reason and emotion; practicality, fantasy, and caprice; norms inherited and values self-discovered. Societies are far more parti-colored. But just as some personal views and practices are wholesome and others unworkable, so in a society some beliefs and practices are crippling or destructive. Barring real danger, it is hardly necessary for states systematically to sift wholesome from unwholesome beliefs and practices. Discriminations of that kind fall into the province, or the lap, of parents who are caring, not just indulgent; educators who teach by example; and writers and artists who pursue truth, not just titillation.

Dignity has no price, but it is a long way from incommensurability of that sort to the notion that moral choices are impracticable, values inscrutable, or community impossible. Plato gave reason the scepter precisely because reason can take a higher good as its touchstone in testing the incommensurable goods of appetite, spirit, and reason itself. The jostling of competing values does not necessitate tragedy. Rather, it suggests how precious judgment is – and how critically any social enterprise needs negotiation. We humans live most of our lives in the space between tragedy and utopia. The goods and ills that compete for our attention and challenge our resolve demand that we optimize: They do not license abandoning deliberation.

Societies do not sing in unison. Nor should they, as Aristotle suggests, resolve every harmony to a monotone, obviating the differences that make complementary roles possible and friendships interesting. Individuals, over time, may win some measure of coherence in the beliefs that frame an identity and the activities that constitute a life. But societies do not depend for their good health on the kind of continuity that an integrated personality requires. Some issues can remain unsettled. Common interests, as Rescher suggests, may prompt individuals to get along well together, even if they do not agree, say, about life's meaning.

I see three basic strategies widely in use in addressing religious differences:

1. Most familiar is a division of faith from practice and, correspondingly, of ritual from pragmatic action: What we do – *if* it affects others – is potentially a public concern, of possible interest to the law. But rituals are expressive acts, safeguarded under the penumbra of intellectual freedom. As symbolic acts they should hardly matter to others, any more than another's thoughts. Let us be pluralists about faith. Beliefs are private; symbols are ornaments. And yet, a burning flag, or cross, or effigy may reach beyond expression. Some beliefs are vivifying, others fatal.

2. An alternative strategy seeks to split essence from accident. *At bottom*, we are told, all religions agree. At least the great world religions do, or (when the work of judgment is handed off to persuasive definitions) all religions worthy of the name. Here pluralism turns monistic: Trappings may differ, but ultimately, we are assured, the great teachings speak with one voice. Splitting hairs only overlooks the inner truth that all religions share.

3. A third approach is to romanticize the religious other, sustain and celebrate presumptive differences, and thus reassert the boundaries. The romantic admires what is exotic in appearance, practices, dress, or presumed attitudes and values. But the noble savage posture depends on keeping one's distance.

The three strategies – balkanize, bowdlerize, or patronize – operate both in the public sphere and inwardly. But religious diversity calls for quite different sorts of response from individuals than from societies. Constitutionalism is needed in the latter case; tact, in the former. Understanding trumps tolerance, but tolerance is a minimum. A tolerant society must exclude organized hatred and discourage the stereotypes that feed intolerance. False rumors spark bloodshed; verbal and pictorial forms of dehumanization are the opening gambits of genocide. Lesser conflagrations flare in corner trash cans, fueled by cruel jokes. So much depends on the ethos. But no ethos thrives on benign neglect, and some extremes demand state action. If pluralism is public policy, hate groups and identity churches deserve no tax breaks; mosques that foment violent jihad are rightly watched or shuttered.

Tolerance rests on respect for human dignity, so it precludes promoting values and norms that break the human spirit. By the same token, it warrants positive actions shown to feed that spirit. So parks and museums, sports facilities, schools, and universities are legitimate and necessary projects of the state. Some pluralists contest the propriety of public efforts to favor toleration, liberty, and human dignity and flourishing. But a pluralism so rigidly constrained as to restrict public support of such projects, practices, and attitudes collapses as a practical program. It just stands gape-mouthed before the sheer fact of diversity, unable to enunciate the grounds for tolerance or to judge what kind of differences matter.

That is not our situation. Where visions of human flourishing grow cloudy or controversial, religious diversity is actually part of the solution. Religions both aid and challenge their milieu through their efforts to mark out the parameters of human well-being. Secularity rightly holds our public institutions aloof from partisanship or pandering to any sectarian ideal. Secularism is a different matter. It seeks to rid society of religious interests and ideas, practices, and values.[15] What pluralism asks for, by contrast, is openness, using the cudgel (and purse) of the law

[15] Cf. William Connolly, *Why I Am Not a Secularist*, 6.

sparingly to restrain what is egregious and to liberate human energies and insights for the pursuit and definition of the best aims of life.

Faith and Practice

So familiar is the division of faith from practice that grew out of the settlement of the seventeenth-century religious wars in Europe that we may hardly notice the questions begged when religions are called creeds.[16] We hallow freedom of thought and expression and prize the freedom to believe or disbelieve in any god or ultimate. Yet religions hardly confine themselves to doxology. Faith is typically seen as a goad to action and a guide to life. Nonbelievers, like believers, rightly cast a gimlet eye on persons of professed faith who breach the bonds of public morals. The devout are expected to be charitable, truthful, honest, not dissolute, and not stained by graft, extortion, money laundering, kidnapping, narcotics dealing, computer theft, or sexual abuse of youngsters – or concealing and thereby condoning and enabling such crimes. If the faithful are found to deceive and abuse their spouses, maltreat their children, perjure themselves, and defraud others, their sincerity or their faith itself will be questioned – or condemned. All religions issue precepts and prescriptions, specifying their expectations with varied concreteness, and no religion divorces faith from practice. Grace may be salvific in Calvinism or Islam, even against the torque of sin. But it is not that sins do not matter. Quite the contrary: It is because sin weighs so heavily that grace, expressed in faith and met by intercession or atonement, becomes vital. Grace is understood to give the sinner strength to battle sin. Only rarely, with the frisson of perversity, is grace said to license revelry in sin.

Sometimes religious norms take the bit between the teeth, yielding ritualism, legalism, scrupulosity, asceticism, and

---

[16] Wilfred Cantwell Smith disliked the word "religion" and preferred to speak of faiths; see his *Faith and Belief*; *The Meaning and End of Religion*. That works, up to a point, for Christianity and Islam, but hardly for Judaism, Taoism, or Confucianism.

discipline for its own sake. In Mimamsa Hinduism, ritual is allowed to overshadow belief, lest thought distract from ritual correctness. In Jewish legal positivism, belief in God is just another commandment – making it hard to see just how legalists can fulfill the commandment to love God with all their hearts and souls and might (Deuteronomy 6:5), let alone emulate God's holiness (Leviticus 19:2). Bahya Ibn Paquda, by contrast, sees philosophical inquiry as integral to piety: The mind must not be left behind on one's spiritual quest. But even the extremes of legalistic positivism or atheistic ritualism do not sunder belief from practice. Even those who meditate on emptiness know how they are supposed to live and what kind of air their meditations are meant to spread throughout their lives. Even antinomians try to live their faith.

The old attempt to decide which came first – ritual or myth, practice or belief – is mired in confusions. In religious life the two go hand in hand: Rituals spawn new stories and sustain old ones, just as stories crystallize in observances. The line between ritual and pragmata is similarly porous, because few rituals are so etiolated as to lack all moral valence. Rituals that disclaim any pragmatic end – such as some of the secular rituals of aesthetics or athletics – still utter a subtext, affirming, say, the autonomy of art or the athletic values that a sport celebrates. Even here rituals powerfully affect participants and observers, as is manifest in the allocation of their energies and resources.

Some religious precepts and prescriptions are problematic. Some are downright wrong. Will a society tolerate polygamy for the sake of religious diversity? What about the withholding of medicines, surgery, or transfusions or the practices of child marriage or honor killings? Is it intolerant to say that piety is perverted by certain acts, that the very idea of honor is dishonored when religious scruples or wounded pride lights an impious, incestuous torch?[17] Faith is hardly confined to Sunday homilies.

---

[17] Kwame Appiah argues that religious and cultural ideals of honor/shame and moral purity can be turned to use as effective barriers to honor killings. *Wall Street Journal*, September 25–26, 2010.

Part of the insistent tug of violent extremes is the desire of the faithful to show others, or themselves, or God a faith and trust beyond mere ideation.

When a Christian Scientist's four year old, treated only with prayer, died of meningitis, the California Supreme Court held that "parents have *no* right to the free exercise of religion at the price of a child's life, regardless of the prohibitive or compulsive nature of the governmental infringement."[18] Jurists say that this decision sanctioned action, not belief. The First Amendment, the courts say, "embraces two concepts – freedom to believe and freedom to act. The first is absolute but, in the nature of things, the second cannot be. Conduct remains subject to regulation for the protection of society."[19] The distinction is precious, yet somewhat artificial. Some beliefs are vitiated if unexercised – the right to educate one's children, for example. Some beliefs have legal implications. A school district, Laurence Tribe argues, would be well within its rights in firing a school bus driver who admired child sacrifice: "the state may act in advance to prevent especially dangerous forms of action based on religious beliefs." Aiming to shore up the precious distinction, Tribe hastens to add, "although the state may in such cases seem to be punishing belief, it is actually trying to forestall action."[20] Still, it is the belief, not actual performance, that warrants the precautions. Jihadists are rightly restricted from air travel, even if all they have done overtly is proclaim a sacred duty to slay infidels.

Some parents sincerely believe their children to be possessed. Many Muslim mothers believe the clitoris sows evil and unchastity. Should society countenance every ritual expression

---

[18] Walker v. Superior Court, 763 P.2d 852, 870 (Cal. 1988). Only in 2010 did the Christian Science Church begin seriously to scale back its demands, making faith a supplement rather than a rival to medical treatments – moved in part by compassion for those whose faith appeared unequal to the challenge of life-threatening disease and in part by hopes that Christian Science healing would be accepted as a reimbursable medical expense. *New York Times*, March 25, 2010.

[19] Cantwell v. Connecticut, 310 U.S. 296, 303–04 (1940).

[20] Tribe, *American Constitutional Law* § 14–16, 1184. My thanks to Charles Collier for these judicial citations.

of a faith? The distinction of symbolic from pragmatic acts helps little here. Jonathan Swift lampoons the disputes between Protestants and Catholics with the parable of unending wars over whether to crack eggs at the big end or the little one.²¹ The dispute was not worth the bloodshed and torture perpetrated in its name – better to bury what once seemed a forced choice. But symbols gain or lose their power by way of what they stand for, and not every symbolic flashpoint is as easily dismissed as one whose flint no longer strikes fire.

Many today who mourn the Taliban's dynamiting of the Buddhas at Bamiyan would never dream of venerating a carved cliffside. Many who take spiritual joy in the music of a mass would never celebrate one. Travel to Afghanistan, and you find believers who do not think much about the uses put to their opium poppies but care mightily about their Hindu neighbors' effigies. Secularity for these believers is not liberation but emasculation, sundering faith from act. Is it culture-bound to frame religious freedom simply in terms of words and thoughts?

A workable, pluralism demands a certain self-restraint and mutual accommodation. Push openness too hard and it turns impotent, powerless to defend itself and without a principle to defend. If a society is to protect religious freedom it is not enough to let bus conductors wear turbans and nurses wear hijabs. There has to be restraint on those who accost men who wear no beards and women with uncovered hair. There needs to be a way of letting children attend school unmolested, and widows sell their besoms. The familiar division of faith from practice will not afford all the protections diversity requires. It goes too far in some ways and not far enough in others. Contrary to the wishful myth, not every faith is tolerable, because not every faith is tolerant. Faiths that foment hatred do not deserve societal support. Faiths that promote bloodshed and incite violence should be curbed. Yet that does not warrant a generic fallacy that treats every "fundamentalism" as a torch alight with violence. Disapproval of a religious teaching or practice is not the same as

²¹ Jonathan Swift, *Gulliver's Travels* (1726) Part I, chapter 4.

uncovering its destructiveness. But genuine destructiveness, in beliefs or practices, must be treated as the enemy it is.

A pluralistic society has moral choices to make: It cannot tolerate just anything. But the attempt to cordon off belief from practice, despite its juridical standing and its historic successes in accommodating a range of religious differences, will not succeed with a wider spectrum of ancient and invented forms of religious diversity (and litigious perversity). It assumes too neat a division where life is full of messy, organic connections.

Religious pluralism is the recognition that more than one spiritual path is validly pursued, since human beings find fulfillment in a variety of ways of life and thought. Those who follow one path need not adopt another to accept that principle. But in any sound and sincere religious commitment, faith and practice go hand in hand. The barriers thrown up between the two prove rather flimsy.

Essential and Adventitious

Toleration, even admiration, may grow from seeing an essential unity beneath surface differences. Beyond the payoff in social harmony or the forging of alliances, there is moral and spiritual uplift in identifying with the religious other. But edifying as that may be, listening too hard for resonances can yield a reductionism of its own. Cantwell Smith, who bridles at the reification of religions and the attendant blurring of differences, loses that subtlety when he discovers a generic core in religions, an underlying unity in faith – ineffable, undefinable, a "universal quality of human life"[22] that imparts "a quiet confidence and joy which enables one to feel at home in the universe and to find meaning in the world and in one's own life, a meaning that is profound and ultimate and . . . stable."[23] Can one canvas capture the variety? The paint looks a bit rosy. Some faiths expect one *not* to feel quite so comfortable in this world. Some foster anger, persecution, or repression. Critics see complacency where

---

[22] Smith, *Towards a World Theology*, 113.
[23] Smith, *Faith and Belief*, 12.

Cantwell Smith finds serenity. Religion can frazzle some nerves. Many people find joy and meaning in their lives without the aid of faith – sometimes by finding ways to keep it at bay.[24] Ecumenism may pursue analogies a bit too joyously, finding unities of spirit that flatten differences that are critical, for some, to a treasured distinctiveness.

Sunyata, in Buddhism, means emptiness. But the connotations are not those that nonbeing might carry in the West. The root idea, as Buddhist thinkers use the term, is the relativity of all that arises, the conditionedness of the transitory. The privileged position of sunyata and the traditional paradoxes equating emptiness with fullness, or conditionality with unconditionedness, set sunyata in some ways in the role of the Absolute in Western thought. But to identify sunyata with God is "too easy," as John Cobb explains.[25] Christians tempted by such equations miss the historic Buddhist disenchantment with the Hindu pleroma. Nontheistic Buddhists like Masao Abe push back: God dies on the cross, he urges, not to save the world, but to empty Godhead of divinity, modeling the renunciation that is the pathway to enlightenment. Quoting Nietzsche on the progression from ancient human sacrifices to the sacrifice of human nature and desire, and finally to that of God himself,[26] Abe finds God's ultimate character in *kenosis*:

God is God, not because God had the son of God take a human form and be sacrificed while God remained God, but because God is a suffering God, a self-sacrificial God through total kenosis. The kenotic God who totally empties Godself and totally sacrifices Godself is, in my view, the true God who thoroughly saves everything, including human beings and nature, through self-sacrificing, abnegating love.[27]

Abe's reduction is just as colonialist as missionary efforts to drape sunyata in godly garments. We still see an outsider claiming hermeneutic rule over realms of meaning already well tenanted.

[24] Cf. Heim in *Salvations*, 57.
[25] Cobb, in *The Emptying of God*, xi.
[26] Abe, "Kenotic God...," in Cobb and Ives, p. 7, quoting *Beyond Good and Evil*.
[27] Ibid., 16.

Those who venture onto the bridges thrown up by such readings may find them crumbling underfoot since they are built on rubble, a Nietzschean or Heideggerian post-Christianity sprinkled with a Buddhist gloss. But Abe presses his salient with calls for an entente of religions, theistic or otherwise, against scientism and nihilism.[28]

Perusing the contested texts, the Jewish theologian Eugene Borowitz hazards modestly, "if I may make a disinterested academic observation, Abe's reinterpretation of Christ's kenosis seems to me utterly to transform it from what I have understood contemporary Christian theologians to be saying."[29] Borowitz gamely offers a few home truths about his own home base:

For Judaism the fundamental human concern is not redemption from sin.... Having no doctrine of original sin, Jews believe that the responsibility and the capacity to turn from evil is given not only to Jews but to all humankind, as the example of the Ninevans in the book of Jonah demonstrates.... For Judaism, the primary human task is creating holiness through righteousness. The responsible deed, the one that simultaneously acknowledges God, others, time, place, nature, and self in Covenantal fulfillment, not only mends the torn but fulfills the promise inherent in existence.[30]

Borowitz declines Abe's invitation to Jews to view the Shoah as an opportunity (like the crucifixion) to rise above "all such dualities as good and evil, holy and profane"[31]:

[T]he caring Jewish community will overwhelmingly reject the suggestion that, for all the trauma connected with the Holocaust, we ought to understand that it *ultimately* has no significance; or, to put it more directly, that *ultimately* there is no utterly fundamental distinction between the Nazi death camp operators and their victims. For most Jews, a response to the encompassing evils of our day . . . cannot properly be made with a consciousness that they are truly second-level concerns, that bringing people to a higher level of understanding is the most significant way to face them. And I cannot imagine them agreeing

[28] Ibid., 4–9.
[29] Borowitz, in *The Emptying of God*, 80.
[30] Ibid., 81–82.
[31] Ibid., 82; see Abe, *Emptying God*, 53.

that the ultimate response to the Nazis would have been for Jews to raise their consciousness from a radically moral to a higher, postmoral level.[32]

Hans Küng welcomes Abe's thought that religions face a common foe in nihilism, but gingerly notes that nihilism has taken a toll not just in the West but also in the Gulag, and even in Japan, where "religion has been replaced by a pseudo-religion (nationalism and militarism) – with catastrophic consequences for Japan's neighbors and ultimately for Japan itself."[33] Küng skates lightly here over the nexus of Tojo militarism to the Nazi Holocaust and to the work of Nishida Kitaro, Tetsuro Watsuji, and the Kyoto school, whose mantle Abe proudly wears. But he does recall that Nietzsche's denunciation of religions did not spare Buddhism, which he called "passive Nihilism."[34] Küng vehemently rejects reading sunyata into Christian theism: Only Jesus, not God, is said to be "emptied" in the text that grounds Christian ideas of kenosis:

Let this mind be in you, which was also in Christ Jesus: Who, being in the form of God, thought it not robbery to be equal with God: But made himself of no reputation, and took upon him the form of a servant, and was made in the likeness of men: And from being found in fashion as a man, he humbled himself, and became obedient unto death, even the death of the cross (Philippians 2:5–8).[35]

For Christians this passage touches the crux of faith: not the idea of God becoming no God but the self-sacrifice of God's only begotten. Any other view, Küng insists, is "unbiblical (in fact, monophysitic or Hegelian)" heresy[36]:

There is no question: Masao Abe's basic intention is dialogic. He isolates key concepts from Christian texts which he then transplants into a Buddhist context, where the concept of kenosis is understood not simply

---

[32] Borowitz, in *The Emptying of God*, 83.
[33] Küng, in Corless and Knitter, *Buddhist Emptiness and Christian Trinity*, 29.
[34] Küng, "God's Self-Renunciation and Buddhist Emptiness," 28–29, citing *Der Fall Wagner*.
[35] Abe quotes the verses in "Kenotic God," 9.
[36] Küng, in *Buddhist Emptiness and Christian Trinity*, 34.

as ethical, exemplary humiliation, but is recast as ontological emptying, an emptying of God, Himself, yes, ultimately as emptiness in general, shunyata.... Just as Christian authors earlier gave a Christian exegesis of Greek or Buddhist texts, so also Abe gives a Buddhist exegesis of Christian texts. He wants in this manner to overcome the cultural and religious gap.... is this an adequate hermeneutic for the inter-religious dialogue? Basically nothing personal is at stake because, even in foreign raiment, one finds only one's own world again.[37]

Küng returns the compliment, leveraging an affirmative metaphysic out of the Buddhist idea that Nothing need not be all negative – because emptiness is the heart of compassion and "a vow to save others, however innumerable."[38] In the spirit of Western piety, where religion is typically at home in some voluntary association, Küng voices a preference for Yogacara Buddhism, in which sunyata bears a positive valence:

Denial is not the end but the means of discovering the hidden reality, the transcendent ground of everything and at the same time the true nature of things as the norm for the true and false. Nagarjuna's great critic, the Vedanta philosopher Shankara (eighth century), who learned so much from him that he has been called a "crypto-Buddhist," thought it consistent to proceed from the "emptiness" of the world of appearances to the true being of Brahman. Shankara was in turn corrected, as we know, by Ramanuja, who defended a modified nondualism, a differentiated unity of the Absolute and the world which is very near the classical Christian position. And even though the Buddhists themselves rejected a "Brahman" or "God," the majority in no way flatly objected to a transcendence which is immanent.

Küng is clearly more at ease with facets of Hindu tradition than with Abe's Buddhist reduction of Christianity. Abe, for his part, matches Küng's distaste for Hegel and the Monophysites with a snub to Yogacara and a patronizing dismissal of Shinran or Pure Land Buddhism (the largest Buddhist sect in Japan), whose followers, he says, seek salvation by merely chanting the name

[37] Ibid., 34–35.
[38] Abe, in *Emptying God*, 58; Ives, in *Divine Emptiness and Historical Fullness*, 52–56.

Amida.[39] Sometimes, the hardest differences to accept are those with the folks next door.

Borowitz makes a buckler of the Torah, citing its text and summoning up his constituents to echo his odium for Abe's postmoral posture. Abe calls up all Asia at his back. He even points to the narrow spit of land that links him to the Pure Land school[40] and casts himself and his interlocutors as spokesmen for their cultures, as if peace among nations depended on the concord of a handful of scholars who cordially concede each other's wisdom even as they parry each other's thrusts. Yet the broad constituencies toward which a speaker gestures, myriads too numerous to count and too voluble to be heard, do not uniformly parse their lives in the abstract categories that learned symposiasts fluently deploy. Religious practice and experience vary greatly and may offer rather slight conceptual footholds. So unity is elusive: Savants seldom reach it by climbing ever higher in the tree of Porphyry, reaching for the generic and universal. The twigs get ever slenderer as they rise, and the people they profess to speak for rarely follow where they climb.[41]

---

[39] Ives, in *Divine Emptiness and Historical Fullness*, 170, takes Abe to task for stating drily, "Buddhism does not accept the notion of a transcendent ruler of the universe or of a savior outside one's self." That ignores Pure Land Buddhism. As Fyodor Stcherbatsky wrote long ago, "When we see an atheistic, soul-denying, philosophic teaching of a path of personal final deliverance, consisting in an absolute extinction of life and a simple worship of the memory of its human founder – when we see it superseded by a magnificent High Church with a supreme God, surrounded by a numerous pantheon and a host of saints, a religion highly devotional, highly ceremonious and clerical, with an ideal of universal salvation of all living creatures, a salvation not in annihilation but in eternal life – we are justified in maintaining that the history of religions has scarcely witnessed such a break between new and old within the pale of what nevertheless continues to claim common descent from the same religious founder." *The Buddhist Concept of Nirvāna*, 36, quoted in Thomas, *The History of Buddhist Thought*, 212–13.

[40] Abe, in Ives, ed., *Divine Emptiness and Historical Fullness*, 28.

[41] Roy Amore calls Buddhism and Christianity "religions of the incarnate god" and cites parallels between precepts, such as "Love your enemies" and "Conquer anger by non-anger." Jesus' disciples "became the 'church,' which is considered the body of Christ; and Gautama's became the 'sangha,' revered as the third of the three precious jewels (the other two are the Buddha and the

Few Catholics today trace the niceties of every papal bull, and as Mary Douglas explains, a young priest's rationales about why one need not eat fish on Fridays do not touch the heart of an old parishioner's lifelong piety. Jews choose their synagogues more on social and cultural than theological grounds. American Buddhists celebrate the O-bon in Honolulu at the temple their parents frequented and bring their children with them. Few hear the thoughtful discourse of the bishop inside, who speaks as the drums beat and the festival crowd circles the towers, reminiscent of a harvest season marked by long departed forebears in the Japan of another era. In America today if congregants have a theology it is often of their own devising, accommodating what they have read or heard. The clergy are glad to see them and rarely press the finer points of doctrine.

Among the intellectually inclined, the conscientious may squelch temptations to poach as Abe does. But it is hard to overlook the alternatives to his vision even within Buddhism. Pluralism needs more than common ground or even a common enemy. It needs to accommodate differences, not paper over them. Diverse cultures and diverse moments within a culture have their own cynosures. Religions may find each other's sore points untroubling or assign them quite different meanings. The differences in how a theology is cantilevered or an epistemology is balanced reveal that outright disagreements are often the least of it in religious diversity.

Nirvana does bear some relation to ideas about God. But nirvana is a state, not a ruler or creator. Structurally it might look more like immortality. But immortality has many meanings, linked to thoughts of God and the good in many ways. For some, it is sensuous; others picture a kind of fusion with the divine. Vulgarly, nirvana is synonymous with ecstasy, but in the Buddha's

Dharma," *Two Masters, One Message,* 46, 55–57. Georg Siegmund writes, "Comparisons between Buddha and Christ seem to present themselves unbidden.... But the parallels that suggest themselves to a first superficial comparison conceal too quickly the decisive differences." *Buddhism and Christianity,* 152; cf. G. Dharmarsiri, *A Buddhist Critique of the Christian Concept of God.*

oldest teachings nirvana meant extinguishing the (transient, hence illusory) self. The Bureau of Standards sets no single metric for gauging the foci of religious interest. God and soul, causality, holiness, beatitude, miracle, life, and eternity are conceptualized quite variously even in philosophies articulated in a single language and milieu – let alone in popular thought. And none of these ideas stands still. Their meanings respond fluidly to new moral and intellectual dynamics as cultures move and change and interact. Such values and ideas are continually taking on new functions, facing or answering new questions and raising still others.

Terms such as "emptiness" are not used in pristine isolation. I remember hearing Gene Borowitz remind a popular audience about the Jewish lost generation of the 1920s and their soi-disant nihilism: "We used to say we believed in nothing," he paraphrased their thinking. "Then we met some people who *really* believed in nothing." Borowitz meant the Nazis. They did not believe in nothing, of course. They had strong beliefs. Some dreamed of a new man, a blond beast, their version of Nietzsche's übermensch, doing philosophy with a hammer and rising above good and evil. What the Nazis meant, one hopes, was quite different from what Abe meant.

Seeing how slippery words such as "absolute" and "nothing" can become, especially in slippery hands, we have to ask ourselves these questions: Is common ground impossible; is inscrutability inevitable? I think not.[42] But we cannot expect every inch of common ground to yield consensus. The ancient prophets foresaw a time when all humanity would use a lucid language and set their shoulders to God's work (Zephaniah 3:9). But clear language does not meld all visions into one. That delusion, my friend Saul Strosberg argues, was the real flaw of Babel (Genesis 11:1) – the false pursuit of unanimity. Human beings, the Bible suggests (Genesis 10:20), already had diverse tongues. But the folk of Babel, in the Torah's fable, bent their minds around one thought. Their project was not God's work – to build a better

---

[42] See Goodman, *In Defense of Truth*, 113–25, 136–41, etc.

life for all, a place where every life would count. Their object was building a monument of dehumanizing scale,[43] a tower to rend the heavens and give their citadel a fame that would subsume the names and lives of all those whose work had built it. Zephaniah's hopes are humbler, more earthbound, but bolder in a way: We will come to understand each other, learning not how to agree but how to listen. Religiously, that could mean invoking the ultimate as each of us best sees it, pursuing the good each in our own way.

Julia Ching, with the grace and wisdom that shone throughout her life, was perhaps a better seeker of common ground than Abe. He was prone to tell Westerners who offered him their hand that a handshake betrays Western aggression and suspicion, because it originates as an assurance that the greeter is unarmed. A bow was humbler, he urged with undisguised pride. Julia's was a gentler humility: "I am an Asian Christian with a non-Christian background," she wrote, expressing pleasure at "the existential and religious 'pluralism' in which we find ourselves." She told of trying to follow the accounts of sunyata advanced by two Buddhist scholars with Western names. She had "struggled to understand," continuously "correcting my ignorance with each reading," hoping "perhaps, eventually" to move on "to the discovery of the 'mind of clear light' – if only at death;" then she added, "Since I may be distant from that goal, I can only grope for light while knowing that it *is* there, and that it is *also* love and compassion; to use words with more Christian resonance, that it is 'loving kindness' (Hebrew: *hesed*)."[44]

Ching's tone strikes a chord. She does not reduce enlightenment to compassion – *hesed*, or *jen*, "human heartedness," as Chinese philosophers call it. It is *also* that, she says, turning to the ethical not to change the subject and waive religion for ethics. She knows that spiritual motives cannot *energize* compassion if they are identical with it. But she sees a link between the two,

---

[43] For the intimidating motives and motifs of Babylonian architecture and beyond, see Lethaby, *Architecture, Mysticism, and Myth*.

[44] Ching, "Response to Jeffrey Hopkins," 133.

as many spiritual teachers have – kindness and generosity as
the surest signs of enlightenment. As Jesus says, *Do men gather
grapes of thorns or figs of thistles?.... By their fruits shall you
know them* (Matthew 7:16, 20).

Yet we cannot gauge diversity in full without recognizing that
some abhor the ethical – or what they call the ethical. For some,
ethics is a stalking horse. Some brand compassion a weakling's
cloak for spite and characterize all pleas for caring as mere false
consciousness and self-deception. Ricoeur sounds a Nietzschean
note: Religions need to get past blame and prescription. Even love
and altruism are inveterate blinds for cruelty and *ressentiment*.[45]
That is hard to see in, say, Levinas. But not every offer of love
is welcomed. Still, even among those who welcome the ethical,
questions remain over how to read or shape its demands: Are
they conventions or laws embedded in the nature of things? Is
the silver rule (Do not unto others what is hateful to you) dearer
than the golden, being less obtrusive?[46] If ethics is to be a common denominator, one must reckon with the diverse ways that
ethics is constructed and construed. Does *laissez-faire* open the
broadest common ground? Epicureans preferred it: Wasn't non-
interference the best *social* policy and not just the high road to
ataraxia? Do-gooders, after all, can be meddlesome. But let-it-be
does readily acquiesce in a not so benign neglect. It can cloak a
sordid selfishness and dig a hidey-hole for the self-serving that
makes eudaimonism baneful to Kant. Choice never vanishes from
the moral horizon. As Nahmanides explains, one can be a wretch
within the bounds of the Law. Any code can screen meanness or
turpitude – as Nazis at Nürnberg hid behind "my station and its
duties," and robber barons behind Mandeville's "private vice is
public virtue."

The face of the other that haunts Levinas's moral vision –
crying out, wordlessly, "Do not kill me!" – must also mean, "Do
not turn away!" But there are thoughtful and thoughtless ways

---

[45] Ricoeur, *The Religious Significance of Atheism*, 75–77, 82–89.
[46] See Allinson, "The Golden Rule as the Core Value in Confucianism and
Christianity."

to reach out and to let go, strengthening the other's hand or turning one's back on the pleading face. Part of what religions can offer ethics, beyond sheer energy, are ways of caring that respect the value and beauty in all beings, and distinctively in persons. Creeds and screeds that negate human worth, be they religious or nonreligious in their underpinnings, are not worth much. Happily, they cannot say much either in their own behalf, without undercutting the neutral or negative ground they seek to stand on.

Moral terms such as compassion, like such freighted words as "absolute" or "empty," bear cultural valences. The Islamic ideal, Ali Mazrui writes, is not liberty but dignity. Connotations here do the heavy lifting, lumbering the idea of liberty with the baggage of license and rampant egoism, and loading dignity not with Kantian reverence for the moral law's respect for persons but with postcolonial bitterness. Compassion, Allah's most prolific epithet, suffers a partial eclipse in this recension. But every confession has its ethos. Adherents may pursue an ideal, cherish, transcend, or disappoint it. But morality is no more fit than theology to unite religions, not just because codes differ but also because morals track religious views and echo religious differences – and are tracked and echoed by them. In the end, neither morals nor religion stands clear of politics or culture.

Given the range of spiritual differences on our planet, the wonder is that we can communicate at all. Openness is the start of an answer. But openness need not be vapid. In matters of belief and understanding, compromise is not always what is needed. On points of principle, it is rarely apt. Readiness to learn from what seems alien or to scrutinize received wisdom shows more honesty and perspicacity. Critical appropriation is the hallmark of wisdom in addressing received traditions. It is also a key to creativity – musical, painterly, or religious.[47] Thoughtful charity is the due of every insight, of any pedigree. It is the joining of open heart with open eyes that gives moral beauty to the

---

[47] See Goodman and Caramenico, *Coming to Mind.*

psalmist's words: *From the rising of the sun to its setting, celebrated is the name of the Lord* (Psalms 113:3). Charity here reads even the idolater's intent in the light most favorable to the ardor and insight of the worshiper. So, Malachi (1:11), echoing the psalmist's thought, finds *incense and pure offerings* to God and in his name throughout the world. Another poet, in other circumstances, can find no gods like his own (Exodus 15:11) or decries alien godlets (Psalms 96:5) – false gods if they demand human sacrifice or solicit temple prostitution. One cannot silence polemics: They are both a sign and an engine of spiritual change and growth. But polemics are not the only mode of interreligious discourse. Indeed, the Septuagint, followed by Philo and Josephus, reads the Torah's ban, *thou shalt not curse the divine* (Exodus 22:27),[48] as forbidding disparagement of *any* god.[49]

The ultimate religious pluralist, rabbinically, is Jethro, the Midianite priest who taught Moses, his son-in-law, how to administer God's law (Exodus 18). How else, the Rabbis reason, commenting on his story, unless Jethro had known their worship, could he have chosen Israel's God above all others (Exodus 17:11)?[50] Abraham frames a covenant with Melchitzedek, king and priest of a supreme God (*el ᶜelyon*). Is this also Abraham's universal God (Genesis 21:33)? The Torah leaves the question open. Melchitzedek blesses Abraham and his God (Genesis 14:18–20), as Jethro will bless the God of Moses (Exodus 18:9–12). The exclusivity of Israel's God most poignantly and pointedly bars the violence and degradation long constitutive in pagan piety.[51]

---

[48] The Authorized Version numbers the verse 22:28 and renders "Thou shalt not revile the gods"; Tyndale: "Thou shalt not rail against the gods."

[49] Philo calls for respect for the gods of diverse cities, even those that are falsely so called; *De Specialibus Legibus* 1.9, 1.53, *De Vita Mosis* 2.38, 2.205; cf. Josephus, *Contra Apion* 2.33, 2.237, *Antiquities.* 4.8, 10, 207; see Wolfson, *Philo,* 2.368–69; Safrai, *The Literature of the Sages,* 140; Urbach, *The Sages,* 1.23–26; but for tyrants as gods, 1.90–91.

[50] Urbach, *The Sages* 1.21.

[51] See Leviticus 18:21, 20:2; Deuteronomy 12:30–31, 18:9–10; Jeremiah 7:31, 19:4–6; Ezekiel 16:20–21, 23:37; Psalms 106:37–38; 2 Kings 3:27, 16:3, 23:10; Goodman, *God of Abraham,* 15–28.

The psalmist bypassed mere courtesy in acknowledging that others too worship the Highest. Still a whiff of condescension persists.[52] Do those others know just what they're worshiping? When Paul identifies for the Athenians the unknown god whose altar he passed by (Acts 17:23), he hopes to guide a misdirected piety. In Psalm 113, at least, the exotic worshipers are far away. The psalmist is not telling them whom they worship but praising God for the myriad celebrations of his name. But he does privilege his own God. So does Malachi, even as he castigates his people for neglecting what other nations implicitly acknowledge. Privileging one's own, for praise or for rebuke, is hardly rare. Plantinga's faith echoes it. Scripture's jealous God will countenance no rival loves. Far-flung devotees, from Mandalay to Kamakura, also think their own gods are special. Inwardness and insularity, the fierce possessiveness and privacy of religious experience, and the communal particularity of religious life fray the threads of unity. Even the most irenic reduction papers over deep rifts and differences. Worshipers can always look askance at the straps and strings outsiders apply to bundle up religious differences in a single packet. They can always say, "That's not what I meant; that's not what I meant at all."

Just who decides what others mean? Philosophers have widely given up the old trick of pulling rank on the laity – so fashionable years ago – of telling those who said "Theft is wrong" that all they really meant was "Those thieves, UGH!"; or of telling people who spoke of God that they meant nothing at all – unless perhaps to voice approval of certain values. Ecumenism may still need to learn a bit about relinquishing such substitutions of judgment: Even the warmest motives do not relieve those who hold a belief or pursue a practice of the primary right (and responsibility) to grasp what it means to them and mark for themselves what they deem essential or adventitious in their traditions. Pluralism demands both charity and clarity. But charity does not obviate critical thinking, and criticism, unlike charity, should begin at home.

---

[52] Cf. the trenchant critique in Katz, *Mysticism and Religious Traditions*.

Eagerness for common ground will not make consensus a sure-fire test of truth. People can err in what they hold most dear, and consensus guards error just as fervently as truth. So common consent cannot certify veracity. But just as risky as the fallacy of *ex consensu gentium* is the notion that one can discount whatever will not match up in disparate religious experiences.[53] Commonalities discovered in the descriptions of diverse traditions are often artifacts of the ignoring of differentia. As van Inwagen writes, reflecting on John Hick's ecumenical impulses,

> I may believe that everything that the Muslim believes that is inconsistent with what I believe is false. But then so does everyone who accepts the law of the excluded middle or the principle of contradiction. What I do *not* do is inform the Muslim that every tenet of Islam that is inconsistent with Buddhism is not really essential to Islam. (Nor do I believe in my heart of hearts that every tenet of Islam that is inconsistent with the beliefs of late-twentieth-century middle class Anglo-American professors is not really essential to Islam.) Despite the fact that I reserve the right to believe things not believed by Muslims, I leave it to the Muslims to decide what is and what is not essential to Islam.[54]

Religions have real differences in truth claims, practices, and values. The differences are not confined to superficialities. Indeed, if a religion cannot be wrong, it cannot be right either, and setting religions above every moral or spiritual error does not accord respect to any.

Good will is just as ready to deny diversity as bigotry is to exaggerate or distort it. Ecumenism is often suspect on these grounds, pursuing mergers in place of understanding, eager to accommodate, greedily reducing exotic commitments to pallid mockeries. Courtesy forbids talk of heresies, and the enlightened do not persecute, at least not in the old-fashioned way.

---

[53] Philip Kitcher argues that religious differences bespeak the falsity of all religions; the historic conditions that prompt religious responses are not of the truth-yielding sort. But this argument, like *consensus gentium*, proves nothing. With any claim one must consider the content and the evidence, not just the provenance – although study of history may help us see the intentions that motivate a claim.

[54] van Inwagen, *God, Knowledge and Mystery: Essays in Philosophical Theology*, 213–14.

Yet, engorgement does distort, especially when it spits out what did not taste quite as expected. Relativism decries essentialism, but with all its vaunted even-handedness, it remains judgmental. What funds its generosity is not evidence for the truth of conflicting views or the soundness of disparate ways but an urge to be deferential – another way of putting others in their place. Hick rocks between the relativistic and the acquisitive, reaching for an elusive essentialism that might let him balance on both sides of the ecumenical seesaw. He readily concedes the truth of a great many religions – and even the worth of some of their more spirited alternatives. But the common theme uniting all that he welcomes is a penchant for the transcendent.

Balking at outright essentialism, Hick pursues family resemblances. But he does single out key differences between religious and naturalistic claims: He is content with the religion of others if it puts them in touch with the Real – regardless of the stories they tell of their encounters. The real test of real contact with the Real is whether one moves forward salvifically. That is revealed in ethical practice, in goodness backed by hopes of limitless improvement. Factual disagreements can be settled in time to come (Did Christ rise? Did Muhammad ride his mount Buraq to the heavens?).[55] Moral differences are finessed. But, like Abe, Hick favors religious sentiments over their naturalistic challengers – although he sees deniers too, even the most strident, perhaps unwittingly "responding to the Real."[56]

I see some truth in that last thought, but also too welcoming a smile. Perhaps one day the Dawkinses and Dennetts will enter to scoff and remain to pray. Didn't Anthony Flew have a change of heart? Didn't Ayer as well, if only in a moment of crisis? It is spiritual imperialism of this sort that gives inclusionary thinking a bad name – even as the relativism that softens Hick's extraterritorial claims cramps the space reserved for his own surviving

---

[55] *Qur'ān* 17; *Mishkat al-Masabih*. Book 26, Chapter 23, tr. Robson, 1264–70. One cannot help recalling Hick's appeal to the hereafter in "Theology and Verification," answering the positivists' charge that religious views are unverifiable.

[56] Hick, in Hewitt, ed., *Problems in the Philosophy of John Hick*, 83.

preferences.[57] One need not travel far to find philosophers who reject the very idea of objective truth, let alone contact with reality. Truth, they charge, is just another guise of God – and claims to objectivity just a power grab. Will the scoffers, still uncleansed, be welcomed nonetheless for their forthrightness? Even their negativity, after all, may be just the quiet working of the Word. No doubt. But don't intentions matter? To evangelical spirits, the depth of any error is the surest sign of ripeness for salvation. But why pester Hume or Ayer on his deathbed? If the man's integrity is indeed God's work, should not one show a little respect and not treat critics as fellow congregants at heart? Deference quite that friendly starts to sound like an old roué trying to win back a former flame by telling her she's lovely when she's angry.

The religious dilettante prizes what the Skeptic or the Epicurean dispraises in religion: the pursuit of transcendence. The Skeptic scents on that track only dogmatism and pretensions to authority. Epicurus finds religion, generically, superstitious and impious for trying to reach up nature's skirts and manage the favor of the gods. He also finds it immoral for invoking norms beyond the inboard pull of pleasure and push of pain.[58] Skeptics scorn attempts to move beyond phenomena: Religion is dogmatic for probing beyond the evident. Epicureans cannot see the freedom that piety finds in heeding a transcendental call – just as naturalists may overlook the possibility that freedom is delegated, that human agency and creativity are gifts of the Divine.

Religious relativists, for all their protestations, are just as unfair. A love as undiscriminating as theirs is tainted by its promiscuity, betrayal of intimacy, and failure of commitment. But professions of openness are tested when persuasive definitions take hold: Poetry I hate is not real poetry; a painting that fails to edify is not real art. The beliefs you profess and the practices that animate your piety are not religious after all. If all religious beliefs are true and all religious practices sound, then every false belief and vicious practice must be nonreligious: Ritual law

---

57 See Mark Heim, *Salvations*, 30–31.
58 See Goodman, *God of Abraham*, 98.

is pharisaic, prayer is superstitious, the murderers of 9/11 were
not true Muslims. All they really hijacked was Islam.

On the contrary, bin Laden's sectaries were devoted Muslims.
Their religion really was Islam – an evil, vicious version, but
not inauthentic. Religions can have illnesses, even cancers. Some
religious practices and beliefs are genuinely evil and no less genuinely religious for that. There is bad poetry. Some music is not
just dissonant and ugly but inconsequent, trivial, or merely noisy,
yet music nonetheless. Just so, there are bad religious ideas and
vicious religious practices. Not every pass at piety attains sanctity. It is no threat to religious freedom to say so. The artist and
the seeker may pursue their visions, but freedom is no proof of
fruitfulness. With any enterprise, as Aristotle taught, there are
many ways to get it right, but far more ways to get it wrong.

The home truth about syncretism (try as it might to fuse dis-
parates in a common mold) is that ideas or practices are not
sure to harmonize just because they express what someone holds
most sacred or most dear. People have trouble enough reconciling their own aspirations. To reconcile the world's religious traditions and inclinations is a philistine's task – often procrustean,
rarely necessary. The early Buddhists who spoke of no-soul were
addressing a Hindu problematic, the vision of this world as a
tangle of self-wrought travails from which many successive lives
might not suffice to free us. Karma wove that field of force, a net
of moral gravity spun from our own acts and choices – and those
of our prior selves. Buddhism sought dissolution of that net by
branding desire, not sin, the source of suffering. Enlightenment
meant relinquishing desire, losing the specious identity that Hindus envisioned as buffeted in cycles of rebirth. Attachment was
a tar baby. Hindus, however, saw Buddhism as nihilism and
answered its seeming negativity with a skepticism of their own.

Buddhists may find it strange that Jews do not idealize letting go. Christians may find it strange that, for many a Buddhist,
immortality is neither prize nor punishment but the bastard child
of desire. Christians who find the core of spirituality lodged
between sin and salvation are often puzzled that Jews are less
concerned with afterworlds than with sanctifying life. But Jews

are bemused by the notion that religion, or even philosophy, is a response to death. Spinoza, as I have often argued, is nowhere a truer child of the Torah than when he writes, "The free man thinks least of all of death; his wisdom is a contemplation not of death but of life."[59] That thought complements Spinoza's distaste for remorse and regret. Death is not denied in the Mosaic ethos, nor are sin and redemption unimportant, but death here is not religion's theme.

There are, of course, diverse ideas of the absolute. There are also religions that dismiss the very idea. Some find the absolute everywhere, not least in the immediate. The Dharma-Body of the Buddha, as one Zen roshi told his eager novice, "is the hedge at the bottom of the garden."[60] Evangelicals preach that Christ is the way – the only way – to salvation. But salvation does not mean quite the same to Christians as it does to Hindus or to Jews. The Hebrew word that Christians read as salvation, the root of the names Jesus and Joshua, often means something more like triumph.[61] Missionaries expecting tribal people to be deeply moved by the story of Christ's passion were shocked when their hearers laughed at the Gospel narrative, calling Jesus a rebel who got what he deserved. Indians in the New World were dismayed at Puritan accounts of hell. Surely, they reasoned, preachers had invented these dispiriting tales just to frighten people into abandoning their ancestral ways.

Religions that address different questions do not directly contradict one another when they differ. That fact scours away one layer of difficulty but exposes another, since religions often differ about what matters most and what they propose to do about it. That leads to all sorts of crosstalk when differences are aired. Dismissal may sting more than disagreement. So how can we learn from each other if our concerns are different? To begin with, not everything we care about is different. Because religions seek to

---

[59] Spinoza, *Ethics* Part 4, Proposition 67.

[60] D. T. Suzuki tells the story, quoted by Aldous Huxley and repeated by R. C. Zaehner, in *Mysticism Sacred and Profane*, 5.

[61] Thus, Psalms 98:1: *Sing unto the Lord a new song, for He has done wonders. His right hand and holy arm have won Him a victory.*

corral core human values, kindred issues do arise, even if they are often framed in instructively different ways and backed by distinctive modes of argument or narrative, ritual or symbolism. The ideas of karma and sin or merit use different grips to grapple with common problems about responsibility.[62] Diverse perspectives take the light in different ways. Dialogue is possible, in part because not *every* difference is bone deep. Just as it is false and uncharitable to reduce whatever others say and do to variants of the familiar, it is misguided to assume that everything foreign is *toto caelo* inaccessible. But we do not need parallels to learn from another's commitments. There are lessons in the strengths and weaknesses of every way of life – traps to avoid, wisdom to glean. If we learn nothing from others' beliefs and practices, we have probably been incurious. But what we learn will rarely just repeat what we think we know already.

Even where we differ sharply, we can usually live and let live, acknowledging what seems vital to another or looms large in another's dreams, even if it does not just now press us with the urgency of an ultimate concern. We need not pretend that all religious differences are inauthentic. Disagreement is not discord. Peace is a lofty enough goal, one that is fortunately not dependent on unanimity or on the erasure of all genuine distinctiveness.

Romancing the Exotic

What, then, of the admiring romantic? A philosopher I know compliments another as a penetrating scholar for describing Asian culture at large, and Confucianism in particular, as "aesthetic" and "intuitive." In contrast, the West is "conceptual" and "analytic." This essentializing is not meant to be acquisitive. The intent is to lean into an admired culture and absorb values that gain charm from their exotic feel – and to urge others to find strains abroad that might be missed at home. Margaret Mead took such tactics to a high pitch. The accusatory *we* comes with the territory: All cultures are equal, but others are more equal

---

[62] See Matilal, "Karma."

than our own. *They* are natural, native, naive – better, for their innocence, in every way, save only their innocence of relativism itself.[63] Stereotypes grow rank here: For "conceptual" or "analytic," read "calculative" or "manipulative." "Intuitive" stands in for Levy Bruhl's "irrational."[64] But cultures are not monoliths. Moral and mental appraisals gain what sense they have from the experience of individual differences, leaving room, one hopes, for complexity of character and outlook, personal growth and change. When applied wholesale to cultures or ethnicities, moral and mental descriptors serve mainly as brickbats, diminishing the other by disparaging his or her kin – or admonishing one's own. In either case surface markers are made signals of cultural attributes and then of virtues and vices.

It is no tribute to diversity to set all members of a group in a single mold. Real groups teem with real differences. We do not know what someone thinks just from the color of her skin or the weave of his cape. Nor do natural languages work like axiom systems.[65] Real people shift their ground continually in the ever ongoing renegotiations of the human conversation – the nonce taxonomies of metaphor, the license of slang, the semantical requisitions of poetry, and the ready remapping of syntax in philosophy. Philosophers may strive to reconcile competing claims on credence or allegiance. But even thinkers of the same school differ profoundly in emphasis or interests, motives, outlook, rigor, and style – not to mention character, affect, and personality, where ideas come to life. Only consider the differences of Peirce, James, Dewey, and Rorty – or of Plato, Speusippus, Plotinus, Porphyry, and Proclus.

---

[63] Heim finds this kink commonly among would-be religious pluralists: "Of the vast religious diversity of the world, the pluralists affirm as fully valid only that narrow segment where believers have approximated the authors' approach to their own traditions.... those without a pluralistic understanding of their faith stand urgently in need of fulfillment and enlightenment. Without such conversion they and their traditions are at least latent threats to world peace and justice, morally dangerous as well as theologically wrong." *Salvations*, 101–2.

[64] See Lloyd, *Demystifying Mentalities*; Goodman, *In Defense of Truth*, 337–53.

[65] Goodman, *In Defense of Truth*, 107–13.

In religions harmony is a hope, continuity a portent.[66] But comity has its costs. Heresy grows from single-mindedness, from too keen a focus here that neglects God knows what elsewhere. Dogma hardens in reaction, bulldozing the hills and valleys, topping the mountain crests, and leaving behind the scars. The unities projected by doxographers draw imaginary lines of varying usefulness and perspicuity. Like isobars on the weather map, they chase constant shifts in the atmosphere. The accords of coreligionists and those discovered across confessional lines are won through conversation. But doxastic and pragmatic accommodations finesse differences. Even in formal creeds and canons, unity bespeaks compromise, not uniformity. Equilibrium in belief or practice is not static but dynamic – as it must be in any living organism or population.

Competing ideals create all sorts of eddies and crosscurrents in a culture, making homogeneity a delusion. Philosophers may broach options overlooked or newly made. Some take sides. Others try to make out a melody in the welter of voices. But any unity attained is a synthetic achievement, not a unison chorus. In any event, what seekers pursue is not always intellectual consummation. The avenues and alleyways they traverse are more often signposted with promises of salvation, privileged knowledge, moral adequacy, or spiritual growth – a taste of transcendence, inner or universal peace, enlightenment, purity, redemption, or acceptance. Long-lived and widely held religions typically offer multiple goals and a variety of meanings for their adherents. Yet the diversity within a religion does not stop insiders and observers from tagging it with a single label and the name or number of its roost in the universal dovecote.

Much the same is done with cultures, genders, language groups, and ethnicities. But a single culture, within its ragged boundaries, may harbor many sects and tongues. A single language may serve philosophers who passionately differ or studiously ignore each other's inquiries. Ethnically charged or

---

[66] See Mishnah Avot 1.1, and Ibn Daud, *The Book of Tradition*; cf. the Muslim doctrine of *ijmā*. "My community," says the *ḥadīth*, "will not agree on an error."

ideologically inflamed warfare, even genocide, afflicts the moieties of a single race or ethnicity. The combatants mark their turf, the better to discern their enemies. Even without bloodshed, ascriptive predicates fly: Women are intuitive, natives think associatively or compactly, Native Americans are in harmony with nature, Confucianists are androgynous. The labels stick like burrs – bearing sophisms useful for prejudging others. Whole cultures get the same dismissive epitomizing that confines another's identity within a factitious crystallization.

Stereotypes are readily inverted: the ugly hat clapped on cheerfully, the invidious tag proudly worn. That trick shows how loosely the masks fit, how sloppily they are made. What pins them in place is attitude. Everted stereotypes can be made glamorous. But because attitudes cannot do the work of understanding, they cannot meet the moral or intellectual needs of pluralism. An admiring sidelong glance is little better than a hasty dismissal: Both are unstable. For condescension, no matter how romantic, retains the contempt that gave it birth.

Viable Strategies

A colleague asks, "If I think Bacon wrote the works of Shakespeare and you think it was Marlowe, we do not feel compelled to go to war over this difference of opinion. Could we reach the same benign indifference with respect to religious dogmas too?" Well, I do not think warfare and indifference quite exhaust the possibilities. Besides, sectarian strife is rarely simply *over* differences in belief. Differences in doctrine and practice often mark communal boundaries fraught with further meanings, objective or ascribed. Some groups become allies; others, adversaries. The cankers can fester tragically. Faith has surely been a factor, but so have ethnicity and class, as well as the ambitions of princes, prelates, dynasts, freebooters, demagogues, and dictators.[67] To

---

[67] In *The Thirty Years War*, C. V. Wedgwood brilliantly analyzes the principals' motives, not questioning their sincerity but often exposing national hankerings, personal ambitions, and credal commitments, mingled with opportunism. Richelieu pushed France into the fray *on the Protestant side*, lest

call sectarian conflicts battles over religious dogma is simplis-
tic, mendaciously echoing an Enlightenment canard born of war
weariness. Intercommunal strife may use creeds and their ritual
embodiments in their battle cries, but a bone of contention is as
often a pretext as a cause. If there is to be a war, any mark of
difference will do to mark the ground.

Human diversity will not vanish, and we should hardly wish
it away, as some did in the 1930s, entranced by Marxian ideas.
Religious differences do stand out, given the role religions play in
canonizing values. But behind old disputes over transubstantia-
tion, say, lay issues about the power and unity of the Church, the
purity or corruption of its priests, the reach and rule of secular
authority, the conscience of the individual, and the continuity of
tradition. It would be nice to think that by now we have settled
all such issues. But it would also be arrogant.

Dismissing religious teachings as dogmas or just calling religions "faiths" reflects the Enlightenment impatience with ritual –
at least of certain types – along with much that religious symbols
stand for. But if it is pluralism we seek – a healthy mix of ways
and thoughts in an integrated society – it is a mistake to try and
forge policy from the wish that religious practices and beliefs
were not taken seriously – wishing, in effect, that religions were
not quite so religious. That is neither possible nor necessary. The
challenge for religious pluralism, like any spiritual task, begins
with ourselves: to uncouple what we hold sacred from threats of
violence and repression.

Clearly, in this age of jihad, religious warfare is not a thing
of the past. But if people defend their lives and lifeways against
mujahidun, it is misguided to say they are fighting over religion.
Most Western societies did give up that sort of battle ages ago.
Even in Ireland, where intercommunal tensions were long con-
fessionally marked, internecine warfare in time grew wearisome,
its rhetoric tedious for many who were expected to rally to its
banners or ferry its bombs. Elsewhere, too, a broad populace is

the Hapsburgs sustain their European hegemony. For the general point, see
Cavanaugh, *The Myth of Religious Violence*.

ready to recognize a diversity of beliefs and practices as worthy
of commitment by their fellows. There is public and private space
for a rich variety of symbols and observances, in limits set partly
by the very project of making room for variety.

The pathways to pluralism begin in humility. Roger Williams
argued wisely that, given humanity's fallen state, as he called it,
it is blasphemous to confuse any earthly dominion with God's
kingdom. But the seed and fruit of humility lie in recognition
of the other: Setting our sights on ultimates reminds us of our
finitude. That in turn can remind us how varied are the interests
and experiences of others and lead us to learn from those who
differ from us, adopting an openness that is too readily confused
with flaccidity. What is limp is rarely limpid.

The workable strategies for civic and civil accommodation
are what they always were. Intellectually, they rest on study and
debate. In the public sphere, they call for public discussion, study
once again, and deliberation – in a framework canted by no one
persuasion but open to the thoughts of all, receptive to divergent
values, not guiltily or slavishly but flexibly. Pluralism means that
no voice is privileged, no argument above critique.

Constitutionalism is guarantarism – a promise of protection
for human rights. Sound constitutions promote accommodation. They argue tacitly but insistently for mutual recognition.
Therefore they welcome the concrete articulation of the broad
if abstract principles they enshrine in the lives and imaginations
of diverse individuals and groups. The principles that underwrite
constitutions are not axioms, but neither can they be mere platitudes. Ideally, they capture values that are universally accessible;
they welcome broad and deep commitment and varied, nuanced
application, serving ever wider constituencies and ever larger
interests than they at first seemed to touch. The dynamic multi-
valency of higher principles should assure us that the struggle to
implement them will not, in any foreseeable future, bring an end
to politics.

Pluralism is far easier for societies than for individuals. Societies do not need to frame a single coherent outlook. A pattern
of living that allows individuals to coordinate their wants and

needs allows, even demands, a variety of lifeways. If only for
that reason, most of the choices we humans make are best left
to individuals. Communities need a pattern of interaction that
is constructive on balance. Division of labor and roles, of styles,
values, and interests is vital. So societies need freedom, social
mobility, appreciation of complementarities, and openness to the
flourishing of their constituent communities. Success in finding
that kind of equilibrium has its best gauge in the flourishing of
individuality and creativity – and not just for the few.

Does that aim demand a common value system? Yes and no,
depending in part on what is meant by a value system. In one
sense, a shared axiology is morally and politically impossible.
There will always be deep differences of vision and values. No
society has ever been utterly homogeneous; it would be tyran-
nous and impractical to try and fashion such a monster. But
much of the diversity that we humans generate is harmless to
the key aims of a state and the attainment of a common civic
and social life. There is no need for a society to cement its people into a single worldview. On a meta-level there can and must
be unity – critically, in higher order values such as the openness of society itself. Yet we do not need unanimity even here.
Still, those who reject openness *do* impede communal life, and
those who reject human growth and freedom will not make
good builders of a pluralistic society – or good candidates for
leadership.

Some of humanity's richest treasures lie in the ideals of the
world's religions. Their variegated accounts and practical artic-
ulations of what counts as love or kindness, honorable peace, or
ultimate dignity may feed rhetorical relativism. But they can also
aid insightful interpreters in finding sharable ideals. As I have
suggested, not everything that is genuinely religious is genuinely
constructive. Anger, fear, and resentment can puff themselves up
into false ideals. Irredentist agendas and vituperative ideologies
do not promote understanding. It is unwise to try to bake a pie of
such bitter fruit. Pluralism undercuts its own ideal when it bows
to the cant of intolerance, as if vice and virtue were moral equals.

Two policy implications arise as we try to draw a moral from
our deliberations:

(1) *Societies (and thus the state, as a society's chief organ) should not only tolerate but also foster religions, pluralistically and even-handedly, in view of the diverse backgrounds and penchants of their citizens – just as wise and prudent legislation seeks to foster the arts, the sciences, learning, and the professions.*

No society benefits when its people lacks character, soul, or spirit. Yet the shaping of character and the nurturing of souls are aims that the state, impersonal and devoted to a vital but rightly minimal agenda of its own, is notoriously ill equipped to pursue. I characterize the state's agenda as "minimal" not to insist that the government that governs best governs least, but because legal sanctions must be used sparingly to remain tolerable or even workable. The perfectionism that a good state fosters lies beyond its powers to define, let alone direct. That is work that individuals are best motivated and most qualified to undertake, and that communities have long and broad experience in fostering. State agencies dare not seek to pry open human hearts and tinker with the individual's highest, toughest, most intimate, and sacred task – the shaping of a life project and vision. The eleemosynary model of indirect support that our polity uses in sustaining the arts and athletic, educational, and research institutions seems most fitting here – far better than establishment, quasi-establishment, or neglect. For this democratic model allows the constituents and supporters of an undertaking to determine for themselves the extent to which and the manner in which it shall be sustained.

(2) *The same humanistic rationales that mandate support of religion also limit the manner and the means of that support.*

Public support here, like public support of the arts, athletics, education, information, recreation, and other spheres of exploration and discovery, is warranted by hopes of human flourishing. It is a mistake for states to become so entangled in spiritual and moral value judgments as to try to weigh up the relative merits of diverse spiritual paths. Openness remains the key. But, as with any law, toleration has its limits, attuned more to practice than to beliefs or attitudes, but recognizing the linkages among them.

In a just society certain ideas should not be fed and certain practices will not be permitted. To specify these ideas and practices is a legislative and judicial matter, too easily politicized or corrupted by communal or personal bias. So liberal legislation wisely draws broad safety zones around religion. There was a time when atheism was beyond the pale, partly because denial of God was widely seen (and sometimes meant) as a rejection of all responsibility. Today atheism may amount to little more than the badge of an assertive naturalism or anticlerical humanism – being morally minimalist or rebellious, metaphysically skeptical or impatient. It can be the slogan of an aggressive or destructive libertinage. But neopaganism too can assume that role. In many of its forms today atheism is not incompatible with the values that sustain societies.

The moral stringency and epistemic chastity of certain forms of atheism resonate with the theological chastity and intellectual honesty that dedicated monotheists demand of themselves when they take seriously God's rejection of bad faith and comforting rationales. Such affinities bespeak a common ground between theists and atheists, despite their many practical and speculative disagreements. The conversation across that terrain, like the ongoing dialogue between skepticism and constructive philosophy, if thoughtfully conducted, can be fruitful, and not just as a sparring floor.[68]

The questions at issue are matters that atheists and theists will continue to debate, just as theists debate the values with which they invest the idea of divinity. But the boundaries of religious toleration today are not between theism and atheism but between religions that open up the soul and those that tend to cut off its air and stymie its growth. Pluralism is of moment here, because it

[68] Cf. Ricoeur, *The Religious Significance of Atheism*, 75–77, 82–89; Masterson, *Atheism and Alienation*; Westphal, *Suspicion and Faith*; Goldmann, *The Hidden God*.

demands respect for individuals and their traditions. But the same warrant sets the limits that keeps pluralism from declining into indiscriminate endorsement or dismissal. Negativities are always to be found among the individual and communal varieties of religion – and of atheism. In an age when even venerable religious bodies can be havens of exploitation and abuse, personal wisdom and public good sense will be gauged by the success of religious and secular individuals and communities in distinguishing ways of life and thought that open windows from those that close doors.

2

Naked in the Public Square

Time was when organizers of a public meeting were happy if people checked their weapons at the door. But in the charged atmosphere of the decades since *Roe* v. *Wade*, self-described liberals may expect those who deliberate on public policy matters to check their ideas too. As Gerald Mara writes, "A number have embraced pluralism not merely as a phenomenon to be recognized within any competent practical philosophy, but also as confirmation of a deeper suspicion that concern with virtue is somehow implausible or illegitimate within political theory."[1] Behind that concern lurks the idea that pluralism itself demands that the state stay silent regarding the character of its citizenry or, indeed, any areas that touch on conscience or fundamental values. But in a democracy all citizens are members of the state, whether active or passive. From that concept stems the thought that in a democracy everyone should not just refrain from doing harm to others but also keep out of others' moral and intellectual space.

In recent years, the work of John Rawls has come to dominate much of the discourse of political theory and political philosophy for reasons not hard to understand. As Robert Nozick, a colleague and rival of Rawls's, writes,

[1] Mara, "Virtue and Pluralism," 26.

54

A *Theory of Justice* is a powerful, deep, subtle, wide-ranging, systematic work in political and moral philosophy which has not seen its like since the writings of John Stuart Mill, if then. It is a fountain of illuminating ideas, integrated together into a lovely whole. Political philosophers now must either work within Rawls's theory or explain why not.[2]

Rawls's later work has not had nearly the impact of *A Theory of Justice*, but it came at a time when many political thinkers had already arrayed themselves as acolytes, and many felt drawn to it, even where its claims qualified or modified the theses of the work that had first drawn them to him.

In that later work, Rawls sought to broaden the core ideas of *A Theory of Justice* so as to make them applicable in a diverse society where many individuals and groups may harbor values at variance with the liberal commitments he expected rational subjects to choose in founding a new society – if only they were unhampered by prior conceptions of their roles, interests, skills, and predilections. Rawls argues in *Political Liberalism* that no religious or metaphysical considerations – no ultimate commitments about truth, reality, or value – have a proper place in core public policy deliberations.[3] Assigning a special meaning to the term "political," so as to distinguish properly political matters from what seemed to him extraneous religious or cultural concerns, Rawls writes,

Political values alone are to settle such fundamental questions as: who has the right to vote, or what religions are to be tolerated, or who is to be assured fair equality of opportunity, or to hold property. Many if not most political questions do not concern those fundamental matters, for example, much tax legislation and many laws regulating property; statutes protecting the environment and controlling pollution; establishing parks and preserving wildlife areas and animal and plant species; and laying aside funds for museums and the arts. Of course, sometimes these do involve fundamental matters.[4]

That last admission leaves the door ajar: It is hard to imagine any political scenario that does not at times alight on some

---

[2] Nozick, *Anarchy State and Utopia*, 183.
[3] Rawls, *Political Liberalism*, 216–26, also *Law of Peoples*, 32.
[4] Rawls, *Political Liberalism*, 214.

fundamental concern. Nor is it easy to see how the political realm can be purged of value judgments that rest on ultimate concerns. Matters of ultimate concern are the heart of religion as committed pluralists have tended to define it, in the most generic terms they could find. And metaphysics, historically, affords the language adopted by those who wish to address ultimate values and realities in suitably nonsectarian terms. As Peter Steinberger remarks, to ask if political philosophy should be done without metaphysics is "to overlook the sense in which political claims unavoidably presuppose serious metaphysical commitments of one kind or another."[5] But Rawls tables to a date uncertain the question as to just what counts as fundamental, following up the words last quoted: "A full account of public reason would take up these other questions and explain in more detail than I can here how they differ from constitutional essentials and questions of basic justice and why the restrictions imposed by public reason do not apply to them; or if they do, not in the same way, or so strictly."[6] As Steinberger observes, Rawls seems torn between *justifying* his liberalism and avoiding metaphysical or moral affirmations, even at the cost of depriving his claims of normative foundation. On the one hand, Rawls writes,

We hope that this political conception of justice may at least be supported by what we may call an "overlapping consensus," that is, by a consensus that includes all the opposing philosophical and religious doctrines likely to persist and to gain adherents in a more or less just democratic society.[7]

But just a few pages earlier he writes, "the idea is that in a constitutional democracy the public conception of justice should be, so far as possible, independent of controversial philosophical and religious doctrines"[8] – as though no controversy were to be expected among the adherents of diverse religious traditions.

[5] Steinberger, "The Impossibility of a 'Political' Conception," 148.
[6] Rawls, *Political Liberalism*, 214–15.
[7] Rawls, "Justice as Fairness: Political not Metaphysical," 225.
[8] Ibid., 223.

Sympathetic Rawlsians rise to defend him from the charge that the constraints (and self-restraints) urged in *Political Liberalism* militate against core liberal values. They count on the dialectic Rawls hoped would yield an "overlapping consensus" to produce a realm of discourse that freely explores a wide variety of live options for open discussion and debate. But for Rawls himself the liberal commitment to free and open debate seems to be trapped against an alley wall by his fears that deliberative discussions in a democracy are inherently and implicitly coercive – because everyone in a democratic society is a ruler in some measure; and any proposal, paean or slur, might influence the formation or implementation of public policy and thus become coercive.

How, one might ask, can *any* deliberative proposal be freed from such fears? But Rawls focuses the high beams of his coerciveness thesis on proposals that he deems sectarian. Genuinely moral suasions, presumably, should always find an open forum, but they must be sharply set apart from the properly political realm where policy is framed and laws and regulations hammered out. The difficulty with this separation of the moral from the political is twofold. First, in a litigious (and individualistic!) society like our own, it is often hard to draw a firm line between moral urgings and policy proposals. Beyond that, law has a tendency (not least in a liberal and consumerist society) to trump morality – as witness today's debates about gay marriage, gambling, abortion, no-fault divorce, and many other socially fraught issues: Legality is widely taken not just to establish a minimal societal norm but also to create an unanswerable social license. Even to dissent from the public relations cause du jour is to brand oneself a bigot. Political correctness does the coercing, whether subtly through self-censorship or more overtly by the kind of silencing that presses a presumptive liberal agenda "all the way down." Rawls's proposal compounds the chilling effect by invoking social pressures and fashions to mute appeals to religious values or metaphysical commitments in the public forum or at the ballot box, the ultimate seat of democratic authority and last refuge of political conscience and consciousness.

Rawls bundles together in limbo the views he deems religious or metaphysical under the general rubric of "comprehensive doctrines." A comprehensive doctrine, he writes, is one that "aspires to cover all of life." As he explains, "if it's a religious doctrine, it talks about our relation to God and the universe" and "has an ordering of all the virtues, not only political virtues but moral virtues as well, including the virtues of private life."[9] A secular comprehensive doctrine, he adds, is similarly overbroad. The disheartening presumption: We cannot really debate politically about the impact on our public lives of what we take to be ultimates. Coming from a philosopher, that sounds like throwing in the towel. But Rawls and others have greater concerns about deliberation than the search for truth.[10] In a democracy, Rawls argues, citizens must anchor their political activity and ground their political speech solely on what their fellow citizens would find reasonable:

> Some might say that the limits of public reason apply only in official forums and so only to legislators, say, when they speak on the floor of parliament, or to the executive and the judiciary in their public acts and decisions. . . . But this does not go far enough.[11]

The limits Rawls sets apply in other arenas as well. For, as he argues, democracy "implies an equal share in the coercive political power that citizens exercise over one another by voting and in other ways."[12] So all speech aiming to steer public policy,

9 Rawls, interview with Bernard Prusak.
10 Comparable views have been urged by Charles Larmore, Bruce Ackerman, Amy Gutman, Thomas Nagel, Lawrence Slocum, and Gerald Gaus.
11 Rawls, *Political Liberalism*, 217.
12 Ibid., 217–18. In *Religious Convictions in Liberal Politics*, Christopher Eberle parses Rawls's objection, dividing the moral issue of respect for fellow citizens from questions of coercion: One may respect one's fellows, he argues, even if one coerces them, as governance may require. But Rawls treats advocacy and even reason-giving in political deliberations as inherently coercive, perhaps confounding coercion with what he finds dogmatic in religious and metaphysical discourse. By dwelling on Europe's religious wars he exacerbates the confusion. As in his avowed intent of breathing new life into the social contract ideal, Rawls seems here to re-fight Locke's battles rather than focus on today's intercommunal concerns. See his interview with Bernard Prusak.

Rawls argues, is ultimately coercive; even voting is not "a private and personal matter." Therefore, a proper self-censorship against appeals to standards not universally deemed reasonable should extend even to one's motives[13]: "Ideally, citizens are to think of themselves *as if* they were legislators and ask themselves what statutes, supported by what reasons satisfying the criterion of reciprocity, they would think most reasonable to enact."[14]

Yet proposals are not legislation, and reasoning, even when compelling, is not coercive in the way that laws are. Rawls seems almost to brand as unfair any appeal to thoughts that others do not already hold. He fights shy of asking everyone to reach identical conclusions, but insists we invoke only grounds that all citizens will find reasonable. What people find reasonable, however, is often what sounds familiar. So, proposals grounded in considerations that might seem novel, revolutionary, even eye-opening can be ruled out of court.[15]

But has Rawls not breached his own standard by urging ground rules for public discourse that many might find unreasonable? His own claims have hardly escaped controversy.[16] Plenty of people find pragmatic or secularist rationales downright offensive. And if political speech is inherently coercive, won't *any* rationale, whether or not it appeals to ultimate concerns, prove coercive implicitly, its blandness hiding an iron fist in a vinyl glove? Isn't some comprehensive notion implicit in any effort to

[13] Rawls, *Political Liberalism*, 214.
[14] Rawls, *Law of Peoples*, 56.
[15] Peter Jones wonders if Rawls's idea of reasonable pluralism is not "disappointingly narrow," perhaps "effective only for those who are already all but converts." Shouldn't "a liberalism worth its salt," he asks, "have something to say to those who are not already disposed to accept it"? "Two Conceptions of Liberalism," 530.
[16] Linda Hirshman writes, "Rawls explains that some people do not endorse justice as fairness because they have other viewpoints and experiences. But his only explanation for people's failure to coalesce around justice as fairness is a list of the opportunities for reasonable people to err. This point seems to weaken seriously his claim to eschew a universal metaphysics of personhood, because disagreements can be explained as the product of error only if all right-thinking people in the relevant human group should agree on his philosophy." "Is the Original Position Inherently Male-Superior?" 1867.

distinguish what shall or shall not be deemed political, religious, or metaphysical, or reflective or unreflective of a "reasonable consensus"?[17] As Richard Bellamy and Martin Hollis ask, "Can a 'political' theory of justice rely on its own bootstraps?"[18]

It is not just in democracies that citizens become complicit in state actions. We are all involved in the public acts we condone. But most speech and advocacy are not state actions. They do not carry official clout, and it seems repressive to treat them as if they did. We cannot deliberate if we do not share and air our views – or deliberate honestly and effectively if we do not lay our cards on the table and spell out our reasons. Naturally it is obnoxious to have dogmas drummed into one's head or to be bombarded with symbols one cannot revere. Such treatment is exclusionary and invidious. Nor is it enough to hope that prudent advocates will spurn parochial appeals. History, including recent history, teaches all too bitterly that chauvinism can win a mass following.

But hasn't Rawls's argument proved both too little and too much? His quarrel in *Political Liberalism* is not with hate speech or public erasure, but with the very utterance of religious or philosophical ideas in the public square. Isn't there a bias showing if we, say, silence arguments against gay marriage that appeal to scripture but permit arguments for gay rights that hold sexual relations to be purely a private matter? Both suasions lean on something like an outlook on life. Is one to be silenced in the public square and the other, well scrubbed in secularity, to be

---

[17] Rawls calls his program "political" and "practical," not metaphysical or epistemological: "it presents itself not as a conception of justice that is true, but one that can serve as a basis of informed and willing political agreement between citizens viewed as free and equal persons. . . . To secure this agreement we try, so far as we can, to avoid disputed philosophical, as well as disputed moral and religious, questions." "Justice as Fairness: Political not Metaphysical," 230. Rawls seems to be trapped in a dilemma: whether to sustain the claim to argue normatively or to sustain the pose of skirting ultimate questions of value or fact – or even questions of what counts as such. Compare his efforts to disengage "moral theory" from moral philosophy, epistemology, and theory of meaning in "The Independence of Moral Theory."

[18] Bellamy and Hollis, "Liberal Justice: Political and Metaphysical," 1–19.

welcomed for its universality?[19] Will we need tribunals to determine which views are comprehensive or likely to seem reasonable to all?

Rawls proposes no philosophical thought police. To prejudge arguments even before they are framed would surely smack of censorship. Rawls's standards seem intended to kick in more on a social than a legal plane. But that makes their impact contingent on the vagaries of moral fashion and the niceties of sophisticated PR campaigns.[20] The standards are still stifling. The holy grail

---

[19] Rawls writes, "I assume all citizens to affirm a comprehensive doctrine to which the political conception they accept is in some way related. But a distinguishing feature of a political conception is that it is presented as free standing and expounded apart from, or without reference to, any such wider background," *Political Liberalism* (2005), 12. The concession, meant to be generous, permits, indeed presumes *inner* commitment to some comprehensive doctrine, but holds fast in reprehending a *public* appeal to any such view. But the surgery proposed belies the nexus of thought to speech critical in commitment, persuasion, and indeed in working out many a new idea. It also ignores the trouble one might have proposing policy ideas without reference to one's core values and sincere beliefs.

[20] Rawls co-signed a "Philosophers' Brief" to the Supreme Court in 1997 supporting physician-assisted suicide. How one lives out one's last days, it argued, should be a personal choice, not dictated by religious or philosophical authorities. Cass Sunstein took exception (*Arizona State Law Journal*, Summer, 1997), citing the controversy provoked by *Roe v. Wade*. Premature Court action, he wrote, could be counterproductive. Rawls called this pragmatic suasion a good argument: One could see sense in the claim that "things would have gone better" had the Court "let the debate play out a bit more," rather than stir up a hornet's nest. Rawls might differ, but he could see Sunstein's point (see his interview with Prusak). As in judicial arguments that hinge on "evolving moral standards" about capital punishment or "community standards" about obscenity, what Rawls acknowledged was a tactical point. But for Rawls the key issue was avoidance of some strong claim about the rights and wrongs of the issue itself. Generalizing, he wrote, "What's important is that people give the kinds of reasons that can be understood and appraised apart from particular comprehensive doctrines: for example, that they argue against physician-assisted suicide not just by speculating about God's wrath or the afterlife." Rawls's examples here drip with sarcasm and paint as rednecks those who might differ with him about the most appropriate conclusion. Michael Walzer's worries that legalized assisted suicide might harm the vulnerable passed scrutiny, perhaps because they raised questions of the indirect effects on others not party to a particular life terminating decision. But Rawls ultimately found Walzer's concerns uncompelling. Appeals to the inherent

here is overlapping consensus. But what folks find reasonable is often driven by their hopes or fears about where a claim might lead, not just thoughts of where it arises. Is polity even possible without dialogue? And is dialogue possible when people may not freely speak their minds about what matters most to them? Richard John Neuhaus puts his finger on the problem at the very origins of Rawls's project:

> Rawls's way of establishing a normative concept of justice contradicts almost every part of the definition of law offered earlier. Law, it was suggested, is the historical, living process of people legislating, adjudicating, administering, and negotiating the allocation of rights and duties. But Rawls's people behind the veil are, in fact, non-persons. They have no history, no tradition, no vested interests, no self-knowledge, no loves, no hates, no fears, no dreams of transcendent purpose or duty. Living persons are distinguished by partiality, by passion, by particularity.[21]

The veil of ignorance was a way of prescinding from such identity-framing, identity-voicing concerns. William Galston caps the point: "It is difficult to imagine that any liberal democracy can sustain conscientious support if it tells millions of its citizens that they cannot rightly say what they believe as part of democratic public dialogue."[22]

Does a liberal society silence public expression of the deepest convictions of its members or of the views that those members expect to resonate most deeply in hearts they hope to win over? To invoke social pressure to limit the range of values to which advocacy might appeal is in effect to squelch thought, speech, and action in ways inherently abhorrent to the liberal dispensation. One may hope that such efforts fall flat, as they often do when confronting deeply held values, but one may also observe that conformity has often aroused and intensified just such pressures.

In titling his book and its program *Political Liberalism*, Rawls redirects the word "liberal" away from urging a generic openness

---

worth or sanctity of each human life, on the other hand, were sectarian and dogmatic.

[21] Neuhaus, *The Naked Public Square*, 257–58.

[22] William Galston, *Liberal Pluralism*, 116.

to independent and diverse thought and expression, making it instead a brand name to be stamped on the varieties of political correctness that shifting fashions will repeatedly redefine as they set the parameters of what shall be accounted reasonable. Like many a reaction, Rawls's secularizing, anti-philosophical steed rears and wheels here into excesses at least as parlous as those that spooked the rider.

Even as regards the state alone, as distinguished from its people, Rawls overrides his goal. It is true that states govern unjustly when they pursue sectarian ends. But Rawls asks for more than nonsectarianism: He insists that the state in no way favor any one comprehensive doctrine over another.[23] Yet some doctrines are wholesome, others palpably evil. Should governments stand neutral and hold aloof among *all* such views and ways, including those that promote hatred, violence, and bigotry? Wouldn't a state that remains cool to all questions and decisions about the good life effectually abdicate its responsibility? Isn't a liberal state false to its charge if it stands so aloof from core value questions that its citizens are left unable to exercise the very freedoms that are its raison d'etre? Just as negative liberties are empty without the material means to exercise them, so is the rejection of paternalism a bitter charade in a society that fails to cultivate capacities for choice. Independent judgment is a mockery in a body of addicts or alcoholics. A populace in thrall to illiteracy, xenophobia, sexual abuse, or superstition – whether by design or by neglect – will find no more meaning in the franchise than the pauper with the same perfect right as the plutocrat to sleep under the bridges of Paris.

Rawls may call his program liberal, but it breeches the core liberal maxim – that individuals be free to choose (and voice!) the grounds of their own choices. Rawls sees a duty, even in the voting booth, to bracket motives not deemed reasonable by one's fellows. His ideal, he admits, may seem strictly to apply to High Court rulings. But the underlying duty, he insists, binds us all, *workably* and in practice, much as the procedural restraints on

[23] Rawls, *Political Liberalism*, 193.

testimony and evidence bind one in a court of law. But isn't the
glory of liberalism the welcome it accords to diversity – including
dissent? Are we utterly to abandon Aristotle's ancient thought
that what makes freedom most precious is the opportunity to
deliberate about the common course?

The alchemy Rawls uses to transmute inner motives, hopes,
and words into public acts rests on his claim that in democracies
it is no monarch but *we* who are the state. Mill's sense of the
power of social pressures pushes the point further, casting as
public discourse even reflections far removed from official policy
deliberations. Granted we should shun not just libel but gossip
and not just censorship but censoriousness. But, as Rawls would
have it, we can injure the social compact even by what we cherish
among our innermost beliefs and purposes. Value schemes that
make, say, honor, altruism, or the public interest paramount are
especially problematic. For Rawls calls on reason to adjudicate
value disputes. But his fear is that rival views of reason's dicta
and its worth may subvert the quest for comity. So, with a bow
toward pluralism and a tip of the hat to the home team, he turns
to culture in his quest for unity:

we assume that all citizens have a rational plan of life that requires for
its fulfillment roughly the same kind of goods. . . . This assumption is of
great importance for it enormously simplifies the problem of finding a
workable index of primary goods. Without restrictive assumptions of
this kind, the index problem is known to be insoluble.[24]

The proposed common denominator here would be money, a
huge stipulation that is made even more striking against the backdrop of Rawls's concession to the notion that the incommensurability of values renders mutual accommodation of disparate goals
in principle impossible. But even confining the issue to material
goods does not help as much as Rawls imagines. For his redistributive norms have hardly generated the kind of consensus he
sought. As Nozick writes,

[24] Ibid., 180–81, n. 8.

If things fell from heaven like manna, and no one had any special entitlement to any portion of it, and unless all agreed to a particular distribution no manna would fall, and somehow the quantity varied depending on the distribution, then it is plausible to claim that persons placed so that they couldn't make threats, or hold out for specially large shares, would agree to the difference principle rule of distribution.[25]

Beyond that, despite its usefulness in equilibrating deserts, few would make money the sole medium and measure of public or private good. Some would place health or education or artistic virtuosity or athletic prowess ahead of income and many another index of well-being. Rawls does broaden his horizon. He includes education, access to public office, and indeed free speech among the goods to be prioritized. These items are constitutive in the liberal canon. But the values held paramount more widely are more diverse. Some privilege simplicity or ecological minimalism or biodiversity, values that may be incommensurate with one another and with those on Rawls's pedestal. All of these goods may compete. And the essence of politics, as we learn from Plato, is adjudication of such conflicts, decision making about how to reconcile and prioritize incommensurate goods – those of appetite, spirit, and reason, say. Justice means making the necessary choices fairly and rightly.

The ideals of piety or learning, humility or self-sacrifice, scientific discovery and artistic creativity and expression have no common measure. Only consider the conflicts of conservationists with animal rights advocates. Individual differences loom large even in the tightest community, and in any real society there are deep group differences as well. There is politics even in a family. Even couples must work out their a way of living together, so all the more so, do the people of a good-sized society. That is why pluralism is a reality that every real state must address. Rawls presumes that life plans may be chosen once the core decisions have been made behind the veil of ignorance. But he assumes that rational choosers would agree on the most basic priorities, giving *lexical* priority to liberty above other goods, agreeing about

[25] Nozick, "Distributive Justice," 95.

what liberty must and must not mean, and accepting like standards about what other goods and ills matter and to what degree. The deliberators of the original position, he assumes, will even agree on the difference principle.

These assumptions, and the posit of a "closed society," its members born into citizenship,[26] turn Rawls's model brittle, exposing its deepest fault: Rawls has canonized a hierarchy of values as elements in a mathematical system.[27] He has drawn up his periodic table of those elements by assaying the nods and frowns of those around him – or those among them whom he finds most reasonable. His stunning turn to the image of a closed society mirrors the airtight cells of the artificial languages in which twentieth-century logicists once imagined they could capture what matters in the living reality of thought and what was worth preserving from the open universe of values – all held fast forever in the amber of canonical, but virtual, systems. The polarized light – here called the light of reason – seemed to shine from within the formal structure of the very idea of law and the symmetries of the crystal latticework of logic.[28] But the unity Rawls finds is stipulative, an artifact of the terms and tools of his analysis, a Whiggish simulacrum, viewed through the loupes of a carefully coopted college of cardinals.

The artificial languages of philosophical logicians mimic the mathematical models of their economist and game theorist colleagues. Formalism was the psilocybin of the mid-twentieth

---

[26] Rawls, *Political Liberalism*, 12.

[27] Cf. Onora O'Neill, *Bounds of Justice*, 170.

[28] Rawls seems drawn to Lon Fuller's view, which he sums up as affirming that "substantive and formal justice go together and therefore that at least grossly unjust institutions are never, or at any rate rarely, impartially and consistently administered." *A Theory of Justice* (1999) 52, citing Fuller's *The Morality of Law*, Chapters 2 and 4. Uniformity, Rawls argues, protects justice by way of "justice as regularity." Rawls does not reduce justice to uniformity. He readily envisions a despotism that skews its rulings "to advance the interests of a dictator or the ideal of a benevolent despot" (208). But he does not place high among his concerns the possibility of a uniformly administered but inherently unjust system of rules. Unwillingness to invoke metaphysical principles such as human dignity may lead him to set more store in uniformity than formal principles alone would warrant.

century, and many an able mind journeyed so deep into the dreams of some closed system as proudly to sever all ties to experience, cutting off economics from psychology or psychology from awareness. Rawls dispenses with the ciphers of symbolic logic and backgrounds the devices of abstract economics, but the formalism persists. Justice has become the product rather than a precondition of agreement.[29]

Feted for reviving normative political philosophy from its post-positivist catatonia, Rawls candles the yield of his thought experiment against what "we" mean by "justice" – as if linguistic analysis had finally proved its worth in settling moral disputes or answering moral skeptics. Small wonder, if usage be the test and the *we* supply the norm, that prescriptivity so readily collapses into local standards or dissolves into appeals to personal intuitions. Rawls skates past the postmodern charge that *we* can be the most vexed word in any narrative.

The intuition Rawls builds on in *Political Liberalism* springs from Ronald Dworkin's case against state favor for any comprehensive doctrine. In the background are familiar words about separating politics from religion – not an intuition universally shared. In fact, as Philip Hamburger has shown, the separation doctrine stands on slippery footing even where it is best known, in the United States.[30] The original demand, written into the Bill of Rights, was for nonestablishment (sometimes, disestablishment) of religion. But some nineteenth- century secularists, seconded by anticlerical and anti-Catholic nativists, launched the notion that the Constitution sets a "wall" of separation (Jefferson's image in a letter to the Baptists of his day) between church and state. That thought begat the notion that any state acknowledgment or sustenance of religion (appointment of legislative chaplains, allocation of funds to confessional colleges, vouchers for religious schooling) runs afoul of the Constitution. But Rawls masks this genealogy, as if he were simply deducing his exclusion from the logic of democracy. The effect is less to guide than to obviate the

---

[29] See Goodman, *On Justice*, 14–15, 24–26, 38.
[30] See Hamburger, *Separation of Church and State*.

tough calls about state interactions with religion that we typically assign to jurists. Blanket formulae sweep the ground, leaving only "neutrality of aim": The state and its rulers (all of us in a democracy) must not take sides as to the goals of human life.[31] "Beyond the requirements already described," Rawls writes, "justice as fairness does not seek to cultivate the distinctive virtues and values of the liberalisms of autonomy and individuality, or indeed of any other comprehensive doctrine."[32] That may seem a backhand slap to libertarianism, but Dewey too might get caught by the same sweeping gesture.

Rejecting the ancient idea of public concern for the ethos, Rawls leaves his proposed society fair game to any influences that may play or prey upon it. So, in the name of liberalism, he clears the decks of all but the most self-serving projects – be they commercial, or political, or even sectarian – if dressed in clothing plain enough to pass for neutral or exotic enough to look nonsectarian. He bolsters his neutrality ideal with a thought from Joseph Raz: The state must do nothing to promote a particular idea, unless acting to cancel or counterbalance the effect.[33] The proviso is redolent of Rawls's notions of compensatory justice: The state, then, does get into the ethos business – but only correctively.

Consider what is excluded then. One might think public education a public good for enhancing individuals' prospects of achieving worthwhile aims and enlarging their experience and capacity to aid and understand others. But a legislator who hopes to promote such ends or even a citizen at a town meeting who urges such designs is promoting a specific view of the human good. So, perhaps, is one who campaigns against smoking, alcoholism, gambling, drug abuse – or incest, pederasty, or polygamy. Public education, public libraries and parks, may be valued as means to make us freer, richer, more competitive, or more equal – but these values are not universally shared and respected. Must

[31] Rawls, *Political Liberalism*, 193–200.
[32] Ibid., 200.
[33] Ibid., 193.

the government stay out of such affairs and democratic citizens keep silent about the merits of the case?

The promise that education might help us grow wiser would seem, now, permissible only for private schools. No such motives could be urged in public fora. Health care aiming to make us safer, saner citizens or better parents – and public programs to build and staff playgrounds, concert halls, or museums, if aiming to help us grow more cooperative, communicative, or cultured, more sensitive to the world and each other – would be left to the private sector. But even there, attempts to serve a public good would be suspect. For even charitable foundations in a democracy like ours are indirectly subsidized through the tax exemptions they enjoy. And taxes are compulsory.[34]

Rawls does offer to limit his constraints to "constitutional essentials" and "questions of basic justice," such as voting rights, equal opportunity, property rights, and religious tolerance. That is no negligible concession, and it is critical to Rawls's distinction of properly political deliberation from illicit appeals to comprehensive doctrines.[35] But does his line of demarcation hold? In a money economy like ours, where revenues are fungible or in a litigious society like that of ancient Athens, or in any society

---

[34] Answering this concern, Rawls seems almost to walk back his severest restraints, but he reinstates them in the end: "public funds for the arts and sciences may be provided through the exchange branch. In this instance there are no restrictions on the reasons citizens may have for imposing upon themselves the requisite taxes. They may assess the merits of these public goods on perfectionist principles, since the coercive machinery of government is used in this case only to overcome the problems of isolation and assurance, and no one is taxed without his consent. The criterion of excellence here does not serve as a political principle; and so, if it wishes, a well ordered society can devote a sizable fraction of its resources to expenditures of this kind. But while the claims of culture can be met in this way, the principles of justice do not permit subsidizing universities and institutes, or opera and the theater, on the grounds that these institutions are intrinsically valuable, and that those who engage in them are to be supported even at some significant expense to others who do not receive compensating benefits. Taxation for these purposes can be justified only as promoting directly or indirectly the social conditions that secure the equal liberties and as advancing in an appropriate way the long-term interests of the least advantaged." *A Theory of Justice* (1999), 291–92.

[35] Rawls's interview with Prusak; *Political Liberalism*, 214.

where rights matter and precedence counts – in any human society, then – it is easy and natural to trace claims to fundamental principles. That is what appellate lawyers do. Christmas trees in the mall, flag burning, lap dancing, school prayer, blood transfusions, exorcisms, health care – all have been claimed as basic rights. It is not just abortion that has been made a constitutional issue. So has the "taking" of property by condemnation *and* regulation; so have "unfunded mandates," the Pledge of Allegiance, security cameras, and traffic stops by state police. The Constitution reaches out and touches seatbelt design and distribution, toys, ladders, scaffolding, automobiles, food labels, drug and cosmetic testing, voter identification, the composition of college athletic teams, educational test design, and health insurance.

Gun rights were a constitutional issue from the founding of the United States, linked not to hunting or personal protection but to the Lockean right of revolution. It is hard to think of any contested issue, from T-shirts with a message to the commitment of the mentally ill, that has not been made a constitutional issue. The more detailed the law, the more ardent the protest. Alcohol earned two constitutional amendments: one for prohibition, another for repeal. Is government financing of sex-change surgery a basic right? Is medical marijuana? Many say it is. Others object when tax dollars are spent on highways or dams – or even on tax collection. Can the environment be protected or public security maintained without the prospect of encroaching on what someone will deem a basic right? Can any law be drafted without raising fundamental questions about the aims and goals of those who will live under it and foot the bill?

Access to restrooms, drinking fountains, buses, and lunch rooms is rightly recognized as a basic right. Same-sex marriage is claimed as well, under the Equal Protection Clause. From prescription costs to tenant relations, disabled access, working conditions, prison crowding, and affirmative action, it is hard to find an area where claims are not called basic rights. Do we share a firm, clear way of drawing a line to contain the category? It cannot be done a priori. That would call for a "comprehensive" doctrine. Litigation has its own dynamic, expanding rights claims to ever new categories – rights for animals and even trees. I prefer to speak of deserts here and to seek their equilibration, rather than make all claims trumps and hunker down for a battle royal over the conflicts of rights that partisans find natural and trial lawyers profitable. But my belief that conflicts can be resolved equitably, that tragedy is not inevitable, and that politics is more than sheer struggle reflects core ideas about justice, truth, and equity unrecognized by lobbyists – elements, no doubt, of a comprehensive doctrine.

Before signing on to Rawls's stipulations we need to ask if we are content that the only arguments acceptable in behalf of public libraries, public education, public parks, or public art must appeal to purely instrumental goods. Good schools, it is said, make good citizens or useful employees; "good citizen" usually means law abiding. Yet good education is not the goal. The state should have no truck with perfectionist schemes aiming to foster the emergence of good persons, of free and thoughtful, independent-minded, sensitive human beings. Such goals are too parochial – but equal access remains a common good, construed by Rawls as the high road to higher status.

Can liberals afford to spurn the Aristotelian idea, taken up by many religions and ideologies, that public institutions are made (and tolerated) because of their help in humanizing human life? Doesn't excluding that idea in effect ban every public effort toward a public good? Without some notion of human worth and some way of fleshing out that notion with open-minded, open-ended visions of the varieties of human fulfillment, does not public policy risk laying all the good that societies can achieve at the feet of some diffuse or impersonal end such as profit – succumbing piecemeal to the sensate but now sacrosanct campaigns of hucksters and healers, with their shiny trays of goods and services and their ersatz ideals from insularity and parochialism to polyandry and eugenics?

Parents, in Rawls's moral world, may pursue the educational ends they choose – but in private schools, and only if the children are not kept ignorant of "their constitutional and civic rights so that, for example, they know that liberty of conscience exists in their society and that apostasy is not a legal crime."[36] That lawyer language paints education as a battle zone or a brig, where intellectual freedom is a right of extreme resort, like habeas corpus, not a lived reality. But surely not every effort to instill values is narrowing, dogmatic, and coercive. Will a curriculum designed to foster critical and creative thinking be excluded from public institutions if its aims and means are framed on premises about what constitutes a wholesome and fulfilling life for well-rounded human beings? Can even the narrower goals of "good citizenship" or marketable job skills escape condemnation, since even such pallid hopes preserve assumptions about human worth and potential? Are minimal and pragmatic expectations any less tendentious and pretentious, any less particularistic?

Many rival claims are made on our public educational and recreational resources. The claims for public support of varsity sports are bolstered by avowals that participation promotes *both* competition and team spirit. Title IX may be devoured by the budgetary demands of football, leaving few resources for fencing, wrestling, or lacrosse. Music and the arts may languish. But Rawls seems, willy-nilly, committed to condemn campaigns for the return of arts education or the preservation of athletic access, if their appeal is to any broad notion of the whole person or the good life. Partiality fares better. There is a seemingly insatiable market for exhibition sports, bingo, beer, or pot. Museums, nature preserves, research institutes, or medals in mathematics, history, or literature may not fare as well as online poker and porn. But woe betide the advocate who says national parks do more for the human spirit or for biodiversity than taxpayer-subsidized arenas. That claim rests on a comprehensive doctrine,

---

[36] Rawls, *Political Liberalism*, 199. Rawls seems ambivalent toward what he sees as the aims of education on Mill's or Kant's account: fostering autonomy and individuality. Does such an education promote a "comprehensive doctrine"? Political liberalism, he writes, "requires far less." Yet Rawls does expect education to "encourage the political virtues," so that students will "want to honor the fair terms of social cooperation in their relations with the rest of society." The liberalism that Rawls finds in Kant or Mill seems more worthy of the name. Education on his view smacks of indoctrination.

and the alternatives can be justified for providing employment. What business has the state in favoring intellectual or cultural goals or wilderness areas? Is compensatory support the due of any alternative vision – grants for graffiti, subsidies for those who would love to play the horses but lack the cash to place a meaningful bet? Recompense will not suffice if it only enables alternatives: It must negate the impact of rival programs. Otherwise, state power has been abused.

Legislators might imagine that day care centers help open up children's potentials and free parents to pursue vocational or educational goals, or simply offer a respite from the demands of child care. Affordable day care can diminish the incidence of child abuse. But policy decisions on that score involve assumptions about what kind of child care is optimal and, indeed, about what might count as fulfillment for parents and their children. Such issues can be controversial. Some people think preschools a positive evil. Can citizens in a democracy deliberate and state their mind about such matters – or about divorce law, or universal national service, or welfare policy – without breaching neutrality? Can we really come together to legislate in the public interest without asking what matters and what should count as a human good?

Despite the rhetoric about reflective equilibrium, it does no good to punt downfield toward "the" culture. Our society houses many cultures, and there are many subcultures in any modern society. There are also many individuals who do not fit the familiar norms that others might use in describing their cultural groups, as well as many whose commitments are unformed or formative. So it does not settle matters to appeal to "our" intuitions, as if they were coherent, uniform, fixed, and dispositive. We humans often differ on value questions, and we may be open to new values and ideas – or a rehearing of old, rediscovered, redefined, or reappropriated ideas. Many of us may expect to profit by hearing one another out, and not just in ways we might have thought rational in advance. But Rawls presumes a static society. He has moved away from Dewey's vision of society as a laboratory, lost confidence in Mill's marketplace of ideas and experiments in living. Above all, he has lost sight of Bergson's hope for an open society.

Where do basic rights find their limit? Would some standard help in defining real differences between, say, injustice and inconvenience? Would some notion of what Norbert Wiener once called the human use of human beings be of use? Conversation might help us justify our "intuitions" to one another – or make better sense of them ourselves. But Rawls rules out such talk in public deliberations. Do game parks that bar aboriginal peoples from their native lands and burial grounds raise questions of basic human rights? Do property rights intersect pollution standards in ways that demand value choices? How are we, as a society, to deal with our thoughts about gender in the military? Presumptively? Can we know the legal rights of Branch Davidians or Scientologists or Jehovah's Witnesses, without asking what should count as a spiritual discipline – or a free choice?

Rawls expects deliberations in a democracy to involve open and equal engagement among its citizens. But he takes back with one hand more than he gives with the other. Wouldn't the exclusion of appeals to religious and metaphysical ideas block appeals to basic rights themselves, unless couched in terms already deemed reasonable?[37] Dialogue that could do us any good in seeking answers or accommodations on vexed issues does not just tell us what we think we already know. New arguments may sound odd at first, especially to those who judge a premise by the conclusion they expect. Fruitful reasoning is often ampliative: It opens our minds to the demands of values we may hold, but perhaps do not hold close enough – or it proposes values we ought to hold. How can it do so without treading on the ground Rawls fences off as the abode of comprehensive ideas?

I think we need *more* appeal to principle in our public moments and a bit less of the assumption that appeals to interests are *eo ipso* legitimate. The philosopher in me would not mind hearing something more, in public policy deliberations, about the groundings of our values. That is what Rawls is striving to

[37] Ibid., 217.

avoid. The equation of justice with the bartering of interests is itself a comprehensive view, but one that obstructs an opening to higher order values that might help conciliate value conflicts or integrate competing interests in some larger good. But it is hard to point out how it can do so if we are not to talk about what makes a good larger.

Moralities, like cultures, are not axiom systems. What was a premise here becomes an inference elsewhere. Real people are much more ad hoc and shifting in outlook than the tintype belief systems, mentalities, and paradigms that some anthropologists construct or philosophers imagine. The thinking of real people is much more open textured and receptive. Debate may unsettle or reconfigure the outlines and color masses of the value map. The landscape of our values, if it could be painted, would not be painted by the numbers. Thoughtful people, free to think for themselves, find all sorts of ideas relevant to the basic issues of democratic governance, but not just as preconcerted moves in a preset game. As they frame their thoughts they may well draw on tradition or lapse into metaphor or mysticism. I would not call the effort to restrain them liberalism.

I cannot quite see how appeals to principle are coercive. Nor do I see any better place for principles than in deliberations. They are needed there, and public deliberations can give them down-to-earth concreteness. It seems bizarre to expect consensus about what is reasonable and to make that expectation the welcome mat of argument, unless reason is diluted to the point of platitude. Even then, consensus is unlikely. Some of us hate platitudes and find mossy nostrums equivocal and vague – and only problematically linked to concrete plans of action. For me even the approach of unanimity sets off warning bells about the sacrifices, logical and physiological, expected to achieve it. Creative deliberation needs lateral thinking and may invoke opinions as yet unheard and unheard of. Complacency is as much an enemy of freedom as coercion, and far more insidious in a democracy.

Rawls does have standards of the reasonable. He knows that political cultures differ. So he calls on thinkers to delve into the culture they inhabit and "unfold" its distinctive features, helping smooth out the overlapping consensus that the reasonable can be expected to endorse. Nicholas Wolterstorff elegantly captures the silliness that results:

The thought, I take it, is this: it would be absurd to require of us that we never choose or advocate a policy unless everybody agrees with us on that policy. Rather, it is the *reasons* for our decisions and advocacies that we must attend to.... As to those reasons, it would again be asking too much to require that we use only those reasons that everybody *in fact* accepts.... all that can be required is that we confine ourselves to reasons *that it is reasonable of us to believe* would be generally accepted.... it cannot be all our fellow citizens whose acceptance is critical. There will be some among them who are not reasonable on the issue....

In short, the reasons that one must use in deciding and discussing political issues are reasons about which it is reasonable for one to believe that they would be accepted by all those of one's fellow citizens who are reasonable on the issue.[38]

The gaping hole that Wolterstorff touches here is the old fallacy of presuming agreement among right-thinking persons. Those who differ are just unreasonable! Rawls has tried for a field goal by shifting from matters of policy to epistemic regions, where he hopes to find kindred spirits. But just as litigators regularly find basic rights to shore up their instant claims, persons who differ about policy often differ over epistemic issues too. Ideas too are fungible. Any democracy large enough to confront constitutional questions will harbor advocates skilled in making almost any stand sound reasonable or at least consonant with a broad consensus of familiar views.

In pub philosophy brawls, *"That's a value judgment!"* used to be a conversation stopper. But in policy deliberations, value terms are signposts marking the places where debate should start. Rawls's demand for reasonable debate among reasonable people puts a new twist into the veil of ignorance and gives a new spin to the old positivist worry about value judgments. Such judgments now seem to be okay – but only so long as they are "reasonable." I have three problems with Rawls's proposal:

---

[38] Wolterstorff, in Audi and Wolterstorff, *Religion in the Public Square*, 93–95.

(1) It impoverishes debate. The obvious snag is Mill's argument, the familiar mainstay of liberty in thought and expression: that all points of view must be actively considered if any are to win conviction. But there is a prior issue. Commitments about reality, truth, and value are often what mobilize our social and political energies. Without these commitments, normative claims may seem to float ungrounded.

(2) The proposal cannot be taken seriously. The likely outcome is disingenuousness – religious motives draped in secular garb, metaphysical principles secreted in the carry-on baggage of logic or rhetoric. Unfamiliar proposals are already too easily ridiculed, branded as outré or extreme – too alien or abstruse to meld with the usual and customary. Rawls's restraints exacerbate the problem by legitimating such dismissals. Real reasons, shunned or discounted in the agora and therefore unstated and untested, grow stale and lose their sting, unhoned and unrevised for lack of critical exposure.[39]

(3) Then there is the *tu quoque* already touched on: Rawls's proposal violates its own principle. Its garb of gray neutrality masks sectarian figure faults. Rawls shapes his category of "public reasons" by branding religious values too narrow and metaphysical thoughts too broad for public use. Political proposals, he stipulates, must be nonsectarian, "no longer just the view of one particular party, but an opinion that all members of a society might reasonably agree to ... understood and appraised apart from their particular comprehensive doctrines."[40] But the image of

[39] Rawls expects that in a society bound by his rules, "some conceptions will die out," *Political Liberalism*, 197. Will they do so without discussion or just without public policy debate? Often, in fact, when a way of thinking or living is deemed unacceptable in its milieu, it becomes hermetic – thus insulated against change. A healthier model is the exposure of all thoughts, including those about core issues of public concern, to the marketplace of ideas.

[40] Rawls, in his interview with Prusak, deems "comprehensive doctrines," by their very breadth, to be sectarian and thus unwelcome to those not signed on

minimalism as a happy medium, a royal road to universality, itself presumes a comprehensive view of things.[41] Meant to rise above sectarianism, it privileges secularity by making a foregone conclusion of the most contentious strictures of secularism. The first fruit of Rawls's minimalism was his reconstituted contract theory of justice. But a corresponding canting of the road persists in Rawls's rules for public policy deliberations.

Here are some further thoughts about these three concerns.

1. Plainly, one desideratum in pluralistic societies is to clear common ground for common use. It is not foundational axioms but shared interests and mutual accommodations that create such spaces, but working together is not quite the same as living together. Without dialogue about the values that support our diverse goals, any mere modus vivendi can become mechanical, even cynical, leaving important differences misunderstood and ripe for demagogic exploitation. The values and ideas that might have steadied pragmatic accommodations drop out of sight. In place of personal encounters and intercommunal collaborations we see the letter of the law, the fine print of the contract, parallel lives that never meet, ships that pass in the night, and relations that reach intensity only in miscues, miscommunications, and the ricochets of conflict.

When business or government, the press, technology, or religious institutions resist probing the values that spur and spark their own workings, the activities lose their lively import for those

---

to the worldview they reflect. Rawls seems fearful that unsuspecting decision makers will be hornswoggled by religious or metaphysical snake oil peddlers and so need protection from them. The lack of trust in people's common sense is in tension with democratic principles and at odds with the liberal aversion toward substitutions of judgment.

[41] Rawls's precept of neutrality teeters atop a steeply canted metaphysic of morals. Responding to the late Paul Hoffman's reminder that "political liberalism" too should eschew metaphysical claims about personhood, Rawls admits to holding a notion of personhood, but one so general as to comport equally with, say, Descartes, Leibniz, or Kant; *Political Liberalism* (2005), 29 n. 31. Would it sit as well with Buddhist or Hindu ideas?

whose labors give them life. Once the aims of an enterprise are no longer questioned or even interconnected (beyond lip service to some nostrum), the enterprise can become a headless monster. Only some higher value – be it truth or thrift, the common good, discovery, fairness, piety, or progress – can keep an institution from becoming an organizational zombie. We need not all sign the same verbatim mission statement – uniformity purchased at the price of platitude. But core values do need to be discussed, not just posted like those vapid motivational flyers that decorate some office walls. Dialogue vitalizes collaborations. But conversations about common goals can and should reach for higher principles that might relate diverse visions. That is where Rawls sounds the alarm in the public square. Yet it is in our big ideas that we humans find ways of integrating thoughts with acts and find structural affinities that may help us link our local truths to one another. The logic of our commitments stands in relief as the family resemblances in our diverse ways of thought and action come into focus. So the cross-questioning of our deep commitments has intellectual as well as moral worth.

Nineteenth-century arguments against slavery, Rawls admits, often cited religious precepts celebrating human dignity or metaphysical ideas of existential worth.[42] Can similar arguments be sustained today, from Mali to Louisiana, Orange County, or Staten Island, without comparable appeals? Can we simply presume an inherited abhorrence of slavery and hope (but hardly

---

[42] Rawls, *Political Liberalism*, 249–51. Abolition was preached in churches and sung in ballads such as "Nicodemus the Slave." Emancipation found a secular, metaphysical crux at the turning point of *Huckleberry Finn*. Young Huck has no abstract notion of existential worth, but he chooses damnation rather than betray a man who has become his friend. It is Samuel Clemens who makes the existential case, using Huck to reach a reader who may have no time for metaphysics. Slavery too found both scriptural and secular rationales – in specious glosses of Ham's curse and tendentious readings of Darwin or the overt teachings of the Smithsonian school. In a political struggle, no holds are barred. Bias can drive the abuse of science just as fiercely as it exploits scripture. The fault lies not in religion or science but in seeking to insulate religion from the moral sensitivity that is a proper fount of spiritual truth, to blinker the open mind of metaphysics, or to bind the sciences to a parti pris.

pray!) that culture and fading historical memory will sustain and transmit the presumed repugnance and block the return of norms widespread not so long ago? The old arguments are unlicensed now. Schoolchildren do not sing the "Battle Hymn of the Republic." How many even know its words? How long before someone paints slavery as a fine and useful thing?

Are we equipped to argue the point – or to object to the chatellizing of women or the abuse of children? Rawls can see the value of religious slogans and homilies in the campaign against Jim Crow or the struggles of the Freedom Riders. But the motives, he insists, must stay secular: pursuit of justice and equality. He does not explain quite how motives are to be disentangled from their religious or metaphysical moorings at the front lines, for those taking the risks. Nor does he have arguments to show how justice and equality will fare once those moorings are slipped. The ideals Rawls treats as ultimates did spring from religious norms and metaphysical projections. Will they escape tarnish or perversion once severed from that ancestry?

Consider Raphael Lemkin (1900–59) and his campaign for the 1948 UN convention against genocide. Lemkin, who coined that term, grounded his understanding of the crime in experience, bolstered by study of the laws and practices of the Third Reich. He was shaken as a youth on learning in 1915 of the Turkish campaign against Armenians. He marked similar patterns in 1933 in the slaughter of Christian Assyrians in Iraq. As a young Polish prosecutor, he offered a paper that year at the League of Nations meeting in Madrid, arguing that "destruction of national, religious, and racial groups" should be prosecuted, like piracy and drug smuggling, as crimes against international law. The League refused to vote on the proposal. The Nazi delegation laughed; starkly secular arguments for race destruction were at the core of *Mein Kampf*. International law recognized no such concept as genocide. Drawing on his own background values, wide reading, and the outlook imparted by a cultured mother, Lemkin secularized religious and humanistic ideas to forge his thesis branding genocide a crime. But the presence of so visible a Jew in high Polish office was unwelcome to many, and Lemkin's outspokenness at Madrid led to his dismissal soon after the conference.

By 1939, Germany and Russia had partitioned Poland, and Lemkin was a guerrilla fighting in the woods. The first phase of the Holocaust – the bloody work of the Einsatzgruppen – was underway. Escaping to Sweden through Lithuania, Lemkin lectured at the University of Stockholm and began documenting the Nazi directives to occupied countries, where the Wehrmacht was setting the political precedent and logistical pattern for Hitler's war against the Jews. Making his way to America through Russia and Japan, Lemkin continued to document the policies that instituted genocide and made the destruction of Jewry a central aim of the Third Reich. With the war ended, he served as an advisor to the Nürnberg Trial judge, but failed to persuade the court to include the word "genocide" in the record. International law allowed guerillas to be shot as *franc tireurs*, but jurists did not find it reasonable to criminalize the annihilation of a people. Was the thought that nations, cultures, races, or religions have destinies beyond those of their members too comprehensive an idea to warrant legislation?

When the UN General Assembly convened at Lake Success, Lemkin was present, pressing for a convention against genocide. Impoverished and ill, unmarried, and bereft of nearly all his family, he lobbied delegates from Latin America and Asia, enlisting every ally he could find, including key church groups. Were their efforts dispensable unless stripped of religious affirmations? On December 9, 1948, despite stout resistance from America Firsters, isolationists, and bigots, Lemkin saw his convention adopted at the Palais de Chaillot. Only in 1988 did Ronald Reagan sign the bill that made genocide a crime under American law.

The language of the convention is not religious, of course. The motives of its supporters were complex and will never be known in full, but they did embed religious and metaphysical assumptions. The notion that such thoughts are out of place in deliberations on core issues of public policy is not just unrealistic; it is also vicious, a short-sighted, narrow-minded attempt to dam up major wellsprings of humanism.

Rawls hedges a bit, ready to tolerate religious motives or metaphysical arguments, so long as secular considerations ride shotgun, to add a universal gloss – as if even the privileging of universality were not itself integral to one particular approach to the metaphysic of morals. But for those who cannot master the self-censorship Rawls calls for and are unprepared to bracket their motives quite so neatly as he asks, his strictures seem to invite disingenuousness and self-deception.[43] Isn't it onerous at best to ask citizens in a liberal democracy to hunt for secular backstops to their deepest values? Some, at least, will be silenced by the restraints. Those who are skilled conceptually may find a way to translate, say, religious values into nonsectarian terms. But they, ironically, are blocked by restrictions on the *metaphysical* principles they might use to reconceptualize their core normative claims.

Can secular arguments safeguard the sanctity of human life or the inestimable worth of peoples and their cultures in the face of genocidal suasions grounded in the professed authority of science, or class interests, or national destiny? History is not reassuring. Can human dignity, let alone the rights of nations and peoples, be defended without appeal to some comprehensive notion of what human beings are and what human lives are for, without some thought as to why persons, or peoples, merit any special regard?

Rawlsian reasons might be sought perhaps, at least in contexts elevated enough to invoke Rawlsian notions. Yet mere appeals to a virtual contract hardly run deep enough or hold fast enough to do the job. And bear in mind that what one thinker sets out as a foundation stone, another treats as derivative, and a third scoffs at as self-refuting. If Rawlsian rationales, when fashions change, are not dismissed as just another piece of comprehensive thinking, what keeps them from being simply dismissed as old hat? Rawls is in vogue for the moment. But many a religious and metaphysical idea shows more staying power. I doubt it is

---

[43] Cf. Daniel Dombrowski, *Rawls and Religion: The Case for Political Liberalism*, 121–23.

prudent to silence them all. Fortunately, and contrary to mid-twentieth-century modernist expectations, that is not a likely outcome.

I have asked if we can speak up for biodiversity without turning to spiritual notions of nature's sublimity or to metaphysical thoughts about the intrinsic worth of plant and animal life. Are all claims to become instrumental, unanchored in any intrinsic good? Is that a less metaphysical claim than holding out for some values as intrinsic? Isn't it a metaphysical claim that to inflict gratuitous suffering is wrong? If the liberty to pollute one's lake or pith one's cat is to be abridged, how can the issue be debated and any restriction warranted without claims about objective values? Isn't there a religious or metaphysical claim about personhood at the heart of the idea that rape and sexual exploitation are wrong? Can we say, without some comprehensive view of things, that such violations are graver when the victim is a minor or a family member? Are incest laws to become dead letters once too few of us can articulate a reason for them without turning to some religious idea of personal sanctity or some metaphysical idea of subjecthood and the delicate cambium of identities emergent in the matrix of the family? Or do laws about such things not regard basic human rights?

Rights are not negotiable, a thought Rawls echoes in his talk of lexical priority – although he does seek to preserve some notion of flexibility or amendment, leaving a sense of vagueness in his account as to just how plastic human liberty is expected to be in his scheme, and where and under what conditions.[44] Freedom, we might argue in response to such waffling or vagueness, is not for sale; dignity cannot be waived. That is what America's founders meant when they called certain rights inalienable and God given. Those men of the Enlightenment freely navigated the passage between the naturalism of "inalienable" and the

---

[44] Cf. Rawls, *A Theory of Justice* (1999), 400–01, where the stability of a just society as its institutions and practices inevitably change is presumed to be preserved in large part by "the sense of justice shared by the members of the community" – and this, despite their acknowledged "great diversity."

spiritual gravamen of "God given." Their mutual understanding on that point anchored *their* pluralism. By rising to a higher
plane of generality, they could take one another's meaning and
see each other's sense, the argument implicit in their Declaration
of Independence: that natural rights are grounded in our urge
to live and flourish and are, as such, the signet sign in creatures
of God's will and work. Both the argument and its premises
are off-limits in Rawls's world – along with the fluency of free
translation from the one idiom to the other.

Inalienable, in the language of the Declaration, pinions the
futility of seeking to deprive persons of the power to defend
their interests. No living being freely surrenders that power.
"Endowed by their Creator" means much the same, since the
laws of nature are God's laws; their stability, the hallmark of
God's sovereignty; the thirst for life and urge to prosper, vivid
marks of grace – far clearer evidence than the suppositious appeal
to the divine right of kings. Metaphysical notions such as that
of natural rights can be compelling. Religious ideas, such as
the creation of human beings in God's image, can be moving.
Combined, the two became watchwords of civil law and rallying
calls of revolution, forging rather than dividing a national identity. Abstractions about lexical priority and thought experiments
about a veil of ignorance have yet to show like power. Calling
rights "trumps" sounds like counsel to a litigator, not a battle
cry of freedom.

Words like "God given" or "inalienable" gain their power
not from the sounds they make but from what they stand for.
Ideas like these two, as they interpret one another, build bridges,
not barriers. What does throw up barriers is the insistent closed-
mindedness that restrains talk of God or nature and forbids frat-
ernizing across the lines that ally sacred and natural obligations.
We humans revere what we hold highest and count as sacred the
norms we keep furthest from the frayed edges of our web of values. So any hint of value differences (even in style!) can compound
our epochal and ethnic diversities and heighten contrasts, real or
imagined. But as long as we inhabit an open society, where no
dogma rules and no presumption suppresses speculation, appeals

to (or against) God or scripture, or any universal idea, carry no more weight than they can muster. In the welter of competing claims their appeal falls back toward their worth. In this sense we do stand naked in the public square: Public rhetoric rings hollow when bare of public interests and deaf to public concerns. That is why it is safe to open our public discourse to diverse speakers, hearing their pleas – not for imposition of parochial rituals or restrictive ideologies, but in hopes of profit from the varied construals our fellow human beings may make of our common human dignity.

The open society is an ideal, not a finished work. Great satchels of dogma persist. Formal metaphysics rarely holds sway in them. Religions are the familiar site, the common centers of moral and spiritual gravity, but dogma is hardly sequestered in churches – which are, apart from cults and claverns, voluntary associations. Secular norms and notions too can be oppressive, giving dogma an afterlife as cant, with conformity its passport. Even so, uniformity is not the hallmark of our world. Too many new and old ideas and norms buffet one another.

Authorities may seek reverence. But their appeals, when heard, are regularly tested against the hearers' good sense. The best place for such testing is just where Mill saw it, in the open air. With issues of public concern, that place means the public forum. Philosophy's charge here is to listen with the open mind it boasts of, testing the logic and pragmatic reach of claims. This work of criticism (easier than philosophy's creative role, but not unrelated) is not infallible. Motives are not always pure. but openness is an ally in assaying religious and metaphysical ideas. Daylight is not the enemy. My plea is for openness. Liberal obscurantism, to give a name to Rawls's paradoxical proposal, is just as sullen as its sectarian rivals. And the hermeticism it breeds robs thinking of the fresh air and sunlight that ideas need to blossom and bear fruit.

Does the internet sweep away obscurantism? That is half a truth. Technical jargon, niche marketing, and affinity clustering create barriers as well as bridges. Fashion is a subtler censor than dictatorship. But argument can dissolve specious claims and expose what is rotten, especially where interests are at stake. The alternative only papers over the decay; it does not open doors. Those who actively engage with one another's thoughts and norms can find more in what a tradition prizes than is seen by indifferent outsiders or parochial acolytes.

The payoff is not remote. When public debate turns to lotteries and other forms of legalized gambling, or to prostitution, pornography, or violent videogames, religious voices may raise concerns unheard from sheerly pragmatic interests. Secular liberals are readily distracted from the regressive impact of lotteries by abstract appeals to liberty or concrete promises of cash for educational or cultural needs, overlooking or underrating the toll of compulsive gambling on individuals and families. Liberals and libertarians may turn a blind eye to the devastation wrought by drugs. They may be swayed by protestations that lap dancing is a form of free expression, a bastion or beachhead of artistic freedom. Inspired by myths of free love, they may label prostitution sheerly consensual, ignoring the coercive exploitation of pimps, the noose of drugs, and the risk of AIDS and other STDs to prostitutes, clients, and the partners and offspring of both parties.[45] Few crimes are truly victimless. But religious voices may see harms that contractual models of human relations fail to register.

Liberals often blind themselves to the metaphysical roots of their own principles. Some tolerate the semiotic degradation of women rather than restrict erotic expression, but mask the absolutes they favor in empirical posits – the harm of hard-core pornography is undemonstrated – as though every act (and not just every person) were innocent until proved guilty. But the tussle with the evidence betrays an a priori sinew. The motives here are not empirical but moral. So it can be wholesome to hear a

---

[45] Constitutional concerns blocked the application of classic quarantine laws to the first AIDS cases; privacy arguments preserved the anonymity of HIV-infected prostitutes. The myth of sexual freedom helped bar the way, seconded by the rationale that the infected would stay silent unless their privacy was protected. AIDS then became a pandemic.

rival voice and fresh thoughts about what to privilege or protect. The humanism that invigorates many a religious tradition is protective of human bodies and spirits. It vigorously contests the notion that we human beings are social isolates with no obligations to self or other beyond what we contractually assume.

Religious texts forbid standing by at another's loss. If concerned voices wax metaphysical or cite scripture to recall that in God's eyes we are all our brothers' keepers, the pleas may prove more clarifying than dogmatic. Yes, metaphysics may sound abstruse, and Godtalk is often startling. Saying that we are all of us interdependent can sound more down to earth. But imperatives grounded in this way are at risk of being read as merely prudential, and they fall far short of universal love. The dramatic irony of Cain's *Am I my brother's keeper?* packs more moral heft than many a well-argued brief. Levinas finds that ancient trope metaphysical. But his graphic evocation of a face whose haunting eyes plead for life – an image intensified by memories of genocide and the scent of fresh graves and the smoke of burning flesh – rouses a stronger plea: Do not kill us – but do not degrade us either. Do not sink us by your silence! Metaphysics can condemn genocide without benefit of law or clergy. But Heidegger can rationalize it, obscenely playing on words like "lightening." Franklin Delano Roosevelt, strictly pragmatic and political, can turn away.

Religion, at its fairest reach, welcomes daylight unafraid of fair debate, even thoughtful probing of its deepest mysteries. But the public has little to fear in religious thoughts and proposals. What is strictly parochial will not win much purchase in an open society. Even mysteries do not explode when opened. People may be reaching for ideals and find sense on more than one plane as they seek a universal hearing. It is because religious values make claims on transcendence that religions can adapt, quietly or grudgingly, revising or discarding values unhelpful to their quest. The highest spiritual values soar above inchoate anticipations and myopic glosses. What is credible in those values will not harm the common good. What moral force they have reflects that good. Any claim to prescriptivity beyond that is deservedly dissolved.

Specious moral claims will always be made, of course. But such falsehoods are flimsy – self-exposed and self-betrayed. Religious demands of harm to self or other wither in the light of day. Fanaticism hates daylight. Jihadis post in the dark; snipers and hostage takers rarely dare to debate as equals with their victims. But open discussion of spiritual and moral maxims can elevate deliberations, encouraging lawmakers to raise their eyes from lobbyists' reports. There is more at issue and at stake than economics in deliberations about the ivory trade. Spiritual leaders, when true to their charge, can breast parochial tides and address universal values in a language of universal concerns. A private ideal, after all, has even less use than a private language. But no culture thrives by learning only what it knows already or hearing only reasoning that it already takes for granted.

The chief fear of those who seek to shield society from sacred texts and inspired traditions is that revelation will infect laws with musty standards unconscionable to many. That worry is selective. Secularists may battle religious claims about euthanasia, abortion, and same-sex marriage, but seek religious allies even in these campaigns; a fortiori, in fighting school vouchers, capital punishment, or world hunger. In efforts to control global warming, religious voices are welcomed – as they were in the fight against apartheid and racial segregation. There are popular and unpopular wars, sweatshops countenanced and sweatshops verboten. Mao and Stalin, while alive, got a better press than Verwoerd. Clerics can be coopted by tyrants.[46] Indeed, they can *be* tyrants. But that means religion's politicization, not the intrusion of religion into politics. What is needed is not a wall of separation between a spiritual conscience and a complacent polity, but a critical voice that knows when and where and how to speak out. That was the charge of the ancient prophets, who challenged priest or prelate, calling a pricked conscience to judge of right and wrong, sacred and profane, beyond the dicta of state counsels or cynical synods.

---

[46] See the telling indictment in David Cymet, *History vs. Apologetics*.

Clearly we should resist the sectarian suborning of state authority, the imposition of religious dogmas and practices whose meanings and trappings are unwanted by those over whom they are cast. But the risks in such a case are hardly just political. The loss of spiritual sincerity is also a great danger. Religious establishment breeds decadence and saps the values that make religions worthy of encounter.[47] There is enough hypocrisy attendant on the institution of religion without the confounding influence of the powers of the state and the privileges at its command. But what follows is the need to separate religious from political institutions, not to isolate policy from thought whenever thinking lifts its eyes above the pragmatic – as if states had no proper interest beyond the instrumental in preventing suicides, say, or promoting healthy births and happy childhoods, and should assign no intrinsic worth to human lives and take no cognizance of the options available to individuals in steering their own lives, or health, or safety. Without religion or metaphysics, education matters only instrumentally; births may add prospective warriors and workers, consumers or polluters, but hold no intrinsic value; and the quality of lives and richness of experience are not entered in the policy calculus but only in the monetary costs of injury or labor lost. But even that narrow gaze, ironically, is metaphysical – and sectarian.

Religions, in their rightful public role, are not arbiters of official values but advocates for the values each hopes will foster human flourishing. The differences among traditions here are not a scandal to be lived down but the emblems of a trial in which each tradition tests and is tested by the rest. Secular thought is nourished when challenged to take off the green eyeshade and look beyond the putative bottom line, finding ways of its own to reckon with higher values – even if the language it must use does ring with metaphysically freighted metaphors.

---

[47] Thelle's *Buddhism and Christianity in Japan* shows how establishment turned Buddhism decadent and despised. Disestablishment allowed it to be taken seriously again.

The profit of the resulting dialogue, or intercourse as it once was called, extends beyond religion. But for most human beings, for most of history, value commitments have been voiced and transmitted, adjusted and revised, religiously. It is in this arena that we humans conciliate our attempts to live our values, weigh the imponderables, and touch the intangibles that enlarge our humanity. Few of us, in fact, pursue metaphysical options very far. Yet even these options are muzzled by Rawls's proposal. That brings me to my second complaint, the invitation to disingenuousness.

2. Consider a case in point. Our adversarial legal system sometimes hauls crime victims and their families into court to testify in sentencing hearings about the harm and pain a criminal has inflicted – lest judges and juries be overly swayed by clever advocates' pleas for the criminal as victim. But when a victim's family speaks of forgiveness (often a religious issue for them), we need to recall that theirs is not the only injured interest. A criminal has offended against the state, the society, and the fabric of the law itself. For crimes are not a wholly private matter. In civil cases parties may reach an settlement, and the state may rightly act as referee. But penal offenses are a public matter and may well involve a message to be sent. Metaphysical questions lurk here at the delicate joint between the forward-looking and backward-looking juridical concerns. But Rawls has barred metaphysics from the core domain of public deliberations.

The procedural protections built into our laws privileging the accused – the presumption of innocence; the safeguards against self-incrimination; the rejection of judicial torture; the privileging of spousal and parental relations and of pastoral, medical, and legal communications – and indeed the very idea of equality before the law are predicated on presumptions of the inestimable worth of the individual, the sanctity of marriage, and of counsel. Those are metaphysical premises, fleshed out in the procedures that give operational meaning to our notions of human dignity. It is these presumptions (and not mere formal uniformity!) that give body to our broad ideals of justice. But such principles and the rules designed to protect them are not safely delegated to the counsels of virtual decisors with nothing to guide them but the presumed rationality of the reasonable – as if consensus were sufficient warrant and warranty of justice.

Many of us know no better way to frame an ultimate concern than in the language religion affords.[48] Religion contributes distinctively, perhaps uniquely, here, because protections of immediate constitutional bearing are readily seen as matters of ultimate concern. Let me offer an example. In *On Justice*, I argued that deserts reflect claims and so cannot be negative. Justice, as Plato proposed (*Republic* I 335), should not diminish those it touches. Just punishments, I reasoned with that thought in mind, should be understood as scaling back privileges presumptively accorded.[49] The presumptions made feasible by our communal and societal engagement are defeasible by violations of the trust that grounds them. That reasoning warrants a retributive account of punishment and underscores its crucial difference from vindictiveness. A retributive account, I argued, must complement the concerns of deterrence and reform, lest forward-looking rationales foster arbitrary and preemptive punishment, even including open oppression, harassment, or "telishment" of the innocent.

My metaphysical story explains why embezzlers and market manipulators should not be trusted with the sorts of instruments they have abused and why sexual predators should not be trusted with the young or vulnerable. Yet, as I have acknowledged, my story does not answer all questions about punishment. Like many Americans, I long opposed capital punishment. Even the worst of us, I reasoned, is in principle redeemable, and it seemed wrong to snuff out even a hopeless life, because such a waste did violence to existential claims. I did not try to rationalize my feelings by arguing that capital punishment is no real deterrent. For it can be that. But even demonstrable deterrence would not justify barbarous practices. We could hardly justify drawing and quartering

---

[48] See Wolterstorff, in Audi and Wolterstorff, 91; cf. Dworkin, *Is Democracy Possible Here?*, 64; Eberle, "Basic Human Worth and Religious Restraint," 157.

[49] Goodman, *On Justice*, 61–72.

even if it proved to deter crime. If executing murderers is cruel
and excessive, perhaps it should be abolished, my metaphysics
seemed to urge. But after the Manson case and the Eichmann
trial, good sense seemed to press the other way. My general theory, which finds the deserts of every being in its claims, did not
seem to settle things. It offered no clear rationale for capital punishment, but neither did it convince me that execution is never
warranted. I had no theory to explain why capital punishment
can be just.

Religious counsels are not irrelevant here. It would not hurt
to listen to papal pleas for mercy, although popes do dip a toe
into politics when they oppose executions worldwide. I would
like to understand their contention better – and to live in a world
where such pleas are no longer needed. The emphatic biblical
demands for capital punishment (Genesis 9:6, Exodus 19:12–
16, Leviticus 20:2) are pertinent too. So is Maimonides' saying
that it is not mercy but cruelty to expose people to violence by
failing to exact justice (*Guide* III 35). I do not see a knock-down-
drag-out argument here. Experience holds me to my stance in
the wake of Manson. I cannot mourn the death of Milosovic's
like, and I regret that natural death spared so many of Pol Pot's
cutthroats and torturers and that many perpetrators and plan-
ners of genocide in Rwanda have gone scot-free. But I would not
silence the Pope. A pope might sway us one day by the power of
his reasoning, even if it does use religious terms or rely on spiritual premises. What Mother Theresa and Gandhi and Schweitzer
have to say matters, even if one cannot agree with every word –
especially if one finds oneself at odds with their positions. Every
philosopher needs to know when to say, "I don't know."

If a thought does not fit our schemata, we are tempted to say
it cannot be right. But philosophies and other skeins of thought
are not logic-tight machines. They do not yield answers that
are incoherent to deny or algorithms that are irrational to question. When we venture into metaphysics, logic offers no such
snap-jawed aid. Many in the twentieth century sought safety by
eschewing metaphysics. However, their policy was largely a posture and a pose. All value commitments are metaphysical. But

banning value judgments cannot work. It amounts to nonsense –
a rule against making rules.

We humans are valuing creatures. Almost every word in our
many natural languages is value laden, including the *if*s, *but*s,
*and*s, and *or*s. Even modus ponens is a norm about how we ought
to reason. Our big ideas – about God, Truth, beauty, reality, reason, freedom, sanity, peace, tolerance, change, *and justice*, of
course – bulge with metaphysical commitments. Like M. Jour-
dain, speaking prose all his life unwittingly, we are constantly
treading on metaphysical ground, whether or not we acknowledge the trespass and seek overt access to its pathways and guidance around its pitfalls and pratfalls. We have eaten of the tree of
knowledge of good and evil; it is too late to spit out the seeds. We
cannot debate practicalities or principles without making metaphysical assumptions; conversely, when we talk metaphysics, we
typically have cases in mind. It is the issues, typically, that puff
up our thoughts to their familiar shapes and sizes.

Questions about the soul, for example, often arise when the
bereaved seek consolation. Arguments once critical in debates on
infant baptism resurfaced in the abortion struggle. Usage does
not settle much. Disputants, like litigants, know how to work
the language or dismiss it. So the winds of policy often drive the
metaphysical premises. Wouldn't it be more honest to reverse that
trend and encourage those who dispute some seemingly recondite
issue to lay their cards on the table and name the stakes – to
explain why, say, talk about the body does not exhaust what
must be said about persons – recovering what scripture means
when it says, in its pithy way, that man does not live by bread
alone (Deuteronomy 8:3)?

That is just the kind of talk Rawls wants silenced in the public
square – metaphysics at its plainest, metaphysics about persons
and the religious language that finds words to voice such thoughts
poetically, using words about life and bread, say, to raise matters
of higher concern than loaves or even the individual lives that the
words encircle. Naturally one can dismiss any text suspected of
being canonical and bracket any insight that sounds too inspired.
But the grounds for doing so might have to remain unspoken,

lest they too sound religious. We can strip from the courthouse walls any plaque or placard that recalls the old belief that God forbids false witness. Such sights might taint the proceedings.[50] But even the exclusion enacts a religious dogma. Even the secular is sectarian.

In Alabama, Susan Pace Hamill, a tax law professor on sabbatical at a divinity school, wrote a paper on tax policy. Published in the Alabama law review, it argued that her state, which boasted the lowest income tax threshold in the Union ($4,600 for a family of four) and taxed infant formula at a higher rate than cattle feed, failed to meet biblical standards of justice.[51] Alabama's constitution skewed the tax laws to favor land owners. Farmers and timber interests paid only 95 cents an acre in property tax. Ms Hamill's article and her talks at churches aroused agitation for change; the clergy in Alabama's 8,000 churches found it hard to remain silent. It is no state responsibility to help the poor, one wealthy layman urged in response: They already benefited from his tithe. But that argument did not travel well. Ms Hamill's biblical appeals packed greater clout than the suasions more familiar in legislative forums and corridors. Were they improper?

Why are appeals to special interests licit and appeals to scripture rejected, if they urge us, say, to hold others no less precious than ourselves before God? Or is the issue one of false abstraction, masking worries about abortion-euthanasia-gay marriage? Are religious opinions welcome in environmental or civil rights causes, but ruled out when attention turns to gambling or alcohol? Should activists accept religiously motivated campaign contributions and volunteer work on matters green, but reject help in other cases, unless the motives are duly filtered – or left unstated?

---

[50] Posting the Decalogue, as I argue in Chapter 3, making it a "monument," trivializes its norms. Jurors today are dismissed and jury verdicts set aside for adverting to religious motives. But the problem is not the intrusion of improper considerations, but the risk of a priorism coloring findings of fact: Legislators, not jurors, are charged with deciding whether and when capital punishment is just. But must the walls of public libraries also be stripped of murals that feature biblical and other religious literature?

[51] *Alabama Law Review*, January, 2003; *Wall Street Journal*, February 12, 2003; *New York Times Magazine*, December 14, 2003.

Political campaigners of all stripes appreciate allies, so long as they can rest assured that their own image (or at times their self-respect) remains unsullied. The motives of prospective volunteers, funders, and canvassers are rarely questioned deeply. There are good, bad, and dubious causes that attract ingenuous and disingenuous varieties of support. But religion is too broad a category (and metaphysics, given its abstraction, can run still broader) to single out for exclusion – even if one could somehow isolate the precise mix of motives that Rawls and others might find generically or categorically inappropriate in a properly political campaign.

William Stuntz, a Harvard law professor and evangelical Christian, pressed a point about the ecology of criminal justice: Tighter procedural protections for the accused, he argued, prompted legislatures to toughen penalties. Funding for prisons and public defenders did not keep pace. With procedural issues eclipsing material justice, prosecutors became leery of defendants with access to fine legal counsel. They pressed for plea bargains where they anticipated procedural trouble. The results, Stuntz argued, rather than discriminating the innocent from the guilty, often reflected racial and class divisions. But thoughts of God's mercy lay at the root of his concerns. Did religious motives render Stuntz's influential policy critiques improper and taint the policy proposals they inspired? Thoughts of mercy do not *need* religious backing, but they are often colored by religious thinking. Indeed, religious arguments might be needed to counter demands for severity, be they secular or religious – amputation for thieves, stoning for adulterers. These are not abstract questions or matters safe in the remote past. Is it best simply to silence religious voices in such policy debates and rule from "our" intuitions?

Rawls's spirited defense of conscience in *A Theory of Justice* stands in tension with the secularism of *Political Liberalism*. His clarion call in the earlier book cites Alexander Bickel and leans heavily on Locke:

In a democratic society ... each citizen is responsible for his interpretation of the principles of justice and for his conduct in the light of them. There can be no legal or socially approved rendering of these principles that we are always morally bound to accept, not even when it is given by a supreme court or legislature.[52]

Wolterstorff spells out the impact of that principle in the matter of advocacy: "It belongs to the *religious convictions* of a good many religious persons in our society that *they ought to base* their decisions concerning fundamental issues of justice on their religious convictions."[53] The familiar terms in which we liberals make our case for conscience and conscientiousness, language echoed in Rawls's plea, are grounded in a metaphysical recasting of the Protestant idea that conscience is God's inner light. That thesis in turn is rooted in biblical ideas of personal integrity, ideas that took on special poignancy in centuries of religious martyrdom. It contrasts sharply with, say, Hobbes's militantly secular version of the social contract – and his attendant apologia for monarchical sovereignty.

Rawls demands that religious motives enter the public square only as neutral principles. Not only statutes but even the debates that shape them must be neutered. Yet, if we learn any lesson from philosophy's checkered career, it is that metaphysical neutrality is illusory. Wisdom thrives on a rich and varied intellectual and experiential diet. It falters when the rival approaches to life's great questions are swept under the carpet, and the bits and pieces that look useful are snitched out again and laundered for reuse until they look flat and gray enough (or flashy and exotic enough) to the unpracticed eye.

3. Our *tu quoque* underscores the inevitability of metaphysics and the ubiquity of religion, evident in awkward efforts to disguise metaphysical views in the common cloth of rhetoric or logic or to conceal religious commitments behind some secular mask. Even the contractual theories of right and justice, once gaily caparisoned to tilt with the divine right of kings, rest on a metaphysic of morals. They presume a natural right to make

---

[52] Rawls, *A Theory of Justice* (1999) 342; cf. 323–35.
[53] Wolterstorff, in Audi and Wolterstorff, 104.

agreements and a duty to keep them. Rawls's thought experiment descends from that lineage. His aim in propounding it, as he avows, was to breathe new life into the Lockean social contract by recasting it as a virtual contract. But social contract theories are not metaphysically neutral. They aim no longer just at monarchy but now more pointedly at natural law by making justice a matter of convention, respecting interests but sidelining appeals to human nature and natural right.

Hence the weakness of such theories. If laws derive their force solely from the logic implicit in some speech act, then either laws would never gain material content but would be left to rest within the cold bosom of their formal structure, or they would remain merely descriptive – or predictive, as some pragmatists believe laws must be. Without some basis in the worth of beings (a subject of religious or metaphysical affirmations), the force of norms is arbitrary at best, ultimately suppositious. The secularism at the root of any a priori or naturalist reduction of obligation canonizes competing and conflicting interests. So it still rests, inevitably, on unacknowledged metaphysical assumptions. But the interests it now canonizes are confined to the tactical demands of individuals, groups, and corporations. And no guidance is allowed in ranking or coordinating those interests. Plato captures the situation brilliantly when he describes the democratic man (*Republic* VIII 558–61), to whom all values are attractive. The democratic man becomes the plaything of the marketplace, if not the courts or the battlefield. Jean Hampton marks a similar irony when she paraphrases Robert Frost, asking whether a Rawlsian could take his own side in an argument.[54]

In our own society, the agencies of tradition and community remain alive and vocal. They have rostra outside our official deliberative assemblies. I am a child of liberalism, so this seems right to me. I do not want some commanding voice to impose parochial visions or particularistic practices – or the whisper of political correctness in my colleagues' ear, for that matter, guiding their every move and prompting their every word like

54 Hampton, "Should Political Philosophy be Done without Metaphysics?" 803.

the earpiece a newscaster wears. But the still small voice that seeks to rouse a larger public to the claims of conscience remains vital in the agora – or the city gates, as the ancient prophets put it. The reminders of our sense of the transcendent – in ancient texts, present exemplars, or poetic visions of the future – are not mere ornaments to be dusted off for perorations or parades. Deliberatively they are of the essence. Liberal theory too leans on them. So does Rawls when he turns for help to a "background culture." Some may find prophetic voices grating and long to silence them. But liberalism in that mood becomes illiberal, the overlapping consensus no longer thoughtful but closing ranks like fish scales or roof tiles or the shields of Roman legions.

To uphold its commitment to individual rights, freedom, and fairness, liberalism must sustain cultural dignity and autonomy as well. The bare ideal of equality cannot specify its own scope or limits. It is empty without some idea of personhood and some vision of value and the possible meanings of human life. Equality, as the term is used in liberal rhetoric and even in what passes for political philosophy, is often just a surrogate for material deserts. Even in talk about choice, the tacit presumption is that choices freely made will generally be wholesome; equality will preserve the choosers. Arguments for dignity similarly presume some schema of the boundaries of personhood and parameters of privacy. Fairness makes sense only against the backdrop of a tacit ethology, a presumptive ecology and economy of society and civilization, a summary vision of the histories in which human identities are rooted and embedded – and from which, at times, they seek and need to spring away. Even the most minimal umpire state, then, cannot perform its designated functions in creating a level playing field – adjudicating conflicts and refereeing competition – without some grasp of the values in play. So even in eschewing the metaphysical it too waxes metaphysical.

But when a state declares neutrality and rejects all claims to judgment about the quality of the ethos, it will follow rather than lead. It will not succeed in banning metaphysics, but will only struggle to promote the substitution of its own rather porous metaphysics, an all too permeable membrane that passes multiple agendas but filters out others, stained by their historic or conceptual associations.

If social interactions dissolve into a quest for cash (the most fluid, fungible, readily hoarded, and transported of goods), the public agenda becomes the regulation of economic interests, fostering trade and industry, overseeing markets and employment – all worthy aims, served well or badly. But these aims (and even educational and economic "opportunity" – again construed in economic terms) hardly exhaust the possibilities or responsibilities of public agency. Should other values – sensate values, say, or those of honor and shame, or pietism – come forward (or wait nearby), the economic state has trouble noticing them or knowing how to address them. Such concerns are not thematized in its laws and institutions or schematized in the philosophies that voice its salient themes. Bureaucrats will stare; theorists will blink. Nothing in their textbooks and working protocols guides engagement here.

The outcome is too familiar. Thousands of religious studies professors cannot, on principle, distinguish cults from sects. The aims and means of mind control that mar and mark cultish authoritarianism elude their analysis. Dedicated professionals find themselves unable to distinguish an open from a closed community, let alone argue a preference for one over the other. Thousands of philosophers and media analysts cannot affirm that sadomasochistic pornography degrades humanity and desecrates sexuality. Instead they calibrate obscenity by degrees of "explicitness" or "offensiveness" to communal standards – as though the harm done by hard-core pornography were a matter of sharp or soft focus, and the damage wreaked in permission giving and degradation of the human image were confined to the mind of the beholder. Even in the realm of practice, their frameworks leave them with little more than a consumerist shrug: "different strokes for different folks." Defense of the ethos is left to freelancers and men in dog collars who then get warned to stay off the public turf. No wonder the ethos is bleeding. In a kind of cultural Gresham's law well known to Spengler, competitive emulation and niche marketing ratchet up the assaults that inure public sensibilities to ever more sensate extremes and demand ever more extreme sensations. Does the public have no interest in the ethos? Wasn't that what Socrates was pointing to when he challenged his fellow Athenians about who was really responsible for corrupting the youth? If the state is the agency entrusted with prosecuting our common interests, hasn't it a proper role in the cultivation of the ethos?

Or are we just to sigh and accept the Sophist's rationale for tragedy's inevitability, making a new gospel of the old canard that decadence is just the price we pay for freedom? If we are to learn from Locke (and from Spinoza, whose ideas Locke quietly built on here), law, not anarchy, sets the stage for freedom. For freedom is not the opposite or enemy of the civil state. On the contrary, each is the enabling condition of the other. As Gerald Mara writes,

> the concern for virtue and the recognition of pluralism are incommensurable only when both commitments are radically conceived. It is not immediately clear that mutual accommodation is simply impossible, even for contemporary champions of each cause, once one moves beyond oversimplified abstractions toward reflective and open discussions of pluralist reality.[55]

No state can flourish without active engagement in behalf of the ethos. Judging by the ham-handedness of state efforts in general and the all too evident risks of confusing secularity with secularism, state agencies are not the most promising protectors of that interest, unless in the most egregious cases, and even then in pretty modest ways. Schools might promote the Pledge of Allegiance, or laws might proscribe flag burning. But ethics in the strict and ancient sense goes far beyond the wishful pieties of what was called good citizenship in mid-twentieth-century grade schools. If wrestling fans are entitled to their frissons, so, surely, is

---

[55] Mara, "Virtue and Pluralism," 30.

the state a legitimate defender of the public temper and temperament. But substantive and extensive state efforts to invigorate the ethos would most likely backfire or fall flat. Jingoism should not sell well, even if it might. And a lowest common denominator, if one could be found, would hardly foster thoughtfulness and caring. Even caring means little if reduced to mawkish gestures and trivial slogans.

Still, a prudently run state would not leave values untouchable or fence off every ultimate that might anchor other values. Therefore it would hardly muffle public talk of values in the public square. We cannot ask everyone who comes to the dance to enter naked – or demand that everyone who comes pretend to enter naked, wrapped in cellophane, as it were, thick enough to obscure any hidden agenda. A good government will foster religious thought and expression and promote metaphysical conversation and inquiry, not hide behind a factitious or fictitious scrim of value neutrality. It will promote all sorts of religious and metaphysical thought and expression that seek ways of affirming life rather than thwart it.

3

Minima and Maxima

Some years ago I took part in an international meeting of philosophers. Of the 180 thinkers who attended, many took the occasion to showcase their values. Socialism was still much bruited in those days, and several speakers scrapped their prepared remarks to sing its praises. Many still imagined, despite Friedrich Hayek's cogent argument in *The Road to Serfdom*, that civil rights and human flourishing could be safe and well served under socialism – or only under socialism. Some thought basic liberties survivable even in a one-party state, where law and politics, the media and means of production, science, inquiry, and the arts, the councils of labor and sources of capital, the vehicles of distribution, stewardship of the land, and regulation of the marketplace were all gripped in a single set of hands. In that forum, I admired Hilary Putnam's courageous confession that socialist promises were "now universally discredited."[1]

Because this was an intercultural meeting, many of the philosophers celebrated relativism and its promised yield in tolerance and accommodation. Bimal Matilal, whom I remembered as a handsome young scholar at Oxford but who was now broken in health and pushed in a wheelchair by his wife, worked with

[1] Hilary Putnam, at the East West Philosopher's Conference, Honolulu, August, 1989.

spirit to distinguish relativism from pluralism. Keenly aware of the variance in the particularities of practice from one culture to the next, he scanned the traditions of India for norms worthy of universal adherence. He singled out respect for life, deference to truth, abhorrence of theft, and rejection of adultery.[2] In each case he drew specific prescriptions from the broad norms he culled from India's rich religious and philosophical array. Although he cited Hindu and Buddhist scriptures and the spiritual wisdom of Gandhi, he strove not to rely on divine prescriptions.

Sectarian bias is not the only risk in the quest for universal norms. American courts can overturn a statute for vagueness, and principles too can fail if framed too broadly. Even when drafted with the best intentions, global formulations may prove culture-bound. But they can also turn vacuous when couched too broadly and fail to pick out what Aristotle called "the doable good."[3] Matilal's four rubrics are noble enough. But they do teeter on the brink of vacuity, begging for the specificity that law or custom might impart – but always at risk of over-particularity and vulnerable to the charge that once pinned down they fail of universality. Do the claims of truth forbid all lies? And if lying is countenanced to spare a fugitive, can we debar other appeals to expedience – to aid others, say, in this world or to help them toward the next? Do we guard verbatim truth but condone prevarication? Or does truthfulness die the death of a thousand cuts and survive in lip service but not in life?

Bracketing for now dramatic doorway confrontations and dropping down the memory hole any thoughts of, say, Lysenko's Stakhanovite violence against the truth, we still must ask: Does love of truth debar white lies and gentle compliments? Where does tact sink into cant or manipulation? When does candor turn brutal or honesty wax crudely literal? Aren't the answers

---

[2] See Matilal, "Pluralism, Relativism," in Deutsch, ed., *Culture and Modernity*, 141–60.

[3] Aristotle, *Nicomachaean Ethics* I 7, 1097a 23–25, Ross translates: "the good achievable by action"; Ostwald, "the good attainable by action"; Joe Sachs, "the good that belongs to action." J. A. K. Thompson seems more apposite in *The Ethics of Aristotle*, 36.

always situational? Can such questions even be asked without at least tacit reference to an ethos – and can an ethos subsist outside a culture or community? But if there is no ethos without an ethnos, can pluralism find any body of moral precepts broad enough to pass as universal yet pointed and concrete enough to escape vacuity?

Matilal's hope was consensus. But consensus regularly pays the price of blandness, and still it may threaten sincerity. Compromise is the stuff of politics. America might never have won its independence or framed its Constitution if the slavery question had first to be settled on principle. But the failure of the founders forthrightly to address that question at the outset set the seeds of a bloodstained Civil War, as Lincoln poignantly confessed in his Second Inaugural Address. If politics is the art of the possible, political virtuosity must lie in framing compromises that build consensus without immolating principle – lest it paper over principled divides so thickly that ambiguity itself becomes a point of law and a juridical tactic, leaving crucial issues to fester.

Not every compromise is worthy or even tolerable. That is easy to see and say but harder to live by, or die for, in practice: There is no proper compromise with Nazis in full spate, or the Khmer Rouge. We have no duty of candor to Inquisitors, or Hutus with dripping machetes, or the KGB, Red Guards, or Janjaweed. The bonds of civility that demand sincerity are otiose, even obscene when civility itself and all that makes it possible are at risk. In this age of suicide bombers, this question forces itself forward: Granted that every culture makes its compromises, are there no overarching norms of life and practice beyond rules announcing hollowly that rules are rules? Foundationally, we need a public commitment to human dignity, enshrined in laws and, more critically, implicit in the ethos. There are many ways of building such commitments – hence the pluralism this book espouses. But not every norm or practice does sustain such dignity. Some subvert it. A rhetoric of rights is no substitute for commitment to their living practice.

Part of what Matilal was seeking was general agreement. But even unanimity reveals little. Consent is a fine marker but is neither necessary nor sufficient to legitimacy. Some whose interests are critically affected by our acts have no effectual say in what affects their realization: the desperately poor, the comatose, the very young and very old, the linguistically or cognitively challenged and impaired, and all those who live outside the deliberative community – foreigners, resident aliens, the disenfranchised, and members of past and future generations, whose projects today's choices may cap or ruin. And consent, regrettably, is not always held apart from markets. There are also always those who – in their eagerness for celebrity or wealth, or a pittance, or a chance at power, real or imagined – readily consent to outrageous abuses of self and others, including those whose interests they should clutch tightest, selling themselves or even their children into slavery or worse.[4]

Some Moral Minima

Moral standards do not need every miscreant's consent, and penal laws are not subject to the felon's veto. Relativists may plead human diversity against moral realism. But to make unanimity the test of justice is a mossy sophism – and a foul instance of the naturalistic fallacy. The many can go wrong, after all. Societies can be unjust – hugely, trivially, tragically, even proudly and self-righteously. Norms, at their most effectual, take root in the thick of life. But many of the particularities that give norms their thickness are not morally critical in isolation. So the differences of culture and character that Sophists flag do not discredit the quest for universal norms. We need to sift style from substance and see through the willful muddling of the two. Honor and disrespect are shown differently in different cultures and received differently by different individuals. But behind the words and gestures are human cares and hopes, flesh, blood, and bone that belie the diverse costumes. Philippa Foot strikes close to home when she pins normative universality to the needs of living beings.[5]

---

[4] See Goodman, *On Justice*, 9–23.
[5] Foot, *Natural Goodness*.

Rawls is right to seek minimal norms applicable in any *decent* society. Among the rights that he deems minimal are "freedom from slavery and serfdom, liberty of conscience, and security of ethnic groups from mass murder and genocide."[6] The grim history of the nineteenth and twentieth centuries overhangs that list. But the rights Rawls canonizes are centered on the need that he holds central: preservation of agency. No affirmation of dignity would be complete without such stipulations as these. But I see more in personhood than agency and choice, which our liberal tradition, for good historic reasons, inclines to fuse with freedom of conscience and expression, privileging cognitive rights and viewing the state as the chief threat against them. Human dignity is larger and needs a more robust array of safeguards against broader threats than those that capture Rawls's eye and dominate the historic manifestos that he celebrates philosophically – the Declaration of Independence, the Bill of Rights, the Emancipation Proclamation, or Mill's *On Liberty*. I would not anchor human rights in the idea of a contract, historical or virtual, but in the claims all beings make. It is these claims that constitute a being's prima facie deserts. Deserts, I have argued, rise to a plateau in the case of persons, where subjecthood warrants the special claims enshrined as rights. One cannot calendar every consideration that persons are due or all the ways in which their interests deserve respect. Rawls knows that no such table of deserts can be drawn up by simply positing the sheer idea of self-interest.[7] The full resources of law, culture, and human tact would be called for even to sketch roughly how human aspirations might fit together. But here I want to single out a few salient areas where the dignity that is the proper goal and worthy core of human deserts is irrefragable.

My listing draws on Jewish sources and experience, although not for the imprimatur of divine command. Ideas of divinity are far too fluid, plastic, and receptive to allow much criterial work to be offloaded in that way. Didn't the Norsemen and Homeric

---

[6] Rawls, *Law of Peoples*, 79.
[7] Rawls, *Political Liberalism*, 214.

Greeks have gods of war? Didn't Vikings have a god of mischief? I would rather start from what we know best and let the sanctity of norms point toward the divine.[8] Moral minima all too readily reflect what is taken to be divine. But human diversity, of values or of gods, is not the cacophony of Babel. Candid conversation can prove morally instructive, especially if we can pinpoint what warrants repugnance for specific acts. So I touch on just a few such categories, not entirely at random: (1) genocide, induced famine, and germ warfare; (2) terrorism, hostage taking, and impressment of child warriors; (3) slavery, polygamy, and incest, and (4) rape and female genital mutilation. Later I reflect on some richer norms that the more minimal set relate to, because even the barest demands of human decency bespeak a moral perfectionism, openly or tacitly.

The maximal norms I single out here are those of the Decalogue. They do evoke a cultural context, and analogous demands might be realized in other ways. But historical particularity does not diminish their centrality. And, as noted, we all can learn from what any moral code proposes. Here is where my pluralism parts company with Rawls. Rawls seeks room for pluralism through secularism and minimalism. But the pluralism I advocate finds its ideal in an ongoing conversation among cultures in all their richness and among individuals in all their uniqueness. Granted, the lively conversation that I envision might also occur under the high, plain arch that Rawls constructs. But the restraints on public discourse and deliberation that Rawls invokes inhibit the conversation. Once made a social norm or political expectation, these restraints would stifle essential parts of it completely. The effect would be more than chilling. A culture in which varied voices of perfectionism have been silenced in the public square, far from transcending particularity, has canonized a deadening ethos of its own, breeding anomie and inviting fanaticism to take up the slack. For human nature abhors a vacuum of ideals.

Both the minima and the maxima I am mooting here presume the inestimable worth of personhood. The minima seek to curb

---

[8] See Goodman, *Love Thy Neighbor as Thyself*, 35–69.

its violation. The maxima inscribe some ways in which human dignity can be fostered. Neither list is exhaustive; both are samplings. Minima are musts. But our maxima are a signpost to one pathway toward an enhanced human life, as pursued in a familiar normative tradition whose resources, even now, have not been plumbed as fully as they might be globally or locally.

 1. *Genocide, Induced Famine, and Germ Warfare.* All living beings make claims to life. The human face, Levinas writes, as if to read the words encrypted in a hesitant smile, urges, "Do not kill me." It says much more if allowed to speak: "Don't shame me, don't pass me by without taking my hand, or offering yours. Don't overlook the chance that we, together, can build far more than anyone can alone – and what we build will be more than we set our hands to, since, as we build, we can cement a friendship and create a community."

Murder is wrong because it destroys a human subject. Warfare is not always wrong; it may be necessary to protect persons. But war is suspect, even beyond the killing, because it slips its leash so readily. Escalating violence strips away moral barriers, as Thucydides clearly saw. The arts of war mask human faces. Helmets, arrow slits, and night goggles keep enemies faceless to one another. Carl Sandburg saw the deadly irony:

In breathing spells of bloody combat between Christian nations the order goes out: "Don't let the men in the front-line trenches fraternize!"[9]

But genocide is both more and less than war; it is more savage, more ready for stalking than for open confrontation. Why is murder uglier when it aims to destroy a group as such? Scale tells part of the story. But there is an impact and intent beyond the tally. Genocide, in today's language, is a hate crime. Hence the "as such."[10] The killers target a race, a culture, a language group or ethnicity, even a class – as Stalin destroyed the kulaks or Mao or the Khmer Rouge branded literate countrymen as class

---

[9] Carl Sandburg, "The People, Yes," in *Complete Poems*, 509.
[10] Cf. May on the "as such" in the UN genocide convention, in *Genocide*, 143–46.

enemies. Beyond the human beings ground to dust or burnt to ashes and chimney smoke are the children yet unborn. The killing is the worst of it, but not the whole of the horror. Genocide targets hope, a people's futurity and way of life. Victims are singled out by some trait, real or ascriptive, that perpetrators use to deny them human standing and to transform them, first in myth and then in policy, into vermin.

Genocide is the ultimate step in essentializing the exotic. It paints in lurid tones what is feared and hated most in the self. Reflected and reversed in the mask that hides the victim's face, the murderers project another in its place, the image of themselves they hope to see once the demon scapegoat is annihilated. The ugly incubus, blown up to cosmic scale, becomes the warrant for the crime. Confounding violence with power, the architects of horror build a regime, unaware that powers built on violence will self-destruct. Hitler, even undefeated, will run out of Jews, gypsies, decadents, and misfits. Tyranny feeds on ever new victims. It manufactures enemies wholesale with the aid of industrial technology and the magic of modern merchandising – as Stalin did, in making state policy of his tyrant paranoia, inventing ever larger classes of "wreckers" – and as jihadis and Salafists do today.

Revolutions regularly fling their fathers and children into the fire. But they burn out in the end, even without the foreign interference that their febrile policies invite and that their crimes against humanity demand. The bonfire collapses of its own weight, but not before incalculable harm is done. Mao's death toll was 70 million souls. He was ready, he bragged in 1958, to sacrifice 300 million, half of China's population, "for the victory of world revolution." Such losses, he reckoned, had "happened quite few times in Chinese history. It's best if half the population is left; next best, one third."[11] The victims of Mao's holocaust, like those of his fantasy apocalypse, were his own people. In Cambodia too, and in Stalin's Soviet empire, the

---

[11] Mao Tse Tung, quoted in Windschuttle, "Mao and the Maoists," 6.

victims were also the executioners. The injuries to China's pat-
rimony and heritage and the crippling of creative imagination
among survivors of the Cultural Revolution pale beside the earlier genocidal enormities of Mao. But even a funeral pyre casts a
shadow.

Yet genocide has its defenders, active and vocal, passive and
tacit. I have sat next to a prominent Buddhist scholar, a pacifist,
and heard him inveigh against the Croats of Serbia, wishing death
on all their kind. Yet ethnic cleansing, as the macabre euphemism
had it, was the purgation he endorsed for his native land. As
long as such hatred burns, responsible people must continue to
condemn it. The agencies most capable of acting against it are
nations and the states they form – one good reason, as I argued
years ago, for the creation of states and coalescence of nations.[12]
The stench of genocide stands chief among the reasons for the
creation of international bodies too. Still, when the calls go out
for intervention, a staying hand is felt. Insistent voices urge that
nations and the agencies they cobble together must set sanctions
ahead of intervention – sanctions strict enough to be felt, but not
so harsh as to provoke an armed response or serious economic
loss. No nation, they urge, should shoulder the risks and costs
of war without a clear international mandate. Even in debating
the wisdom of sanctions, those who speak for intervention can
expect to be branded neocolonialists, cowboys – or manichaeans,
the special sobriquet reserved for those who distinguish right
from wrong in affairs of state.[13]

---

[12] See Goodman, *Judaism, Human Rights and Human Values*, Chapter 5. *Bien
pensant* projectors place faith and hope in world government – international
courts and international law. But the embryonic, often half-hearted, all too
easily suborned efforts of the United Nations do not build confidence that
such agencies will mount a credible alternative to national efforts, lumbering
and ill considered as they often are. We may be told to wait for more effective international "peacekeeping." But the record thus far is uninspired and
uninspiring. Performance is consistently too little and too late.

[13] Lest we forget, Srebrenica was under notional UN protection in 1995. Even
as 8,000 Bosnian Muslim men and boys were rounded up for execution
there, Ratko Mladic, the general behind that act of genocide, executing the
policies and plans of Slobodan Milosevic's Serbian government, was deep

If some national interest influences countervailing calls for military intervention to halt acts of genocide, does that motive tar the intervention and impose a moral hold, lest action seem insufficiently disinterested? Jean Elshtain offers a fair answer: "If we accept that all human motives are a complex admixture, a humanitarian intervention is not perforce invalidated if it overlaps other motives."[14] Indeed, because wars are shared acts, motives *must* be mixed, or there will never be the collective will to hazard even the most pressing rescue. Could America have freed its slaves had the Union faced no threat? Elshtain's Augustinian realism is a fitting rejoinder to the moralism that demands purity in politics before approving humanitarian action. A moralistic case that proves deaf to moral pleas amounts to special pleading. The world stands guilty for failing to act swiftly and decisively against Hitler's Holocaust and the genocides of Cambodia, Rwanda, Serbia, and Sudan. The member states of the United Nations mock the founding dream of an international voice and force of conscience when they problematize action against genocide, when they temporize, obfuscate, and change the subject.[15]

---

in consultations with high-level UN and NATO officials about the fate of "the Srebrenica population" – as his hidden diaries, tapes, and records reveal. He was plotting with Croatian leaders to kill many more. *New York Times*, July 11, 2010. Even when that story broke years later, Mladek remained at large. The Serbian leader, Radovan Karadzic was on trial at the Hague. But Milosevic died in 2006, frustrating a verdict in his trial for war crimes.

14 Elshtain, "There Oughta be a Law," 85.

15 After visiting memorials for 800,000 dead in Rwanda, UN Secretary-General Ban Ki-moon called it "high time to turn the promise of the responsibility to protect into practice." He voiced frustration with those "who try to change the subject or turn our common effort to curb the worst atrocities in human history into a struggle over ideology, geography, or economics." This was in response to the former Sandinista foreign minister Miguel D'Escoto Brockmann, a Catholic priest and then General Assembly president, who echoed Noam Chomsky's charge that "responsibility to protect" is neocolonialism. Brockmann invited Chomsky and others to address the General Assembly and argued that genuine efforts to combat genocide depend on global economic redistribution and restructuring of the Security Council. *New York Times*, July 23, 2009. In April, 2011, the flailing dictatorship of Muammar Khaddafy sought to make Brockmann Lybia's ambassador to the United Nations.

Along with genocide comes induced famine, typified in Stalin's starvation of the Ukraine, covered up by Walter Duranty, a reporter warm to the march of communism. Here, as in Matilal's thoughts, truth comes into play, speaking out against expedience. Duranty, the *New York Times* Moscow correspondent, actively concealed Stalin's punitive famine, writing in euphemisms and spreading Stalin's smokescreen that blamed "wreckers" for the "serious food shortage." Duranty denied in cold print that there was "actual starvation" and parroted Stalin's gag line: "you can't make an omelet without breaking eggs." Privately, at a 1933 British Embassy party, Duranty admitted to Ann O'Hare McCormick that at least 10 million had died that year. His reporting was honored with a Pulitzer Prize, citing his "scholarship, profundity, impartiality, sound judgment and exceptional clarity." Malcolm Muggeridge, who tried to report the truth about the famine, was blackballed in retaliation.[16] Stalin's vindictive apocalypse was a form of genocide. So was the famine Mao and his henchmen inflicted on China in the Great Leap Forward: Some 36 million to 45 million human beings were worked to death, starved to death, or beaten to death.[17] Germ warfare joins the roster of crimes against humanity. So does Saddam's genocidal air war against the Kurds, Shiʿites, and Marsh Arabs.

The apparatus of a modern state and the mythos of misinformation spread and made fashionable by corrupted and controlled media and made plausible, even respectable, by bought and coopted politicians make hatred a political tool, focusing energies and uniting followers, as Orwell saw. Once tyranny directs a people's eyes to an object of hatred, every struggle becomes a victory. Even defeat becomes a tragic call to further sacrifice. Iran was Saddam's enemy before he invaded Kuwait or set his gaze on the oil wealth and sacred cities of Arabia. Many

[16] Luciuk, *Not Worthy: Walter Duranty's Pulitzer Prize and the New York Times*; Taylor, *Stalin's Apologist: Walter Duranty, the New York Times Man in Moscow*. Duranty was quoting Stalin's words about omelets, although Stalin, whom Trotsky had called the "outstanding mediocrity of our Party," did not originate the bloody apothegm.

[17] See Frank Dikötter, *Mao's Great Famine*; Yang Jisheng, *Tombstone*.

an Arab and Muslim leader from Nasser in Egypt to Bin Laden to the radical imams of Indonesia has used hatred tactically, to distract a nation even from its most pressing needs. American wealth and power and Israel's very existence become goads and cankers, firing resentment and distracting a populace from the hard work of social and economic development, ecological reconstruction, spiritual growth, and moral self-mastery.

2. *Terrorism, Hostages, Child Warriors.* The targets of terrorism are almost random, but as in genocide, a mystique of violence lights the fuse. For some, the bombs that kill and maim unsuspecting victims are pieces of expressionistic theater intended to vent fanatic frustrations with the course of history. Reflecting on tyranny and playing with the thought that the rebel may win a kind of righteousness by risking self-destruction, Camus, in his play *The Just* (1949), pictures the terrorist Kaliayev rejecting his first chance to slay Grand Duke Sergei if it means killing the nobleman's niece and nephew in the same carriage. The saboteur derailing a train might demand of himself what he extracts from others. But the frisson of such thoughts does not efface the ugly lie that romances indiscriminate carnage. Rebellion, Camus urges, may affirm human solidarity. But "any rebellion which claims the right to destroy this solidarity" loses its claim to nobility and becomes "in reality an acquiescence in murder."[18] The means deface and disgrace the ends professed.

Can the targeting of innocents escape that consequence? The real root of terrorism, laid bare by Camus' argument, is nihilism: "Young disciples try with bombs and revolvers and their bravado marching to the gallows, to escape the contradiction and create the values they lack."[19] Dostoevsky saw this clearly at the heart of any murder: The horror of Raskolnikov's crime dissolves the motives meant to justify it. Terrorists negate what they pretend to fight for. Innocent blood blurs and blots the ends proclaimed to justify the slaughter. It is not uncommon for an end to be desecrated by the means deployed in its behalf. Once

[18] Camus, *The Rebel*, 22.
[19] Ibid., 15–17, 305.

those means become a tactic, even a way of life, the blasphemy is complete.

Kaliayev's readiness to die to slay an uncle of the Tsar may have seemed a noble gesture before the routinization of suicide bombing – before the Tamil Tigers learned and taught others how to blow themselves up in the marketplace; before imams and disaffected engineers made an industry of martyrdom, offering glory in the streets and solace in God's garden to recruits too eager to erase their past and simplify their future by shredding busloads of children, strafing wedding parties and holiday gatherings with backpacks of ball bearings and nails, or crashing jetliners into office buildings; before Serbs were paid twenty-five cents a pop for shooting passersby from the upper stories of derelict buildings in Sarajevo; before indigent Iraqis got twenty bucks for lobbing a grenade or planting an IED and Saddam Hussein paid bounties of twenty-five thousand to the families of Palestinian suicide bombers.

To the professional, terrorism is a technique, not a cry of despair. It feeds on the sanctity of life and clogs the media eye with gobbets of sensation. It blackmails democracies, intimidates populations, impoverishes workers, and threatens travelers, students, diplomats, medics, aid workers, and educators. But a kind of Stockholm syndrome entrances the academics, journalists, and even some governments that might have given the victims a voice. The terrorist machine promises a hero's death, but turns out martyrs with the same sweatshop technique used in counterfeiting designer brands, ersatz medicines, or cooking methamphetamines. By sapping civil confidence the strategists and engineers of terror aim beyond their immediate victims. Yet the object is not a voice in the counsels of responsive governance, but imposition of control through threats and bloodshed.

Terrorism spreads because it works, not in righting wrongs but more like a viral contagion, hobbling economies, shifting votes, rending alliances – and winning sanguinary recruits eager to believe that God or history, class or racial destiny, anger, shame, or the sheer horror of fire and blood will vindicate its violence. But even victory does not bring it to a halt, as the

Soviet Gulag, the Cambodian killing fields, the Nazi Holocaust, the Iranian terror, Tiananmen Square, and Taliban beheadings testify. The sequel to a terrorist victory is a bloodbath of the innocent and guilty followed by no opening to light and freedom but instead the fiat of a warlord or opportunist – mob rule – and then repression by some clan, or junta, or thug kleptocracy. When inevitable defeat arrives, the old tactics, now made policy, have become constitutive in a regime's sense of identity and purpose. Hitler and his minions ran the trains all the faster and sped the ghastly work of the death camps when they knew the Reich was doomed – as if that and not the work of governance were the raison d'etre of the state. Defeated in the first Gulf War, Saddam fired the oil wells of Kuwait, lashing out against humanity at large and baring the nihilism at the heart of his megalomania. Terrorism may begin with a tagline or battle cry, but like genocide, it is insatiable – violence made an end in itself, without pretense of a rationale.

Why is terrorism wrong? An answer is worth spelling out, since sophists regularly shift blame to the victims and twist the appraisal from *turpis causa* to *dubia causa*. Terrorists become "militants," their affiliations and funding sources cloaked in referential opacity with phrases like "classified as a terrorist group." Apologists and sympathizers, meanwhile, class terrorism as *honoris causa*. Perpetrators are feted, their acts of murder and mayhem justified and even sanctified.

Terrorism is the willful targeting of noncombatants, aiming for maximal psychic impact. Terrorism is a war crime, because war, if just at all, seeks only to destroy an enemy's power to make war. Terrorism finds a military use in sapping the will to resist. Its intensity comes from its flagrancy. The more helpless and innocent the victims, the more lurid the light. But, like other sensate acts, terrorism seeks ever higher sensations as public sensitivity is leathered over: The more devastating and inhumane the carnage, the more avidly is it sought by terrorist strategists and ideologues. When media outlets and academics soft-pedal the moral issues (even as they play up the horror), presenting terrorism as a natural response to presumptive desperation, they obliquely endorse the tactic.[20] When they cite the need to address (and redress) "the root causes," they become complicit with the aim of wringing political profit from the blood of innocents. Delicate sensibilities that blanch at thoughts of the carbon footprint of the fruits and vegetables their neighbors eat respond with troubling calm to the notion that exploding an airliner or bombing a nightclub, a pizza parlor, or a marathon finish line can be right if it commands attention.[21] Tender souls who would never knowingly buy a blood diamond cover their eyes and call terrorists "freedom fighters" or urge sitting down with them to understand their motives, instead of standing up to parry their attacks; they too easily forget that some tactics discredit the motives pled to justify them – and that the higher the motives, even at face value, the sharper the discord between ends and means.

Theorists, in a sorites, may call terrorism "no more atrocious" than warfare, because war too may target civilians.[22] The excesses of battle give color to their claims. But today's rather precise munitions undercut the argument: If the ethics of warfare changed when sabers gave way to Gatling guns, they must change again when precision ordnance obviates carpet bombing. Granted, warfare has often breached the line protecting noncombatants, but that line is all the more critical for that. Claims that a military response may be counterproductive and preclude negotiation privilege terrorist attacks, granting terrorists a standing that negotiation alone would not have won. Pleas to see the terrorist's point of view, as if it were unknown, pretend to ignorance of the widely bruited aims of most terrorist attackers. A concomitant readiness to sweep aside the fate of victims ill assorts with this conversational gambit. Rarely are these victims responsible for those wrongs, real or factitious, that terrorists claim as motives.

---

[20] See the journal *Critical Studies in Terrorism*.

[21] Najibullah Zazi, confessing his plans to bomb the New York subways: "I would sacrifice myself to bring attention to what the United States military was doing to civilians in Afghanistan." *New York Times*, February 23, 2010.

[22] See McMahan, "The Ethics of Killing in War." Robert Goodin, among many others, blurs the line between terrorism, counterterrorism, and warfare in *What's Wrong with Terrorism*.

Victims and often nominal "root causes" as well are chosen not for relevance but for salience.

Some terrorist acts, including many of the most heinous, are expansionist, triumphalist, irredentist, sectarian – or provocative, aiming to incite intergroup bloodletting. The drug lords of Mexico are often indiscriminate about their targets. The Shining Path in Peru killed many campesinos, thought to be insufficiently appreciative of the Maoist sunrise. Sunnis in Iraq and Pakistan target Shiʿites, aiming to destabilize the country. The methods are ugly. The motives make them only uglier.

Rationalizations, even the mildest, abet the hideous work, because terrorism feeds on second-guessing. But not every apologue pursues moderation. Just days after the September 11, 2001 attacks, Ward Churchill, then teaching at the University of Colorado, cast a moralistic pallium over that criminal act of war. He called the "technocratic corps" in the World Trade Center "little Eichmanns" – aping Hannah Arendt's lucubrations about the banality of evil. Branding an entire civil populace with the execrated name of Eichmann only bares the genocidal motives of many a terrorist act. Were the young pastry chefs from Hawaii who worked at "Windows on the World" and died in the 9/11 attack "little Eichmanns"? Were the secretaries and accountants, financial analysts and traders? Were the first responders, the firefighters and police? Does work in an industry or service to a society demonized by hatred, or mere presence in or near a building emblematic of a prosperous pluralistic culture, make everyone a little Eichmann?

Hostage taking and the use of child warriors parallel the terrorist ethos. Hostages are chosen for the impact of their seizure. If they are tortured or brutally executed it is not because they pose a threat but because the violence can punctuate or amplify a claim. The world, again, is made a spectator to this theater of cruelty.

Like slavery, the use of child warriors violates personhood, making the child victims means and not ends, objects and not subjects. Peter W. Singer estimated that there were some 300,000 child soldiers – voluntary, semi-voluntary, or coerced,

under arms in a recent year.[23] The International Criminal Court
has branded recruitment of children under age fifteen a war
crime, but no one has yet been convicted of it, and child soldiers in guerrilla and warlord forces are impressed as young as
nine or ten. Often drugged, made sex slaves, or used as cannon
fodder, they are set to commit atrocities in ragtag armies that
exploit a child's relative physical and moral helplessness and
fearlessness; they live in conditions of penury, alienation, anger,
or isolation. The child warriors grow up educationally destitute
and emotionally scarred by all that they have done and suffered.

3. *Slavery, Polygamy, and Incest.* Slavery methodically negates
human subjecthood, making a person a tool for use. Kitsch too
is manipulative, but it does not violate our freedom. Murder is
destructive, but slavery keeps its victims alive while robbing them
of agency – transferring the choice of ends to others who do not
share their interests, as Aristotle recognized even as he affirmed
the worth of slavery. Yet slavery means more than alienating a
person's agency – and far more than unpaid or inadequately com-
pensated labor. It diminishes personhood, whether the sense of
subjecthood is vested in one's freedom of choice or in command
of one's time and energies, the chance of leisure, expression of
one's sexuality, or simply personal pride.

There are an estimated 27 million slaves today of both sexes
and all ages, but the majority are women and children. The
U.S. State Department cited evidence near the start of the mil-
lennium that between 700,000 and four million persons were
trafficked annually across international borders, including some
50,000 into the United States.[24] More recently, the numbers have
increased in the global economic downturn. A 2009 UN report
estimated some 12.3 million persons were trafficked annually[25] –
men chiefly for agricultural or construction labor; women and
children for prostitution, domestic servitude, or sweatshop labor.

---

[23] Singer, *Children at War.*
[24] U.S. Department of State, Trafficking in Persons Report, June 5, 2002; Miko,
    "Trafficking in Women and Children"; Finckenauer and Schrook, "Human
    Trafficking"; Richard, "International Trafficking."
[25] *New York Times,* July 17, 2009.

False promises of marriage or employment, torturous burdens of debt, sequestration of immigration papers, and exploitation of fears of immigration authorities are frequently used tactics. So are violence and threats, and to these are added the burden of unhealthy and unsafe workplaces and living conditions, and, for the sexually exploited, the risk of AIDS and other STDs.

Many victims from Thailand, Vietnam, China, Mexico, Russia, or Eastern Europe are brought to Asia, the Middle East, Western Europe, and North America. Burmese girls are sold into prostitution or forced marriages in China in response to the shortage of women resulting from China's one-child policy. Slavery in Africa and the Middle East often slips under the radar. The UN Office for the Coordination of Humanitarian Affairs found children in Chad regularly sold to Arab herdsmen for the price of a calf. Despite government denials, Tuaregs in Mali continue to enslave Bella people, and travelers report overt slave markets in Timbuktu. In Mauritania Arab overlords force women and girls into concubinage or agricultural slave labor. An estimated 600,000 black Mauritanians, some 20 percent of the population, are held in bondage, often hereditary. Although slave ownership was banned in 1981 and criminalized in 2007, the laws remain unenforced. Slaves are taught that disobedience forfeits paradise, and a prominent imam ruled in 1997 that emancipation would violate a core Islamic precept by expropriating legally acquired property.[26]

Niger outlawed slavery in 2003, but local rights workers found some 870,000 still in bondage. One study estimated nearly 8 percent of the population were slaves at that time. Civil war and genocide greatly expanded slavery in Sudan: Boys from Christian and animist groups were kidnapped in the south and pressed into northern militias, and girls were made domestics, field workers, sex slaves, or forced brides, with open government support and unabashed appeals to Islamic norms. In 2000 slaves were commonly sold for $50. A 2003 study found about a thousand children trafficked annually to the Middle East from rural

[26] Ronald Segal, *Islam's Black Slaves*, 206.

Ethiopia – the girls as sex slaves, domestics, or prostitutes and the boys as weavers or cattle herders.

Traffickers to the West include small gangs, major crime syndicates, and drug cartels. Recruiters, abductors, transporters, safe houses, forgers, debt enforcers, brothel owners, and sweatshop operators line the pipeline of misery. Fraud, extortion, racketeering, money laundering, bribery, narcotics abuses, and gambling are related crimes. The victimizers find human cargo easier to ship than drugs; the crimes are less severely punished and more lucrative. As one official put it, "Drugs are sold only once. Humans can be sold multiple times."[27]

Despite rosy dramatizations, polygamy too exploits – not usually as heinously as slavery, but similarly. Apologists claim that multiple marriages, where countenanced, are freely entered, freely left, and well protected by law or custom. Would it were so. The daily interactions that touch a couple's welfare and happiness depend more on custom than on law, but personal character and individual familial practices weigh still more heavily. Women are particularly vulnerable where the law and other societal agencies have their most limited reach. Marriages are paradigmatically private. Partly for that reason sanctioned polygamy has an impact far beyond those who practice it. It affects the status and relations of both men and women, and of their children as well – but most strikingly, it alters the tenor of women's lives.

Is it intolerant to ban polygamy? After all, polygamists do not restrict monogamy. The argument, of course, is sophistical. Polygamy is an invidious system, regardless of the preferences of some practitioners. It diminishes some persons in the presumed interest of others. Regardless of the conditions that may once have favored its institution, it turns women into trophies, objects of pleasure, means of reproduction, and providers of child care and domestic labor. As they age, first wives often become drudges, unless they can exploit their status to dominate younger

---

[27] INS official interviewed December 20, 2002, in *Human Trafficking: International Criminal Trade in Modern Slavery*, Regional Organized Crime Information Center, 2002.

wives and impose subordinate roles on them. Testimony from happy co-wives about their sisterly relations does not ease the structural constraints that foment rivalries for a husband's favor and the status of offspring.

Advocates of many a social change often fail to anticipate their impact. They take for granted existing goods or freedoms even as the framework that secures them is destabilized.[28] Polygamy transforms social and economic relations among men.[29] More palpably, it transforms marriage, making parity and partnership rarer and harder to achieve. But it is chiefly because polygamy is bad for women that it is bad for humanity. Relativists may call romantic love and companionate marriage recent inventions that are culture-bound and fraught with troubles of their own. Granted, no human institution is without its troubles. The love of couples may indeed seem new, especially if one ignores ancient texts and narrowly defines emotional bonds. But to say that an institution has a history or cultural setting does not make just any alternative equally humanizing. Casual or solicited accounts of happy multiple marriages, like the antebellum stories of happy slaves, do not efface the structural invidiousness: It is impossible, given the realities of our nature, for three or more human beings to share the intimacy a couple can build. That is the basic problem too with "free love" and "open marriage." The best intentioned experiments of this sort only depersonalize or commodify intimacy. Polygamy denatures marriage. The impact verges toward an extreme when ego-driven fantasies touch earth in the harems of cult leaders.

Just as temporary marriage and serial monogamy sap familial and social stability and erode the soil in which emotionally

---

[28] The physician Ibn al-Nafis (thirteenth century) reads the prominence of homosexual relations in his own Islamic society as a natural consequence of the sequestering of women and their engrossment in polygamous marriages; *Philosophus Autodidactus*, 65.

[29] The Fundamentalist Church of Jesus Christ of Latter Day Saints was charged with banishing boys as young as eleven or twelve on pretexts such as attending movies, so as to reduce the competition for multiple wives. *Salt Lake Tribune*, June 21, 2006.

stalwart personalities take root – not just among children but among adult participants as well – polygamous relationships diminish the participants by corroding the trust that undergirds monogamous commitment. Polygamy diminishes husbands by depersonalizing what might have been their closest relationship. It diminishes wives more gravely by making them less sharers and more like possessions, to be used and kept, and perhaps one day shelved or discarded. Those who cite our society's present spotty record as regards marriage seem disingenuous in proposing a remedy that only aggravates the trends they expect their hearers to view with alarm.

Incest too breaches privacy, but more damagingly than polygamy, because the victim is typically a minor. Daughters are the chief victims, although most cultures define incest more broadly. But why speak of victims when incest (in rare cases and in theory) may be voluntary? The answer lies in seeing what it is that incest prohibitions seek to protect: the integrity of the family, surely – but why? Why are incest restrictions found in every culture when no one, to the casual eye, need be harmed? Utilitarians sometimes have trouble seeing incest laws as more than ornamental. I see them as foundational. Relativists, from the early Sophists on, flaunt the cultural differences in kinship laws or even their imagined absence in remote lands. But no society leaves sexual relations unregulated, and the salient outliers – say, ritual royal incest in ancient Egypt or pre-contact Hawaii – were symbolic displays of power and concentrations of *mana* fed, in part, on the frisson of the violation.

Some biologists and anthropologists ascribe what they quaintly call the incest taboo to an instinctual aversion rooted in the risks of heightened homozygosity.[30] The risk is real, but in moral terms the issue is more complex. It is true that offspring of

---

[30] Arens, *The Original Sin* critiques Edward Westermarck's aversion thesis and includes detailed ethological accounts of ritual royal incest. There is evidence that children raised together, as in a children's house on a kibbutz, tend to marry outside their experiential sibship. Yet incest, as caseworkers in every community know, is far from rare.

close kin lose much of the protection of a diploid genome: The paired genes that closely related parents inherit from a common ancestor too often match, leaving no workable back-up for a damaged gene. Genetic defects increase in frequency as the coefficient of inbreeding increases, so the incidence of genetic diseases and disabilities accelerates when kin marriages are frequent. The tragic effects in consanguineous families and inbred communities are well known. But why raise the specter of genetic diseases if some incestuous unions yield no offspring?

Beyond the toll of inbreeding, social and moral concerns underlie and underscore the widespread abhorrence of incest.[31] The moral issue is the need to protect emergent personhood in the familial matrix. A growing youngster's sense of self, as we have observed, is deeply invested in an emergent sexual identity. Invasion of that space is inherently violative, troubling the waters in which a new face can see itself and bring into focus personal desires and hopes, a vision of adult life. So societies rightly guard the boundaries of privacy within the family. Just how they do so is indeed a cultural matter. Kinship laws define as well as protect. But no society seems to miss the point: The aim is not just to maximize gratifications or minimize pains but to protect the delicate chrysalis of personhood.[32]

4. *Rape and Clitoridectomy.* So why is rape wrong? It is not just a violation of another's will. For statutory rape is as much a crime as violent rape: A minor is presumed to lack the judgment needed for valid consent. Nor is injury the sole issue. Not every rape involves physical harm. Rape is wrong because it crosses the line on the scale of commitment from affirmation to negation, from the supportive and creative to the destructive and abasing.

---

[31] See Liebermann, et al., "Does Morality have a Biological Basis."

[32] Hume, polemicizing against moral rationalism, argues that incest prohibitions cannot be matters of reason, since relations deemed "criminal" among humans "have not the smallest moral turpitude and deformity" among animals (*Treatise* III I 1.24, ed. Selby-Bigge, 467). But animals do not have personalities in the way that humans do, so the need to protect the emergent sexuality in which a personality is invested does not arise in the same way.

Of all sexual acts, rape is the most alienating – exploitative and
objectifying, yes, but also violative, not just of another's body
but of personhood.

It often used to be said that rape is not a sexual but a power
crime. There is support for that impression from studies that consult rapists' motives, which may aim to humiliate, to strip away
the persona that guards personal dignity. But denying that rape is
a sexual crime has another resonance that rings false, echoing the
modern myth that there is no bad sex. Regrettably, there is bad
sex. Rape is a paradigm case: an act of hate and exploitation, not
love and trust, striking out against the intimacy that gives eros its
natural and transcendent meanings. Intimidation is often of the
essence. The scars run deep, psychically and socially, attesting
to the centrality of sexuality in founding human character and
anchoring identity.

It is not true, of course, that no act has an inherent meaning.
On the contrary, kissing has natural meanings. So does love making. Rape perverts such meanings and overlays a passionate or
passionless violence on sexuality. The rapist violates a victim's
psyche even as her bodily integrity and self-image are abused.
That may help explain why rape is so prevalent in genocidal
wars: The object in such wars is not just to snatch land, kill
troops, or spike weaponry but also to humiliate and unnerve.
Rape is wrong. Always. No circumstance can make it right.[33]
Rape is not, as some feminists pretend, coterminous with het-
erosexual relations. The rhetoric of that canard aims to infect
heterosexuality with the violence that the normative and natural
bonds of loving couples vigorously belie.

What has this to do with cliterodectomy? Only this: that ritual
removal in girlhood of the chief organ of a woman's sexual gratification and orgasmic satisfaction robs the victim, in adulthood,

---

[33] In June, 2002, a Muslim village court in Pakistan ordered Mukhtar Mai gang
raped, as punishment for her twelve-year-old brother's reportedly walking
with a girl from an influential tribe. Raped by four volunteers she was dis-
played naked to hundreds of village onlookers. *Pakistan Times*, March 6,
2006. It is hard to think of a better argument for the need to separate what
may be socially sanctioned from what must be deemed vicious.

of a vital source of joy, self-esteem, and warm relations available to other women. Cultural norms that link the intact clitoris with promiscuity or sexual excess are rooted in fears of women's sexuality and are bathed in insecurity about their fidelity. Such fears confuse liberty with license. Confounding male circumcision with cliterodectomy, as if it too were a mutilation, is another invidious confusion, because circumcision – whether hygienic or spiritually symbolic – does not hamper sexual satisfaction in either partner.[34] It is not mutilation. But cliterodectomy and the more extensive cutting that may accompany it clearly are.

Rawls's Whiggish account of the minimal demands of human decency fails him here, because it appeals solely to choice and agency and prescinds from any substantive account of the good. As Rawls writes,

What are to count as primary goods is not decided by asking what general means are essential for achieving the final ends which a comprehensive empirical or historical survey might show that people usually or normally have in common. There may be few if any such ends; and those there are may not serve the purposes of a conception of justice.[35]

As Andrew Koppelman notes, Rawls may feel appalled by cliterodectomy, but his "constructivist" theory, which seeks to derive the norms of justice from the logic of choice, "cannot generate a basis for condemning it." The case is paradigmatic. Indeed, Rawls balks at a blanket condemnation of slavery, because he can think of worse fates.[36] As Koppelman urges, "A satisfactory conception of human rights must draw on some normative source beyond that offered by constructivism."[37]

I have not tried to spell out all human obligations to self or others or to list every form of wrongdoing. But I do see a thread

---

[34] See Ed Schoen, "Circumcision Updated – Indicated," 860–61; *On Circumcision.* See also Weiss, Quigley, and Hayes, "Male Circumcision and Risk of HIV Infection in Sub-Saharan Africa."

[35] Rawls, *Political Liberalism*, 308.

[36] Rawls, *A Theory of Justice* (1999) 218.

[37] Koppelman, "Can Rawls Condemn Female Genital Mutilation?"

linking the few minima I have listed as candidates for universal
concern: All the wrongs I have cited involve some violation of the
truth. Not that truth telling is somehow the arch imperative from
which the rest are somehow to be deduced. The truths violated
here are those of human personhood – the dignity we have in
common, despite all our individual and group differences in its
articulation. Genocide denies and rejects our common humanity.
It raises the horror of murder to a higher power by negating a
group's hopes and aspirations, seeking to cut them off at the
root, along with every individual hope and dream. Famine and
germ warfare strike at the shared core of our biological being.
Gratuitous hatred is the motive; denial of the life principle is
the modality. With terrorism as with rape, demoralization – to
crush a human spirit that seems intolerable to the assailant – is
the aim. Hostage taking, similarly, seeks to trade in a loss of
spirit. So do human trafficking and enslavement: All of these
negate the claims to freedom that enliven human subjecthood.
Polygamy, cliterodectomy, and incest thwart human sexual and
marital fulfillment – incest, by bruising the psychic roots of a
confident, often emergent, sexual identity; genital mutilation, by
excising the somatic focus of a woman's erotic gratification; and
polygamy, by subverting the intimacy that makes marriage more
than an economic or procreative arrangement and allows it to
blossom as a union of two souls and the bodies in which those
souls flourish.

The Ten Commandments

The moral minima I have proposed have universal human application. But no one lives in a world so austere as to be ruled
by rules bare enough to safeguard just the realms these minima
may outline. Even a far longer and more systematic list of minima would be too thin for living use. We all live in communities
with norms of ethical practice and social convention that can
guide our choices and smooth our relations. Communities foster thick beds of norms that concretely construe human dignity,
supplementing the minimal norms that aim to protect humanity
at its most vulnerable. The well-known tablets of the Decalogue

stand out in one such network, specifying the demands of dignity and responsibility in ways that reflect what Rawls would call a comprehensive doctrine. Rooted in theism and the history of Israel, the network branches out into a luxuriant code, the warp on which the fabric of a way of life has been woven. But even at its starkest, bare of that rich weft and the patterns embroidered over, around, and through it, biblical theism fosters a humanism that commends the Decalogue in universal terms.

The biblical code in full, encapsulated or prefigured in the Decalogue – from the institution of the Sabbath to the broad imperatives to champion the widow and orphan, deal kindly with the Egyptian, and love the stranger – reflects Israel's experience of liberation from Egyptian bondage. The historical embeddedness of its norms allows the Torah's commandments to build an ethos as rich and thick as a way of life requires while retaining the universality that has enabled those norms to breast the centuries and appeal to individuals and cultures far removed from their original setting. The Decalogue is a paradigm case of what a concrete code of norms, rooted in cultural and historical particularity, can contribute to a way of life.

Like the 613 commandments traditionally counted in the Torah, this subset has a prologue. The Rabbis, like Philo, read the biblical account of creation as setting the stage for God's Law. But the prelude to the Ten Commandments is no cosmogenic narrative or patriarchal history, but rather the affirmation of an existential bond: *I am the Lord thy God who brought thee out of the land of Egypt, that slave house* (Exodus 20:2). God here is Israel's liberator, affirming a historic bond with Israel as the keeper of the people's destiny. The affirmation is fraught with normative significance, not least because the fresh memory of liberation speaks to the sanctity of personhood in the human individual, where God's image shines.

Parataxis is often pregnant biblically. The Decalogue, tellingly, is revealed on the heels of a visit. *Jethro, priest of Midian, father-in-law of Moses, hearing of all that God had done for Moses and Israel his people* (Exodus 18:1), brought Moses' wife Zipporah and their two sons to Israel's camp. Moses and Jethro embrace. Jethro blesses the God of Moses, and Moses tells his story. But the next day, watching Moses at work, Jethro is troubled: *What is it that you are you doing to the people? Why do you sit alone with the whole nation standing about you from morning to night?* (18:14). Moses explains: *The people come to me to consult God. If they have an issue, it comes before me, and I judge between one person and the next and inform them of God's rulings and guidance* (et huqqei ha-Elohim ve-et toratav) (Exodus 18:15–16).

Torah here is not yet law but direction. God guided the exodus and led the people through the desert, campsite by campsite (Exodus 13:17–18, 20–22, 14:1–2). Moses now judges case by case. Had the people no notion of a fixed rule? How could that idea have escaped them in a land like Egypt? Clearly they expect to follow God's guidance. But will that mean imitating Moses, as Muslims will one day canonize every gesture of their prophet? Perhaps God has new demands for every juncture, and every case demands new oracles. How does one know what actions might be normatively neutral or where one risks offending God? Jethro has no hesitation in criticizing his son-in-law:

What you are doing is not good. You will exhaust yourself and this people as well. The task is too heavy for you. You cannot do it alone. Listen to me now. I will advise you – God be with you! Do represent the people before God. Bring their cases to God and apprise them of his rulings and directions, inform them of the course to take and the practices to follow. But cast your eye among the people as a whole on able men who fear God, men of integrity who hate ill-gotten gain. Make them magistrates of thousands, hundreds, fifties, and tens, to judge the people continually and bring any major issue to you; but judge all lesser ones themselves. Lighten your load; let them share it. If you do, and God so charge you, you'll be able to persist, and the whole nation will reach their destination safely. (Exodus 18:17–23)

Moses takes the advice, and the Midianite priest returns to his homeland. Jethro speaks forthrightly, as an older man giving practical counsel informed by experience. His worry is not that Moses will turn tyrant by hoarding power, but that he will waste himself, ruin his mission, and exhaust his people. Appealing to a leader's sense of responsibility, he warns Moses that it is unfair to keep everyone on tenterhooks, awaiting rulings that will typically prove trivial. For why would a just God use inconsistent principles? Wouldn't it be better to teach the people prospectively the general rules to obey? Moses will still judge the hard cases, those not yet settled in principle. Lesser matters are res judicata, safely delegated to reliable appointees. God himself, Jethro trusts, will agree. Moses thus rises from judge to teacher. God's *torot* are no longer casuistic but juridical, addressing not situational particulars but principles of law.

Soon after seeing Jethro, Moses is called to the mountain. There God gives him a new charge, recalling to him how God bore Israel *on eagles' wings* and promising a covenant that will make Israel *My treasure among all nations... my kingdom of priests, a holy people* (Exodus 19:4–6). That promise frames the Decalogue and proclaims its goals. These laws are given by the Creator of heaven and earth, the universal ruler and judge. But they are not imposed on the world. They represent God's covenant with Israel, a national constitution, as it were. Their principles will unfold into a system of law. Later comers, seeing the universal ideals embodied in these precepts, will sign on to elements of the covenant.[38] But for now the aim is to sanctify Israel through the way of life prescribed for them.

1. *I am the Lord thy God, who brought thee out of the land of Egypt, that slave house* (Exodus 20:2). Is there an imperative in the first of God's ten points (Hebrew, *devarim*)?[39] There is, Maimonides says. How can God's Law be binding until his sovereignty is established? But doesn't the Torah become circular, Crescas will demand, if God's authority is among its edicts? Maimonides anticipates such concerns by stressing that

---

[38] Ernst Renan wrote that the Ten Commandments "are for all peoples; and they will be, during all the centuries, the commandments of God." Not a parochial hope.

[39] So they are called until the second century, following the Torah's own usage (Exodus 34:28; Deuteronomy 4:13, 10:14). Today's name, *Aseret ha-Dibrot*, is from the Talmud; the term "Decalogue" comes from Clement of Alexandria, ca. 200.

all Israel heard God's declaration for themselves (Exodus 20:15–18; Deuteronomy 5:4–7; B. Makkot 24a).[40] How does that help? Does a direct command have authority that is lacking in a relayed order?

God does not literally speak. So direct hearing here must mean that Israelites grasped God's reality for themselves and saw the imperative in it. How so? Either by intuiting the unity of absolute reality with absolute perfection – a perfection that invites love and the aspiration toward self-perfection, fulfilling our humanity and inviting us to rise beyond our limitations – or by seeing the grace and wisdom of creation and recognizing in nature the hallmarks of transcendence, summoning us, so far as we are able, to "walk in God's ways" – to emulate his generosity and pursue the moral and intellectual perfection in ourselves that brings us closer to God's own perfection.

Inferentially or intuitively, then, if not by tradition, God is known even as his laws are given. Those who cannot directly link perfection with reality can see the nexus of divinity with justice, grace, and mercy: God bestows being, light, life, and liberty. His sanctity defines and guards the sanctity of personhood; his generosity bespeaks the justice and mercy of his Law, whose norms and narrative affirm the worth of being. The first of the ten

---

[40] Weren't *all* ten commandments heard by all the people, Nahmanides asks. For we read: *God spoke all these words* (Exodus 20:1), and when Moses retells the event: *These words did the Lord speak to all your assemblies on the mountain, from the midst of the fire and cloud and thick darkness, in a great voice not heard again. He wrote them on two stone tablets and gave them to me* (Deuteronomy 5:19). Nahmanides replies: If Israel heard God's voice throughout the epiphany at Sinai, they understood only the first two items. The rest were relayed by Moses: *When you heard the voice out of the darkness, the mountain burning fire, you came to me, all the heads of your tribes and your elders, and said: The Lord our God has shown us his glory and greatness; we have heard his voice from the midst of the fire. This day we saw that God may speak to a man, and he yet live. But let us not die now. For this great fire will consume us. If we hear the voice of the Lord our God any further we shall die. For what mortal has heard the voice of the living God speak from the midst of the fire, as we have, and lived? Go nearer yourself and hear all that the Lord our God says, and relate it to us. Whatever the Lord our God tells you will we listen and perform* (Deuteronomy 5:20–25).

commandments, then, enunciates, in God's own voice, as it were, the absoluteness implicit in God's I AM. It bespeaks a perfection inviting emulation. The imperatives of the Decalogue, elaborated in the remaining biblical laws, unfold norms by which the human likeness to divinity can be lived. The perfection to be striven for does not remain an abstract or unreachable ideal. It is realized in human character and relations, wisdom and understanding.

2. *No other gods shalt thou have before me* (Exodus 20:3). God's second article demands exclusivity. Divine jealousy (20:5) is not a passion but a call to intimacy. In the opening words of Genesis, the implicit metaphor makes God a king who has only to speak for his will to be done. But here God is a lover, the beloved of the Song of Songs. Even in thought, Ibn Ezra explains, Israel must revere no other. Ideals and archetypes – Epicurean, Jungian, New Age figments – are unworthy of adoration. This law, like the first one, is spiritual, yet profoundly consequential and life changing: Israel's constitution is a marriage contract with God.

Before in the verse means *instead*. The Torah says *before*, Rashi explains, not *zulati*, "none else," because it would be demeaning even verbally to acknowledge that God might be rivaled. The Aramaic of Onkelos renders the Hebrew as "alongside Me" – a universal exclusion, because God is everywhere. Ibn Ezra, citing Genesis 11:28, where *ᶜal penei* means "in his lifetime," draws a similar inference, because God is eternal. More literally, *before me* means "to my face" – like a brazen, cheating spouse. Nahmanides highlights that nuance, citing the challenge at the onset of Job's troubles – that this perfect man, once stripped of his blessings, would curse God to his face (Job 1:11). The exegete hears a note of spite in alien worship; hence God's reference to *those that hate Me* (Exodus 20:5). Alien worship bears a moral valence. Throwing over God means rejecting life with him, abandoning his ways. Those who hate God follow Baal or Moloch, seeking divinity in acts of horror. Recalling Malachi's words – *From the rising of the sun to its setting my name is great among the nations. Everywhere incense is burnt in my name and a pure offering is given* (1:11) – we feel the force of "pure" here:

It is in offerings untainted with the blood of innocents that God sees a pure intent.

Nahmanides classifies three objects of pagan worship:

(1) The celestial intelligences or star souls that philosophers see as the reality behind the idea of angels. When scripture acknowledges the gods of other nations (Exodus 15:11, 18:11, 6:14, 10:17; Psalms 97:7), Nahmanides sees a form of henotheism, one god presiding over others, the spirits that govern the fate of nations (cf. Daniel 10:13, 20).

(2) The heavenly bodies themselves, which some may think divine and charged with the nations' fate (Job 38:33; Deuteronomy 17:3; Jeremiah 8:2; Isaiah 27:9). Rulers swept up in such beliefs search for visible gods in the ascent of a monarch's star (see Ezekiel 28:2; Isaiah 14:14; Exodus Rabbah 9:7).

(3) Demons and specters – the false, fantastic gods abhorred in scripture for the vicious practices used in their worship (Leviticus 17:7; Deuteronomy 32:17; Job 4:16).[41] Here Nahmanides finds no shadow of true divinity.

Still, his scheme exempts the nations from God's demand for exclusivity, for the very text that bans star worship to Israelites proclaims that God assigned the heavenly host to all nations under heaven (Deuteronomy 4:19). To the ancient rabbis this meant that each nation has its constellation – that is, all but Israel: *Ein mazal le-Yisrael* (Shabbat 156a; Nedarim 32a). Israel has no sign but answers directly to God. Thus Micah's pluralism, following close on the heels of his vision of every person under his own vine and fig tree with none to make him afraid: *For every nation follows each in the name of its God. But we walk in the name of our God, forever* (Micah 3:5).

[41] The biblical abhorrence of idolatry reflects abhorrence for the practices of pagan worship, recrudescent in New Age cults all too eager to celebrate what seems striking and to gain distance from the tamer, saner values of moral monotheism.

In Jewish tradition, the words that follow in the Decalogue spell out the demands of the second commandment: *Thou shalt make no idol nor image of anything in heaven above or earth below, or in the water beneath the earth to bow down before and worship. For I, the Lord your God, am a jealous God, visiting the sin of the fathers on their offspring to the third and fourth generation of those that hate Me, but showing favor thousands-fold toward those who love Me and keep my commandments* (Exodus 20:4–6). Sacral images of any natural or mythic being are debarred, as a corollary of God's exclusivity. Nothing on earth, in the heavens, or the deep may be worshiped. The ban breaks with pagan syncretism, but there is no prohibition of representational art as is at times imagined.[42] What is rejected are all attempts to capture God's ultimacy in an artifact.

The sanction warned of marks the issue as a matter of culture: God visits the sins of parents on their offspring, not by some vicarious taint but through the persistence of vicious ways. The Talmud (Sanhedrin 27) underscores the point, and Onkelos builds it into his translation: Forebears' crimes rebound against later generations "when they continue sinning as their fathers did." As Saadiah explains (at Job 21:19), later generations *decline in their fathers' sins* (Leviticus 26:39) – that is, by following them. But sound ways etch the ethos more deeply: For those who love God, favor (*hesed*) is requited *thousandsfold* (cf. Tosefta to Sota 4). Each generation, then, is a custodian of the ethos.

3. *Thou shalt not take the name of the Lord thy God in vain* (Exodus 20:7). The offense that God *will not excuse* (20:7), I have long maintained, is not making what were once called profane oaths, but instead taking evil as a pole star, disguised under one of God's many names.[43] Voegelin, relying on the etymology of the Hebrew pejorative *shav'*, renders this commandment, "Thou shalt not invoke the name of YHWH thy God to evil intent."

---

[42] See the thorough discussion in Bland, *The Artless Jew*.
[43] Goodman, *On Justice*, 113; *God of Abraham*, Chapter 1. Although citing the familiar glosses, Hertz writes: "*in vain*. lit. 'for vanity,' or 'falsehood'; for anything that is unreal or groundless"; at Exodus 20:7, p. 296.

He explains, "The commandments . . . prohibit fallacious conduct that would obscure the nature of the God who has revealed himself as the *ehyeh asher ehyeh*."[44] Tyranny, not perjury, casts the shadow that darkens Voegelin's page here: The state or race or party, armed with tools of terror and torture, perpetuates the pagan confounding of power with violence. The falsehood condemned biblically is exactly what our moral minima denounced: crimes masked in the false absolutes that unleash rapine and bloodshed. For, as Genesis insists (9:6), to violate humanity is to blaspheme against God, whose image each human being bears. Our bare minima take direction from these higher maxima and fix on the sanctity they safeguard, imputing incalculable value to personhood. Liberals may call rights trumps, but theistic humanism puts the case more strongly, not taking life to be a game.

There is another way of abusing God's name, however, beyond the erection of false absolutes: through wrongs done by those who profess piety or hold some sacred office or affiliation, calling into question not just their own sincerity but also the very authenticity of the ideals to which they pretend allegiance. Here lies the category that Jewish moralists call *ḥillul ha-Shem*, desecration of God's name, again a far broader rubric than a merely verbal slight.

4. *Remember the Sabbath day, to keep it holy. Six days shalt thou labor and do all thy work. But the seventh day is a Sabbath to the Lord thy God. Do no work on it, thou and thy son and daughter, thy servant and maid, thy beasts, and the stranger in thy precincts. For in six days did the Lord thy God make heaven and earth, the sea, and all they hold, and He rested on the seventh day. That is why the Lord blessed and hallowed the Sabbath day* (Exodus 20:8; cf. Deuteronomy 5:12).

A friend tells me that he became a Jew, and indeed a rabbi, in good part because he was inspired by the beauty of the Sabbath and the richness with which its observance perfuses one's life. There are both positive and negative liberties here: One is freed from labor and freed to enjoy and attain spiritual and intellectual

---

[44] Voegelin, *Order and History*, 1.426.

growth and fulfillment. Tradition links these two sides of Sabbath liberty by the ways in which the commandment is worded in the Decalogue and as recalled in the discourse of Moses in Deuteronomy: *Remember* sets out a positive commandment; *keep*, a negative one. *Keep* regards the Sabbath restrictions; *remember* invites one to its joys and emulation of God's all-sufficiency. For, as the rabbinic Sages say, Sabbaths are a foretaste of immortality.

A famous midrash smooths over the verbal difference between our two formulations: *Keep* and *Remember* were fused in a single divine utterance – a mystical topos (Mekhilta, Bahodesh 7) enshrined in the liturgical epithalamium *L'chah Dodi* welcoming the Sabbath as a bride: "*Keep* and *remember* were brought to our hearing in a single word by the God who *is* Unity." Ibn Ezra responds: "Heaven forfend that I correct the Sages. Our minds are dwarfed by theirs. But our contemporaries take the Sages' words at face value." Two words cannot be heard at once; the sounds would only blur and slur. The Sages' intent – that what fuses are the two facets of meaning – is missed if one fixates on the marvel of a twice-heard word. Deuteronomy states plainly (5:1–5) that Moses was paraphrasing the Sinai revelation.[45]

Rashi elaborates on the nuance added by the notion of remembering: The act of remembrance can extend weeklong, inviting us, if we acquire anything delightful, to save it for the Sabbath. Still, Nahmanides notes, the Rabbis do not try to resolve *every* discrepancy between the two texts of the Decalogue. If *zakhor*, "remember," bespeaks a positive duty to sanctify the Sabbath, and *shamor*, "keep or protect," prescribes a negative one, the unity addressed in the midrash bespeaks a complementarity: The restrictions also sanctify; the celebratory sanctifications also set Sabbaths apart from the workaday routine.

Sabbath rest is complemented by the stipulation, *Six days shalt thou labor and do all thy work* (Exodus 23:12; Deuteronomy 5:13), an affirmative command: Work is an obligation. Everyone must contribute to the human project. One's work may be

---

[45] Ibn Ezra, *Commentary on Exodus*, tr. Strickman and Silver, 395, 399–400, 404.

ennobling, it may be a calling, and it may be of critical value. But even before they needed to labor to sustain themselves, Adam and Eve were to tend the garden. Noah was charged to build the ark and save the animals. Neither task was left in God's hands. All human beings have an obligation to preserve and perfect the world, to look after one another and promote the general good. Our responsibility for nature and culture emulates God's creative and sustaining work, just as our rest emulates his consummate perfection. Our lives find their distinctive purposes in the ways we discover to fulfill this obligation. Just as Sabbaths clear a space in our minds for souls to grow in, work gives substance to our identity and meaning to our lives.

But Sabbaths portend a more existential truth than the need for rest or even a mission. They are emblematic of human dignity, a remembrance of Israel's liberation, and a memorial of God's act of creation. Like God, we are not the creatures of our roles. We are free to be creators of our projects, but we are not to be welded to them. The same liberty belongs to men, women, and children; native and stranger. Even servitude, in the ancient biblical society, cannot efface God's image. Rest is a gift not to be declined. It nests protected within the rhythms of the weekly cycle. And that cycle is itself no fact of nature, but a modality pointing beyond the calls of the natural or the social world.

Deuteronomy, our first commentary on the Mosaic code, underscores the moral stroke: *Remember, thou wert a slave in the land of Egypt, and the Lord thy God delivered thee from there with a strong hand and an outstretched arm. Therefore did the Lord thy God command thee to make the Sabbath day* (Deuteronomy 5:15). Sabbaths are made, not found. They matter most to those whose days are not wholly their own. The memory of liberation drives home the point: No one may be made a mere thing. Even animals are not to be worked without respite; they too have a share in God's rest. The principle is extended even to the land (Exodus 23:10–12). But the cynosure is human Thus the agrarian release includes the remission of debts and the freeing of bonded servants (Deuteronomy 15:1–3, 12–15). Yet Sabbaths are not just for the downtrodden. They open a window on transcendence, offering, as the Sages put it, a fore-taste of immortality in the taste of liberty. The Torah in the fourth commandment hallows dignity not in abstract terms but in the earthy difference between labor and leisure.

5. *Honor thy father and thy mother* (Exodus 20:12). As in other biblical laws about parents and offspring (Exodus 21:15, 17; Leviticus 19:3, 20:9; Deuteronomy 21:18, 27:16), fathers and mothers are equal here. And as in the second and third commandments, a sanction is mentioned, which is not civil or criminal but communal. The reward, long tenure in the land, is not a gratuity but an outcome constitutive in the ethos the Law seeks to foster. The verb *ya'arikhun*, Ibn Ezra notes, is transitive: not "that thy days be long" but "that they (your parents) may prolong thy days." The matching texts (at Deuteronomy 11:9, 22:7) have *that you may prolong*. In both cases culture is the vehicle: Filial honor sets an example – a life-preserving model, Saadiah argues. A nation where parents are honored long after parenting is done merits long tenure and stability in its homeland and strengthens the bonds that enhance that possibility.

Sociobiologists propose that parents care for (and care about) their young for their genes' sake. But here offspring are charged to honor their parents – not for their usefulness or even in appreciation of their care. The commandment does not presuppose exemplary parents. Nor is age the issue. Parents need not be elderly, and respect for the elderly is commanded elsewhere: *Rise up before a hoary head* (Leviticus 19:32), a duty both broader and thinner than filial piety. Rather, the obligation to honor one's parents marks the sanctity of the relation. Malachi, as the canon closes, speaks poignantly of parents and children turning toward one another, a kind of epitome and consummation of interhuman harmony at its most elemental (3:23). But the filial obligation set out in the Decalogue finds its warrant not in social stability or even in social harmony. We honor parents not to build a special bond but to acknowledge and solidify the bond we have.

Cant remarks and stereotypes about a generation gap, snide jokes and cruel conventions about overbearing mothers and dod-dering or oppressive fathers, reflect an ethos hostile to the moral

bonds between generations. If well tended, those bonds are chan-
nels of lasting caring and communication. In one rabbi's gloss,
honor thy father and thy mother must also mean honor the
father or mother within you by preserving, protecting, educating,
and enlightening your children, raising morally and intellectually
strong adults – a heritage deeper than genes can build.

6. *Thou shalt not murder* (Exodus 20:13). The Hebrew does
not say, "Thou shalt not kill." That would blur the critical distinction of murder from manslaughter (Exodus 21:18; Numbers
35:6–34) and mire the Law in inconsistency, since it does not
ban but mandates capital punishment (Exodus 21:12, 15–17,
22:18, 31:14–15, etc.), anticipates just warfare (Deuteronomy
20, 21:1017), and permits deadly force against a home invasion
(Exodus 22:1) or a heinous crime.[46] The Law does not confuse slaughtering an animal with slaying a human being. But it
does expand rabbinically to forbid injury to another person and,
homiletically, even to forbid shaming another, causing the blood,
in effect, to drain from another's face.

Murder is the intentional, efficacious, and wrongful use of
deadly force against another person. Blood payment is no remedy (Numbers 35:31). Capital proceedings are hedged with strict
procedural safeguards of the accused (Numbers 35:30), but a victim's kin may not waive punishment. Society, as we have noted, is
also injured, but it too has no standing to set aside the penalty of
this ultimate affront to the sanctity of law and life. Reconciliation
does not efface the enormity. As Maimonides wrote,

if criminals were not punished, crime would go wholly unchecked, and
those who contemplate wrongdoing would be undeterred. No fool is

---

[46] "These may be saved from sin even at the cost of their lives: one who pursues
another to slay him, or who pursues a male or a betrothed girl – but not
one who desecrates the Sabbath or commits idolatry" (Mishnah Sanhedrin
8.7). The law fuses self-defense with the protection of others, relying on the
command, *Nor shall you stand idly by the blood of your neighbor* (Leviticus 19:16). Those who can must act to prevent murder and rape, but only
with the force needed to protect the victim – and save the aggressor (*rodef*)
from committing an irreparable crime. For the ethos, see Fletcher, "Talmudic
Reflections on Self-Defense."

more fatuous than one who calls it humane to abolish punishment. That would be the height of inhumanity and the ruin of civil order. What is compassionate, in fact, is to do as He commanded: *Establish judges and magistrates in all your precincts* (Deuteronomy 16:18).

Impartiality marks the rule of law (Exodus 23:3; Leviticus 19:15).

7. *Thou shalt not commit adultery* (Exodus 20:13). Ibn Ezra argues, with his usual linguistic flair, that what this commandment forbids, under the name *ni'uf*, are all forms of wrongful sexual congress. Thus Jeremiah (3:9) uses this term when he inveighs against the people of Judah for whoring *even with stocks and stones*. Jeremiah's vivid imagery refers to the idols espoused in place of God. Ibn Ezra's gloss broadens the charge. But halakhically adultery is a man's intercourse with another's wife. The penalty is capital for both parties (Leviticus 20:10; Deuteronomy 22:22). As Hertz writes, "There is to be no double standard of conjugal morality in Israel."

The biblical grounds are not those commonly cited in later glosses. The aim is not to preserve the lines of paternity, prevent incest, or safeguard filial piety.[47] Nor does the Law, as some feminists imagine, make women chattels. Biblically, as we have observed, there is no capital penalty for property crimes. God promises that following his laws will spare Israel the diseases they knew in Egypt (Exodus 15:26). But the suffering wrought by adultery runs deeper, bringing heartache, feuds, even the death of innocent children. The Torah will help *purge this evil from your midst* (Deuteronomy 22:21), by addressing not just the act but the ethos.

The biblical norm sharply contrasts with an imagined genetic imperative to be prolific through promiscuity. Hezekiah ben Manoah, called the Hizzekuni after the title of his commentary on the Pentateuch (ca. 1240), inveighs against the specious morality of serving one's race by impregnating as many women as possible. Such notions, he writes, do not build the world, but tend only to its destruction. Genghis Khan, who fathered countless children, was not a builder but a destroyer. Better to raise and

47 Cf. Philo, *De Decalogo* 121–31.

relate to a few children than to scatter many. Biblically, sexual love is sacred, but eros per se is not. What is sacred warrants reverence and must cohere with other core values such as love and respect, and not be made public and promiscuous.

8. *Thou shalt not steal.* The normal sense of the Hebrew, as Ibn Ezra shows, is to forbid taking another's property by force or fraud. The standard penalty for theft, as we have observed, is restitution in a multiple of the value taken. Maimonides sees the excess as a deterrent; Abravanel, as compensation for the attendant pain and suffering. But why is theft even mentioned in the Decalogue? Is the offense grave enough? Isn't theft separately forbidden in Leviticus, along with fraud and mendacity (19:11)? The Talmud (B. Sanhedrin 86) reasons that mere larceny would not be tabled with capital crimes such as murder and adultery: The concern must be with persons (*nefashot*). So the issue would be man stealing, potentially a capital offense (Exodus 21:16).[48] Onkelos translates accordingly, and Nahmanides concurs: The concern, as with murder, is protection of God's handiwork, although the commandment is extended to every property crime.

9. *Thou shalt not bear false witness against another* (Exodus 20:13). This commandment sheds light on the third: If the reference there were to oaths, this ninth might seem to overlap it.[49] Leviticus 19:11 bars lying broadly. Here the setting is a court proceeding. Moshe Greenberg explains that, in the law of the "scheming witnesses," conspirators are liable to the fate they devised for their victim. But that law (Deuteronomy 19:16–19) addresses only cases of personal injury. "The scope of this Commandment is much wider, since witnesses also play a role in civil matters." Here the aim is "to protect the validity and reliability of the judicial process."[50]

[48] Kidnapping, as Ibn Ezra notes, is a capital offense when the victim is a child or a mute, unable to raise the alarm.

[49] At Deuteronomy 5:17, the word *shav'* is used in place of *shaker*: What is prohibited there is groundless testimony against another. Here in Exodus the proscription forbids a damaging lie.

[50] Greenberg, "Some Postulates of Biblical Criminal Law," 296.

Ibn Ezra comments: "For years I asked myself why the text has *ᶜed sheker* (false witness, instead of *ᶜedut sheker*, false testimony). I've come to believe that Scripture here addresses the false witness: Do not testify if you are a false witness!" All must internalize the values that undergird the system for justice to be served. Only consider the impact of the presumption that the machinery of justice must be adversarial and the expectation that the accused may or even must do anything to protect his presumptive interests. Rabbinically, the prohibition of every class of verbal injury to others is sheltered under this commandment.

10. *Thou shalt not covet* (Exodus 20:14). If any commandment reveals the Decalogue as a moral code aiming to help form a holy people, it is this one. As Mordecai Kaplan writes, "'Thou shalt not covet' cannot be classed with the legal prohibitions or duties which constitute the other commandments, since it cannot be enforced by societal action. It deals with the inner disposition which no one but the individual himself can in the last instance bring under control." Yet this commandment is critical: "Unless a man masters his own disposition so that he shall not covet what belongs to others, no amount of external enforcement will secure the complete observance of the other commandments."[51]

Law and morals intertwine here, because intent is mother of the act: *Thou shalt not covet* reaches into the heart – or calls each of us to do so. Deuteronomy (10:16) generalizes poetically: *circumcise your hearts*. Behavioral conformity does not suffice. We must plumb our intentions and make our motives worthy not just of the Law's indulgence but also of God's pride. The tenth commandment speaks to each conscience – but the ethos it informs when publicly pronounced may help keep one out of courtrooms. It does its work in the inner forum, where one stands alone with oneself before God – but the outcomes of that inner conversation, multiplied many times over, are visible in the community the Law seeks to build.

Each imperative of the Decalogue, as exegetes observe, is framed in the second person singular, addressing the individual.

---

[51] Mordecai Kaplan, Introduction to *Mesillat Yesharim*, xix.

So these prescriptions function timelessly as a fount of personal norms. But to do so the tablets must do more than vaguely gesture toward an ideal. If their imperatives are to be effectual, their proper place is in the heart, in the actions and intentions of those addressed. The original stone tablets, tellingly, are shattered (Exodus 32:19), and the back-up copy is lost – just as no one knows where Moses was buried. The Decalogue, then, is not an archive. As the Torah says of its law in full: *It is not in heaven, as if to say, 'Who will go up to heaven for us, and get it for us and let us hear it, that we may do it?' Nor is it over the sea, as if to say, 'Who will cross the sea for us, and get it for us and let us hear it, that we may do it?' The thing is very close to thee, in thy mouth and in thy heart, to act on it* (Deuteronomy 30:12–14). The *thing* here is nothing mysterious, but as plain and direct as the choice between life and death, good and evil (Deuteronomy 30:15). It is a way of life, a law set out in the Mosaic manner, as the command of the living God.

The United States not long ago was treated to a courtroom circus about hanging framed translations of the Decalogue on the wall in public places or mounting the tablets on a courthouse lawn, as a sort of cenotaph of standards long admired but at risk of being forgotten or recalled only as quaint emblems, like hexes painted on old barns or sun catchers in a shop window. But the Decalogue is not a wall hanging or memorial. Indeed, the Hasidic master Mendel of Kotzk teaches that the biblical ban on idolatry includes making idols even of God's commandments, substituting outer form for inner intent. The Kotzker enriches Maimonides' ruling that biblical verses are not to be used as ornaments or amulets.[52]

Familiarity, here as elsewhere, still breeds contempt. To reduce God's laws to decorative motifs, even as a pretext for securing their place in public space, brackets their commands in referential opacity and dims their intensity, much as Ku, the Hawaiian war god, is diminished when reduced to a luau decoration or a resin key fob with green rhinestone eyes. An aumakua was a

[52] Maimonides, *Responsa*, ed. J. Blau, no. 268, 2.510–15.

tutelary god, lesser than great gods like Ku, yet still an object of awe, imbued with ancestral spirits and a marker on one pathway toward transcendence. We may differ about what warrants reckoning as holy. But pluralists must respect and not diminish what another holds sacred. Holiness is desecrated when an aumakua becomes a patio ornament or restaurant sign. A court that posts the Decalogue as an icon has not restored but sapped its force, making it mere signage like the barely noticed EXIT sign over the door.

The Pledge of Allegiance is turned vacuous by legal fictions calling its invocation of God "ceremonial deism" – civic mumbo-jumbo, lodge ritual, historic, perhaps, but spiritually empty and operationally null. The Decalogue, summoning hearers to self-transformation, can be secularized, of course, like Santa Claus. A creche in the park, by those standards, becomes mere decoration. "Bismark is a herring," as Yip Harburg wrote. The Ten Commandments are a plaque. "DuBarry is a lipstick . . . Queen Mary just floats along from pier to pier," and "Venus DeMilo is a pink brassiere. . . . Yes, my honey lamb, Swift is just a ham. Lincoln's a tunnel; Coolidge is a dam. The Czar of Russia is now a jar of caviar" and "Cleopatra is a black cigar!"

4

The Road to Kazanistan

When Rawls is credited with restoring normative discourse in politics, the praise might mean that his example freed theorists long afraid to buck the positivist tide that ran so strong in the first two-thirds of the twentieth century. Or it might mean that his work broke the hold of the machiavellian equation of realism with realpolitik so often attached to the idea of value-free social science in the study and teaching of politics, history, and law. There is some truth in those claims. Rawls did help make normative claims respectable where they had been shunned. He must share the credit, of course, with Watergate, which provoked widespread calls for a new infusion of moral concerns into public life and for the teaching of morality to future leaders and professionals. Such spirited calls seem innocent of the ancient recognition that virtue is learned more from practice and example than from precept and tuition. The fond hopes for moral education externalized the infamy, ducking the admission that Watergate, like many another scandal, was not just a violation of the ethos but also an ugly caricature of it – spit and image of the practices long modeled in the Lone Ranger's forays into villains' safes and offices: Conscientious subterfuge was fine, so long as it stayed sub rosa. The jig was up when Nixon was caught sending men into the Watergate sniffing for evidence of Cuban ties to the Democratic Party. The same moralists who voiced shock at the burglary lionized Daniel Ellsberg for leaking the Pentagon Papers. Plato's lesson was hard to learn and easy to forget: It was not Socrates but Athens who formed the character of Alcibiades.

Morals, for much of the twentieth century, were readily and willfully confused with moralism. The Vienna Circle – their shadow grown tall by mid-century, silhouetted in the glow of scientistic optimism – shunned value talk. They had seen the rhetoric of idealism carried off by extremist ideologues to misty metaphysical heights and then restored, deflowered and led captive by dubious and dangerous causes. Positivism looked clearer and cleaner. Pragmatism felt more down to earth than overt metaphysics. And utilitarianism, at least, seemed naturalistic and forward looking. Or Marxism – if one could trust its promises and ignore the noises off from the dungeons and the Gulag – bruited itself as scientific and progressive, the wave of the future.

Even before Nazi officers and officials stood in the dock at Nürnberg trying to shelter behind a dossier tagged "My Station and its Duties," *duty* had been marked a four-letter word. The flood of war works that philosophers turned out during or soon after World War II – T. D. Weldon's *Vocabulary of Politics*, William McGovern's *From Luther to Hitler*, Karl Popper's *The Open Society and its Enemies*, and many others – damned absolutism as the root of totalitarianism.[1] In doing so, they stretched

---

[1] Ralph Barton Perry's *Our Side is Right*, a notable exception, turns Perry's thesis that value is the object of any interest into a stern condemnation of tyranny: "If 'right' is to be used as the predicate of a sentence which is true or false, then 'right' must have a meaning. In spite of the moral skepticism which has run riot in the world during the last century there is little disagreement as to what that meaning is. The right act is the act that best satisfies all claims as they are viewed by a disinterested and sympathetic bystander" (12). Totalitarian regimes systematically deny the legitimate claims of persons, so they are wrong. Perry forthrightly rejects moral relativism: The view that "all moral convictions are equally right" is a "way of weakening men's moral convictions." Yet liberals are "extremely vulnerable" to the notion that one must "respect the other man's belief even though it be a belief in slavery and intolerance." So "the more pure and scrupulous the liberal is the more surely can he be counted on to befriend the enemies of liberalism. And once these are morally befriended, and their code is given an equal standing with our own, it becomes ridiculous to fight them on moral grounds. There may still be other things to fight about,

the meaning of "absolutism" to cover any affirmation of objective differences between right and wrong. Philosophers, with an aw-shucks twang and a tug at the forelock, confessed that democracy was just their prejudice. That posture survives in Rorty's dismissal of philosophy and his free admission that his own constitutional preferences are just his biases. It also survives in Rawls's appeals to tradition and his pleas to silence "comprehensive" doctrines in policy debates. But Rawls did help dispel the fear of normative talk in politics. He did this, almost magically, without visible appeal to a comprehensive doctrine of his own or any apparent violation of Hume's warnings about moralists who pull an ought out of a silk hat full of *is*-es. He did it, in fact, by telling a story.

Rawls's colleague Harvey Mansfield deserves some of the credit as well for finding the moral subtext, an appeal to civic virtue, that Spinoza had sensed in Machiavelli's politics.[2] But the work of another colleague, Robert Nozick, attests to Rawls's success in breaking the positivist spell. For Nozick answered Rawls's case for redistribution by citing the moral authority of possession: What right, he asked, in *Anarchy, State, and Utopia*, has anyone to take what is mine to aid someone else? That moral question has a moral answer: Spinoza's recognition that private means and personal sympathy fall far short of meeting grave human needs. Beyond that stand Maimonides' twin theses: that charity (one face of justice in the Mosaic canon[3]) must give of the best one has, and that the highest form of charity aids others to self-sufficiency. Spinoza's reasoning does cast a safety net,

such as life, property, and territory, but the moral motivation is gone" (10). The "muddle," Perry writes, "For muddle it is," stems "from a failure to distinguish between a moral difference and a merely emotional difference. There is a moral difference between ourselves and the Nazis because we believe that freedom is right, and they believe that slavery is right." Perry's words still resonate regarding not just the neo-Nazis but also their genocidally motivated avatars in Iran, Pakistan, Waziristan, the Philippines, Guinea, Somalia, Indonesia, and Afghanistan – and their apologists.

[2] Spinoza, *Tractatus Theologico-Politicus* 5.7, tr. Shirley, in the *Complete Works*, 700.

[3] See Goodman, "Mosaic Liberalism."

and Maimonides' guy wires give that net spring and bounce. But Nozick's claims show how far the worm has turned since philosophers dismissed normative discourse as nonsense and rarely or barely held back from branding it as nasty nonsense too.

Rawls's story is about a social contract. He shields it from Hume by frequent reminders that the contract is imaginary. Imagine, he proposes, a group of rational persons meeting to choose the rules that will govern them.[4] They must make their choices under a veil of ignorance, not knowing what roles they will play in the new society nor even what talents, skills, or preferences they will have when they come to birth as citizens. With no idea whether they will be rich or poor, wise or simple, artistic or prosaic – no notion of their values beyond what Rawls thinks implicit in the bare idea of rationality, a disposition to pursue their own interests, and a resolute intent to define those interests for oneself – they would choose a mode of governance, Rawls argues, that would safeguard their liberties, allowing them to continue to make choices in the future. And knowing and desiring their own advantage, in parceling out goods and ills they would choose a system that maximizes equality, allowing only those inequalities that would benefit the least advantaged among them.[5] Despite the veil, then, Rawls's choosers seem well

---

[4] Rawls, *A Theory of Justice*, 11.

[5] Rawls's "Difference Principle" for basic "social and economic inequalities" is that "the higher expectations of those better situated are just if and only if they work as part of a scheme which improves the expectations of the least advantaged members of society." *A Theory of Justice* (1999), 65. One difficulty here lies in the assumption that effort and merit have nothing to do with determining who is "better situated." Everything is assumed to be a matter of good or ill fortune. Rawls writes, "the intuitive idea is that since everyone's well-being depends upon a scheme of cooperation without which no one could have a satisfactory life, the division of advantages should be such as to draw forth the willing cooperation of everyone taking part in it, including those less well situated. The two principles mentioned [equality of basic liberties and the difference principle in allocation of goods and opportunities] seem to be a fair basis on which those better endowed or more fortunate in their social position, neither of which we can be said to deserve, could expect the willing cooperation of others when some workable scheme is a necessary condition of the welfare of all" (13–14; cf. 63–64). So all rights, goods, and opportunities

schooled in Pareto's equilibria and disequilibria. Further, Rawls argues, rational choosers would give lexical priority to the first of his two principles over the second: Formal rights will always trump material entitlements, for only so is free choice preserved.[6]

What Rawls's thought experiment reveals, he says, is what we would call justice: "Justice as Fairness," as he labels the concept. That was the title of the 1955 article in which he broached his idea – a title he preserves in the 2001 volume summing up his stance. By then an estimated million words had been written about *A Theory of Justice*, in which Rawls elaborates his claims, seeks to answer and anticipate rejoinders, and lays out means by which his theory might be put into practice. What the thought experiment reveals, Rawls urges, tallies with tradition – with Aristotle, Locke, Rousseau, and Kant – and with "our intuitive conviction of the primacy of justice."[7] The appeal, ultimately, is to the social contract idea, since ancient times a powerful test of legitimacy and in early modern times a powerful fumigant against the divine right of kings.[8] But the

---

here are *bestowed*. None are intrinsic or innate, and there are no earned deserts. Further, Rawls assumes that his choosers would give preference to themselves and others like themselves. Rawls's choosers "are conceived as not taking an interest in one another's interests" (12). Yet self-preference is hardly a matter of logic and is inconsistent with some versions of rationality. But Rawls is no pluralist about rationality. His rational man, indeed, tends to equate leadership with advantage and opportunity with power. But even selfish individuals might see advantages in yielding leadership to bright, generous, or hard-working others or to those whose values they approve. And access to material goods is not the sole yardstick that rational decision makers might choose if unaware of the values they would come to hold.

[6] Yet the priority of liberty over life is no analytic matter. Nor is it a lead pipe cinch even assuming an advantage in keeping one's options open. Real people often weigh things differently. Recall the "better-Red-than-dead" debate of living memory. When people are asked to risk their comfort or their lives for liberty, much depends on the (comprehensive) views they hold as to the place of liberty (or other special values) – how they regard those for whom the sacrifice is to be made and how they expect liberties dearly bought to be used.

[7] Rawls, *Law of Peoples*, 4, 10–11.

[8] Rawls seeks to dispel the mythic aura of the contract idea by speaking not of actual but of virtual consent. But as I argued in *On Justice*, 9–23, consent, whether actual or virtual, although a good index, is neither a necessary nor a sufficient criterion of justice.

disappearance of monarchy or the dissipation of its once mordant moral claims robs the contract idea of its once revolutionary punch, just as voting practices (including initiative, referendum, and recall) bring the idea of consent down from the mythic empyrean into the realm of prosaic political practice.

Rawls's appeal to shared intuitions is not meant to reduce his theory to a mere analysis of usage. "This theory," he wrote, "is not offered as a description of ordinary meanings."[9] Rawls was making normative claims. Yet he rested them on a seemingly empirical premise: that the principles that his thought experiment sought to distill from a welter of competing notions about justice would be recognized by reason as the ones rational persons *would* choose in the conditions he specifies.[10] There is a tension here, of course, between abstraction and reality.

Rawls invokes an economist's notion of rational choice to give pith to his idea of rationality. Yet it is crucial to his case that rationality in his model present a relatively thin profile. It is not clear, for example, that the choosers in the original position would know just how steep a curve to tolerate in allowing inequalities – that is, *just how much would the least advantaged have to benefit to justify a given degree of inequality?* It is also not clear that rational persons deprived of knowledge of their future levels of altruism, or risk aversion, or sense of community (beyond Rawls's posit of class consciousness) would have any idea how to answer such a question or reach agreement about such things – or even what to count as a basic good. So it is not clear that these mannequins would be able to make the choices Rawls calls on them to make.

Still, it is important to Rawls to keep their decision making free of any specific ordering of values, lest his instrument for situating justice decline into obvious circularity. Just as Kant strove to derive the end-in-itself formulation of the categorical imperative from the universal-law formulation, and just as Lon Fuller sought to derive thicker norms from the very logic of

9 Rawls, *A Theory of Justice*, 10.
10 Rawls, *Law of Peoples*, 16.

the idea of law, Rawls hopes to unpack the idea of rationality to yield a view of justice that readers will recognize as their own. But, *insofar as the appeal is empirical*, the approach does run afoul of Hume's critique and does slap up against G. E. Moore's open question method. We humans are fallible, after all. Our notions of justice might be sadly mistaken or half-baked. The point is not academic. Past theorists and common folk as well have accepted many a practice that now seems manifestly unjust. Remember Huck's tormented conscience when he helps Jim escape an owner, who, as Huck ponders the case, never did Huck any harm. Much that we accept today might one day seem grossly unjust to our successors. Yet, *insofar as Rawls's argument is analytic*, it becomes trivial, merely spelling out the implications of his stipulated conditions.

Rawls coined the term "reflective equilibrium" to describe the dialectical process by which, he hoped, the rough edges would be rubbed off discrepant ideas in the search for justice:

We begin by describing it so that it represents generally shared and preferably weak conditions. We then see if these conditions are strong enough to yield a significant set of principles. If not we look for further principles equally reasonable. But if so, and these principles match our considered convictions of justice, then so far well and good. But presumably there will be discrepancies. In this case we have a choice. We can either modify the account of the initial situation or we can revise our existing judgments... By going back and forth, sometimes altering the conditions of the contractual circumstances, at others withdrawing our judgments and conforming them to principle, I assume that eventually we shall find a description of the initial situation that both expresses reasonable conditions and yields principles which match our considered judgments duly pruned and adjusted. This state of affairs I refer to as reflective equilibrium.[11]

Rawls's account of reflective equilibrium strangely mirrors the mystic's idea that higher knowledge is won, doubts overcome, and epistemic problems dissolved when thought proceeds in isolation. But here dialogue displaces seclusion, and the ancient

---

[11] Rawls, *A Theory of Justice* (1999), 18, citing Nelson Goodman, *Fact, Fiction, and Forecast*, 65–68, for the model of reflective equilibrium.

worry – that dialectical suasions may match up without winning their way to truth – is forgotten. Yet "generally shared" principles and convictions can be horribly wrong. What emerges may be dogma, complacency, or confusion. Much depends on what is deemed "rational" and who counts as "we." Dialectic *can* correct mistaken ideas, but it can also fragment or polarize disparate views. Rawls presumes shared standards of validation. But despite the faith we philosophers vest in dialogue, it need not yield consensus, and many a hard-won consensus turns ugly.

Rawls's theory was criticized on many grounds. Popularly, its redistributive claims seemed to many supporters and critics alike a belated manifesto for George McGovern's platform. Philosophically, the word "rational" introduced a sea of troubles. If choosers behind the veil of ignorance are presumed rational enough to seek their own interests and interested enough to preserve their liberties and pursue entitlements (presumptively, material goods and the means to secure them), why are they not rational enough to imagine that other goods might mean more to them than possessions – more than power or even liberty itself? As I asked in *On Justice*, "how would those who know nothing of their own values and have no experience of the testing of liberty against rival urgings and exigencies understand liberty?"[12] Has Rawls freighted his idea of rationality with personal and familiar preferences while excluding values that seemed to him secondary or inconsequential but that others might cherish?

Rationality in Rawls's theory boils down to a species of egoism. His original choosers, as Amy Eckert notes, "do not take an interest in each other's interests." Do they even care what others think of them? Their presumptive goals are narrow, like the aims accountants presume in preparing tax returns. Does that leave room for a life based on the Buddhist teaching that all suffering stems from attachment? Or for Stoic indifference to externals? Such persons, Rawls holds, are free to pursue their ideals in the new society. But how, in ignorance of the attitudes they may later hold, can they found a society not inimical to those values?

[12] Goodman, *On Justice*, 18.

Does rationality rule out ascetic or spiritual or pietistic or even chivalric priorities?

Some say, in Rawls's defense, that his intent is to presume the least about human nature and (thus) to assume the worst. But there is a difference between minimal and cynical premises. Diminished egoism, some defenders add, would only strengthen Rawls's case – for redistribution, that is. But altruists might want opportunities for responsibility (rather than property or income) to be shared more widely. Buddhists would set detachment at the core of their desiderata. To chivalric or Nietzschean choosers, equality might be of minimal concern. They might well risk penury or peonage for a shot at knightly or even royal glory.

Describing Cretan society as attuned to warfare (*Laws* I 625–26), Plato suggests that any polity might be understood as centered on some core thematic. Rawls introduces such a thematic when he prejudges the interests of his deciders. A society attuned to eros or erudition, valor or valetudinarianism would reach vastly different results from those that Rawls expects. But in a real society, where individual and group diversity are taken seriously, the very notion of a uniform thematic falls to the ground. That is one difference between a real and an imagined society, and its relevance points to the core of what gives pluralism its claim to legitimacy.

Partisans of Rawls, when asked whether values other than those he calls rational might actually be freely chosen behind the veil of ignorance, tend to answer that the master's goal was to define the core principles of a *liberal* society. Indeed, Rawls often uses the words "liberal" and "rational" interchangeably. But here his argument turns circular, and the thought experiment becomes not a means of discovering the character of justice but just a way of stipulating one favored version of the liberal ideal.

Rawls's rational founders are blinkered (by hypothesis) to the possibility that they might prefer a society oriented toward agape, anarchy, adventure, beauty, candor, caring, change, charity, creativity, dignity, discipline, domination, domesticity, dynasty, elan, energy, entertainment, ethnicity, fertility, filial piety, grandeur, gratitude, gender equity, health, holiness, honor, idealism, knowledge, love, militarism, nobility, novelty, obedience, piety, propriety, purity, quarrelsomeness, querulousness, revolution, risk, ritual, science, self-sacrifice, style, truth, unbelief, victory, virtue, virtuosity, wisdom, xenophobia, youth, or zeal. I could instance many more, each with countless foci, variants, degrees, alloys, interactions, and interpretations. Rawls may bracket such values as lifestyle preferences, choices that liberalism facilitates. But for those who prefer aestheticism or athleticism, dandyism or dadaism even above liberty, what is chosen is not a lifestyle but a life. How (without question begging) would anyone in the original position know that building a society around such values is irrational? Can we concede even the letter *J* to Rawls, when Jains, Jehovah's Witnesses, and Jews are not given permission to frame a way of life but simply told that they are free to find a place in Rawls's polity? We already know how deeply committed to secularism and not just secularity that polity proves to be.

Many people have spurned Patrick Henry's noble thought (and Nathan Hale's noble act), by preferring life to liberty. Many have surrendered liberty for security – often in the bourgeois sense popular in the 1950s. Many still do. Others have sacrificed life or liberty for their children's sake or safety, or for reputation, comradeship, or a cause. Rawls expects his founders to privilege liberty, so as to remain free to choose among the values they will encounter.[13] He eases the choice by abstracting from all forms of constraint – although positing that resources are not unlimited – and, of course, maintains the premise that choices (for some reason) must be made and that the basic rules, once chosen (for some reason), must be obeyed.

One should acknowledge that material goods are often valued (at least in part) for making choices feasible. But those who sacrifice personal interests for others's sake, or for a principle, or to safeguard symbols or ideas they hold sacred do not fit the mold imposed by Rawls's argument. It is hard to say that sheer rationality would privilege liberty above all other goods when choosers who *knew* their preferences might have valued honor

---

[13] Rawls, *A Theory of Justice* (1999), 37–40; *Law of Peoples* (2000), 150–51.

or national pride or royal privilege ahead of liberty, as many did in the past.

Rawls, as Thomas Nagel puts it, hopes "to provide an Archimedian point," the uncontested fulcrum of all further choices as to "any of the fuller conceptions of the good that lead people to differ."[14] But, as Nagel asks, "Why should the parties in the original position be prepared to commit themselves to principles that may frustrate or contravene their deepest convictions, just because they are deprived of knowledge of those convictions?" The veil of ignorance is especially unfair, Nagel adds, in barring the knowledge that choosers might have preferred a life grounded in well-defined social or economic structures or in concerted efforts to realize specific goals or perfect specific virtues, capacities, or skills.[15]

The assumptions built into Rawls's method discount "conceptions of the good that depend heavily on the relation between one's own position and that of others."[16] So family and fellowship are ranked secondary, a priori. Rawls worries about the damage that certain practices may wreak on the self-esteem of some. But practices that might enhance self-esteem meet no similar concern. The veil of ignorance, as Rawls weaves it, screens myriad paths of excellence central to motivation, whether we seek virtue, virtuosity, fame, holiness, or community. Persons may choose such paths once the veil is removed, but they may not structure a society to foster such enrichments. The bias is unseen by Rawls because he projects his limiting assumptions onto the rationality of his primary choosers.

Neutrality here is not neutral. What the model counts as reason is mainly a desire to keep one's options open. That is not irrational, but neither is it the whole of reason – or liberty. Restricting the field of view to a narrow slit creates an iridescence: The colors of liberty shift from the game theorist's choice to keep the chance to choose, to the value that some may choose

[14] Nagel, "Rawls on Justice," 8.
[15] Ibid., 11.
[16] Ibid.

to die for – a liberty ranked above other goods not in order of abstraction but in substance and enriched with visions of the life that the exercise of liberty will open to those for whom the sacrifice is made. The shift from the liberty of decision theory to the liberty dear to patriots seems a bit of a bait-and-switch.

We can see what Rawls is after: No one, he hopes, will be trapped in untutored choices. But there is an exception: Every one of Rawls's choosers is locked in a society structured by Rawls's idea of reason. Liberty itself cannot be sold or sacrificed – a welcome outcome, especially if the liberty to be safeguarded is soundly and sincerely fleshed out in practice. But that is a big if, since notions of liberty vary and gyrate between socialist and libertarian extremes. But not everyone favors liberty, however bodied forth. Some prefer discipline or duty. Rawls leaves them free to make their way *within* the society that (*ex hypothesi*) they have chosen. But they are not free to build a social system based on values of their own. That is a problem. For isn't it in setting our own priorities, not just personally but politically, in deciding what we value and how to implement our choices in a public sphere, that we are most fully free? The paradox in Rawls's argument is that by making liberty paramount, he has recognized our need to build a value system for ourselves, to share in building a community. But he has also closed off a wide variety of choices in the public sphere that a chooser might have valued.

Some might find the society extruded from Rawls's thought experiment far too vanilla But even vanilla is still a flavor, and not neutral or transparent. Yet some of what Rawls's social contractors might choose might be pretty florid. Do they countenance group marriage or group sex? Some think such arrangements critical to liberty. Others find them degrading, meretricious, and exploitative. Is family structure to be worked out once the ground rules are set? I would argue that rules about family come first. The point may be disputed, but that is just the trouble here. Liberty comes in many flavors. The idea needs to be interpreted before it can be ranked. But fleshing out ideals is the work not of law but of culture, just the sort of thing that the veil of ignorance is meant to obscure.

The dynamic of cultures tests our more abstract assumptions when cultures bring to life the values we espouse. Abstract models regularly if tacitly lean on a background culture but overlook its distinctiveness. What is familiar looks clear as air, so it is easy to forget its presence or to presume it is unchanging, impervious to loss or interference, steady as the sky or sea – as though they too were invariant. As a participant and exponent, I am interested in exploring, defining, and developing the culture I have called Mosaic liberalism, because I find in that heritage some concrete ways of celebrating and protecting human dignity. Liberty is central in the Mosaic culture, not alien to it. But abstract liberty does look a bit pallid next to the protections persons may need to thrive and flourish. The abstract ideal of liberty cannot clearly tell me whether incest is a sound or unsound choice, although cultures generally take a pretty strong stand on that question and biblical norms draw a pertinent margin of privacy around our personhood. Formal talk of equality says nothing of a sacred obligation to treat our fellow humans with the same regard we hope for from others. Mosaic liberalism and its daughter traditions do espouse and seek to flesh out that ideal and work to instill it in our character and institute it in our practices.

Rawls's deliberators "must decide once and for all what is to count among them as just and unjust."[17] *Basic* principles, Rawls writes, must be (virtually) inviolable: "Being first virtues of human activities, truth and justice are uncompromising."[18] To champions of change such as Dewey, the notion of fixed principles may look uncomfortable. Would it be irrational for someone who did not know if *change* would prove to be his or her paramount value to reject such principles? Rawls thinks *some* kinds of change must always be available. So here, as in any real society, there is always room for disputing just where constancy belongs. But sheer instrumental reason knows little and cares less for the values Rawls holds sacrosanct. It does not know when to prefer flexibility over stability and continuity. That is one more

---

[17] Rawls, *A Theory of Justice*, 12.
[18] Ibid., 4.

effect of taking "reason" now abstractly and now in a sense more concretely.

Liberty by itself cannot say whether *Roe* v. *Wade* should be upheld, overturned, or qualified; whether gay marriage should be a constitutional right; or capital punishment should be sustained or rejected. Specific recensions of the idea of liberty address such questions in historically and culturally situated interpretations – but the responses differ. Many of America's founders saw the surest promise of liberty in the right to bear arms, but not everyone endorsed the Lockean right of revolution. Whether to count slaves as persons or as property was a vexed issue in the writing of the Constitution and proved critical, as Lincoln saw, not just to the nation's survival but also to the meaning of its mission. Questions about who may marry or whether fetuses have rights are no less basic. But these issues are not thematized in the U.S. Constitution or addressed by the bare idea of rationality. Capital punishment and abortion have both been called constitutional issues. Does the sanctity of human life demand or preclude either or both? A theory of justice that remains silent on such questions has settled nothing, but questions like these cannot be answered by culturally blind surrogates.

There were deep divisions over the *Dred Scott* case and again over the "separate but equal" doctrine. The Torah, in striking contrast, rules clearly as to fugitive slaves: They are not to be returned (Deuteronomy 23:16). It does not ask, as Taney's Court was asked, whether slaves have legal standing. But even so fierce a foe of slavery as John Quincy Adams thought that property rights trump claims for emancipation. The Torah bans mistreatment of Egyptians. The reason: *thou wert a stranger in his land* (Deuteronomy 23:8). In formal terms, that is a non sequitur. Here it makes an argument. An opposite inference might equally have been made, yet scripture here is not applying a rule but modeling a practice. An ethos of caring puts the argument through and generalizes it:

When a stranger dwelleth with thee in thy land, ye shall not wrong him. You must treat the resident stranger the same as the homeborn. Thou shalt love him as thyself. For ye were strangers in the land of Egypt. I am the Lord your God. (Leviticus 19:33–34; cf. Exodus 22:20, 23:9; Deuteronomy 27:19)

God's self-affirmation punctuates the command, underscoring its absoluteness and gravity. History is invoked to resolve any ambivalence or hesitation. Formal principles alone cannot do that. Both *Dred Scott* and *Plessy* v. *Ferguson* were argued and decided on libertarian grounds, guided by presumptions that seemed unproblematic to the Court's majority. Missing was the affirmation of the inestimable worth of the human person.

Individuals and cultures can set quite a variety of goods high in the constellation of values. Would Che Guevara's quest for perpetual revolution seem irrational from behind a veil of ignorance? Che and his friends might not sit down *at all* to draw up lasting, structural plans. But revolutionaries do make plans, even laws. What disciples of perpetual revolution reject with contempt is Rawls's "once and for all." For them the constant is revolution. When the patina wears off the revolutionary icon and the charisma that grows from the barrel of an AK-47 is routinized, we hear the Mexican oxymoron: institutional revolution. But romantic rebels cherish instability. Such men are no liberals. That contrary and contrarian outcome blunts Rawls's argument and bends it back toward circularity: If liberalism is a given, just what is proved by Rawls's thought experiment? Does it yield any normative claims or just a stipulative definition? Even Jefferson spoke fondly, although not presciently, of the blood needed to water liberty's tree. History taught us that ballots can do what bullets cannot – that governments can be changed without dissolution of the state. So life itself may instruct reason about liberty. Hobbes took what reason teaches in one way, Burke in another, Robespierre and Emma Goldman in other ways still. Without history, liberty in any language is just a word.

Did Aristotle give equality the same weight Rawls did? Did Hume, when he called its pursuit "extremely pernicious"?[19]

---

[19] Russell Hardin, speaking at Vanderbilt University on March 14, 2004, argued that Hume *would have* embraced equality had he known how effectual democracy could become, thus conquering his fears that equality must mean

Aristotle saw reciprocity as a core political need (*Nicomachaean Ethics* V 4–5, esp. 1132b 32–1133a 5). But understanding is the summit – a good in itself and our best guide to living. A thinking life, however, Aristotle reasoned, demands the leisure that only free men can enjoy – and attains it only at the expense of slaves. Aristotle clearly preferred and would choose a world where some are slaves, so as to ensure that others may live fully human lives. He would rather risk slavery (the ever present risk of sea travel in his time) than live in a world where all are free, if that meant that everyone must descend to gouging minerals from the earth, plowing a field, shoeing horses, or chaffering in the agora. Automata, he reasoned, would obviate the hard choice between enslaving others and foregoing the good life. But automata are not readily at hand,[20] and the idea that *all* should enjoy a day of peace

"leveling down." Perhaps. But I suspect Hume loathed equality as an inevitable enemy of excellence, unstable if attained, and corrosive even in the offing: "historians, and even common sense, may inform us, that, however specious these ideas of perfect equality may seem, they are really, at bottom, impracticable; and were they not so, would be extremely pernicious to human society. Render possessions ever so equal, men's different degrees of art, care, and industry will immediately break that equality. Or if you check these virtues, you reduce society to the most extreme indigence; and instead of preventing want and beggary in a few, render it unavoidable to the whole community. The most rigorous inquisition too is requisite to watch every inequality on its first appearance; and the most severe jurisdiction, to punish and redress it. But besides, that so much authority must soon degenerate into tyranny, and be exerted with great partialities; who can possibly be possessed of it, in such a situation as is here supposed? Perfect equality of possessions, destroying all subordination, weakens extremely the authority of magistracy, and must reduce all power nearly to a level, as well as property." *An Enquiry Concerning the Principles of Morals*, III II § 5, ed. Nidditch, p. 194. Hume has less trouble with the idea that people would or should die for king and country. He liked rationality no more than equality. Among the many who have hated equality, Nietzsche may take pride of place. But he too would have dug in his heels at paying deference to rationality, in place, let us say, of passion. How to parse such concepts as liberty, equality, or excellence so as to take cognizance of Hume's or Nietzsche's warnings without falling into their traps is again a cultural matter – and one that not just any cultural strategy successfully resolves. No purely formal notion effectively grapples with it.

[20] The lack of automata in Aristotle's time, we are told, resulted not from technological weaknesses. Clockwork mechanisms were made for use in toys and temples. But slave labor was just too cheap to warrant investing capital and ingenuity in automata.

and contemplation is foreign to Aristotle's culture. Sabbaths, we have seen, can humanize, even divinize our lives. But their institution rests not just on a higher order reciprocity (like Gandhi's requirement that everyone in his ashram provide massages to all the rest) but also on the recognition of the sanctity of the individual, a thought alien to Aristotle (partly *because* of slavery). Sabbaths are also a norm that Rawls's choosers might never have addressed and that Rawls himself would bar from their deliberations. To him a universal sabbath would look parochial; its enforcement would violate core liberties. So which does reason deem more basic: the right to rest or the right to self-exploitation? Rawls is ill equipped to answer. But is Aristotle irrational because his views on freedom sort out differently from ours? That is a strange call and a pretty heavy charge to make against a mind like Aristotle's, especially if it is meant to follow from the thin notion of rationality with which we began.

We *should* differ with Aristotle about slavery. But when we do, the issue is our priorities, not his rationality. It was he, after all, who taught us much of what we know about the means and ends of reason, and he did so without Pickwickian definitions. To part company with Aristotle over slavery we need recognition of the inestimable worth and dignity of all persons. That recognition is not implicit in an abstract idea of liberty: It is part of what that idea is abstracted *from*. How often when we speak of equality or liberty do we *mean* existential dignity and worth, but sidestep saying so – much as youngsters say "democracy" when they mean constitutional, representational government. Values fleshed out by experience and culture are just what Rawls professed to leave behind in projecting outcomes behind the veil of ignorance. Like his positivist predecessors, he fights shy of visions of human purpose, no matter how open-ended, lest his project seem sectarian. Hence the magic show, drawing substantive standards of justice from a seemingly empty high silk hat, the sheer idea of rationality.[21]

---

[21] Onora O'Neill detects "a number of unargued idealizations" in Rawls's premise: "from adopting 'the concept of rationality standard in social theory,' to ruling out the motive of envy, to ascribing desires for more rather

Substantive norms, anchored in positive commitments about the ultimate character of things or the ultimate worth of persons, are just what the veil of ignorance was meant to hide. But it is a mistake to banish from deliberative discourse all talk of human nature and its possibilities. The error compounds when such considerations are silenced in constitutional deliberations. Laws address human beings, not algorithms. That is why the Torah prefaces its prescriptive program with cosmological and historical preludes, viewing creation as a good and life as a gift, and forthrightly teaching that men and women are not alien to each other but of one flesh – allies and counterparts, rightly loyal to each other even above their parents (Genesis 2:18–24).

Culture counts not least in norms about home life. So Susan Okin, like Jane English before her, rightly asked why rationality in Rawls's original position stands outside the family door and does not enter to speak of fairness there.[22] Are family relations somehow less than basic? Rawls stipulated at the outset of *A Theory of Justice* that his thought experiment

> may not work for the rules and practices of private associations or for those of less than comprehensive social groups. They may be irrelevant for the various informal conventions and customs of everyday life; they may not elucidate the justice, or perhaps better, the fairness of voluntary cooperative arrangements or procedures for making contractual agreements.[23]

> than less of each of a short list of primary goods to each agent, to thinking of agents as 'deputies for a kind of everlasting moral agent or institution,' to assuming that an account of justice can in the first instance be worked out for the case of a 'bounded society.' Some of these assumptions could perhaps be justified as no more than simplifications of – abstractions from – empirical truths; others probably could not. In any case, the strategy of working with a limited and minimal set of supposedly merely abstract claims about human agents is one that Rawls set aside in his later work.... Rawls in his later writing hinged his theory of justice not on the abstract, indeed idealized, construction of an original position, but on the ideals of citizens of liberal democratic societies." *Bounds of Justice*, 72, 150. Rawls leans toward the empirical when seeking application for his model, but counts on abstraction when seeking to bind its premises to his inferences.

22 Susan Okin, Vanderbilt lecture, February 9, 2004, a few weeks before her death, citing work by Jane English from the 1970s. Okin's text was published as "Justice and Gender."

23 Rawls, *A Theory of Justice*, 8.

The admission seems damning: Rawls's core standards gloss over much that lies at the beating heart of human lives – let alone the power to enter into an agreement and the duty to abide by it once made. Rawls responded to Okin by arguing that family relations answer to different standards from those invoked in founding a society.[24] But she still felt that his model of justice was wrong to sideline the family. Onora O'Neill, echoing Okin, Carole Pateman, and others, spells out the issue: Rawls "pre-empts the question of intra-familial justice . . . not by crude insistence that heads of families must be men, but by taking it as read that there is some just form of family which allows the interests of some to be justly represented by others. . . . This is idealization indeed: it buries the question of gender justice rather than resolving it."[25]

How central do we take familial relations to be in the norms that structure a society? It is prudent, in the interest of privacy, to restrain state interference in family life – but is hardly wise to ignore the delicate connective tissue between public and private lives. Only consider the disastrous attempts of Soviet and Communist Chinese authorities to implement Marx's distaste for the "bourgeois" family. The preservation and protection of the family are not topics that founders of a society can successfully ignore. But Rawls's veil of abstractions and stipulations withholds from his notional founders the cultural tools that might address such questions. Liberal theorists have long assumed that marital and filial relations float airily above the real nuts and bolts they whiggishly construe in commercial and contractual terms. As Jean Elshtain writes,

By failing to come up with a vocabulary rich enough to account for the centrality of the social relationships of the family, even as they "depoliticized" these relationships, the thinkers within the liberal tradition adopted a set of assumptions which required the "setting aside of the fundamental facts of birth, childhood, parenthood, old age, and death."[26]

---

[24] Rawls, *Law of Peoples*, 158.
[25] O'Neill, *Bounds of Justice*, 153.
[26] Elshtain, *Public Man, Private Woman*, 106–7. The embedded quote is from Robert Paul Wolff, "There's Nobody Here but Us Persons," 133.

Rawls polishes the Lockean loom to a high gloss. But the cogs, clutches, and cams that allow the mechanism to engage or disengage without elisions and collisions are not the design of untutored reason.[27] The humanistic traditions of monotheism, which underwrite the liberal dispensation (despite all efforts at erasure), penetrate more deeply because they sustain contact with the persons the machine was made to serve. They find the family at the root of any social structure and do not exclude the less tangible dimensions of human dignity from the core concerns of law.

When an ethos is strained by social change or crisis, the private realm becomes a precious refuge. Such times may look exceptional to those experiencing them, but they tend to be pretty typical historically. In troubled times, informal relations such as those of the family are critical to the maintenance of peace and equity. That makes marriage and divorce, parenthood and sibship, always critical to the intimate work of constructing personhood, and all the more vital in sustaining social institutions.[28] Without equity *here*, within the family, liberty is a sham and formal social structures are, at best, under threat.

So if the veil of ignorance obscures the values that might safeguard the sanctity of marriage and the boundaries of equity and excess between partners, if the choices made in the original position fail to shelter personhood and to afford space and create opportunity for the emergence and expression of personal identity, they have not safeguarded liberty. But even to notice such concerns, choosers of basic laws must slip the blindfold somewhat to let in some light from beyond the framework of economically modeled choice.

The light that human flourishing requires in fact is colored by our living conditions and is invariably cultural. Once it pierces the veil of ignorance, rationality is no longer a formal exercise. That is where the work begins, as individuals and communities link hands with predecessors and successors to articulate a value scheme and social system infused with richer, thicker, more concrete visions of personhood and choice than abstract rationality alone can draft.

[27] Cf. Elshtain, *Public Man, Private Woman*, 116–27.
[28] See Goodman, *God of Abraham*, 219–23.

We have seen how Rawls freights rationality with the outcomes he asks of it, even as he stretches taut the veil of ignorance to exclude unwanted values. We have also seen the virtual contract at risk of slighting the many interests potentially elided or underrated by its signatories: future generations and the unborn, the comatose and gravely ill or compromised, foreigners and would-be immigrants, outsiders and outliers. Compactors might pledge to guard such interests and might sincerely mean to do so. But Rawls's premises hardly situate such concerns at the normative center of gravity. Do the signatories even know what their attitudes will be about promise keeping – let alone about outsiders, infants, or the unborn? How would they protect such interests, when unaware of their views until the sociopolitical die is cast? Would they care about individual animals and plants, species, ecosystems? Rawls does expect them to preserve such things: The protection of territory and its environmental integrity, *in perpetuity*, he argues, is the real reason for the institution of property. This oddly backhand claim – curiously metaphysical at bottom – seeks to extract environmental interests from an interest in ownership by deriving property rights from environmental interests. Rawls covers himself by couching the concern in prudence: Even veiled choosers would know that ownerless land or goods go to ruin[29] – thus presuming the very interest he means to derive, at least in terms of usufruct. Evidently the veil is sheer enough for signatories to read Garrett Hardin's "Tragedy of the Commons" through its fabric. The concern must remain instrumental, lest it wax metaphysical. There will be no acknowledgment of intrinsic worth. So do we have a way of settling disputes between the primacy of sentience and the claims of biodiversity? Can such issues be negotiated behind a veil of ignorance? Or are relations between humans and other species, and between our species and the environment at large again not basic enough?

We have already asked how Rawlsian founders can assign worth to anything without invoking some comprehensive

---

[29] Rawls, *Law of Peoples*, 8.

doctrine. Even instrumental value is lost if unanchored in intrinsic worth. Rawls's talk of the "environment" does gesture toward some intrinsic value, perhaps in human life. But allowing that faux pas to pass, how are human wants and quality of life to be balanced against nonhuman needs? Such questions must remain moot in the original position, their answers obscured by the veil of ignorance even if they may seem too basic to be left open.

Rawls thinks he knows where rationality would fix the starting point for a society. But even in the few decades since his first sketch, popular attitudes have shifted and diverged. On almost any issue, some have found his expectations too demanding; others, too slight. As his book aged, its scheme appeared increasingly parochial, less a theory deriving the idea of justice than a position paper delineating the shared preferences of a certain "we." Pluralism seemed slighted, de facto diversity kept under wraps. Pressed by feminists and communitarians, ecologists and libertarians, Rawls added caveats and codicils, epicycles and eccentrics. His Lockean lean-to became a cavernous train station. *Political Liberalism* sought to acknowledge communities and subcultures while assuring the secularity of the state by building secularism into its ethos. Liberalism itself was no comprehensive doctrine, we were assured – as if it bore no gene or meme from its ancestry or its past. It had never been a half-secularized ideal or harbored any project of becoming an all-embracing way of life and thought.[30]

In Rawls's version, liberalism bites its own tail. In the name of liberty Rawls promotes a rule as brittle as those once imposed by prelates and princes. The initial irritant, perhaps, was religious opposition to abortion.[31] But philosophers like to speak in universal terms, even at the cost of over-generalization. In Rawls's

---

[30] For the roots of liberalism, see, e.g., Becker, *The Heavenly City of the Eighteenth Century French Philosophers*; Pangle, *The Theological Basis of Liberal Modernity*; For liberalism as a way of life, see, e.g., Dewey, *The Public and its Problems*.

[31] Cf. Robert George and Christopher Wolfe, "Natural Law and Public Reason," 66.

case that means reserving the word "political" for specific secular dimensions of civic life. Rawls's nod toward community in *Political Liberalism*, as a result, conjures in my mind memories of the Tongan children I once saw performing dances of their archipelago. Squatting on tapa mats, they ran through their hand gestures, closely watched by their bespectacled ministers with well-worn, leather-bound Bibles in hand. Authentic enough to be what they were, the dances preserved no steps or body movements. Did they mime the hollow forms of now some forgotten ritual? Was I witnessing deracinated hulas? The cultures that show their faces in Rawls's scoured public forum, stripped of any open savor of faith or philosophy, bear the faint if telling scent of naphtha and formaldehyde.

A similar scent follows when Rawls goes international, proposing a new league, not of nations but of liberal and non-liberal but "decent" peoples, whose representatives gather, chattering in their many languages, bearing the trappings of their cultures and the memories and histories of national trauma – perhaps even wearing their colorful costumes – but stripped of comprehensive doctrines. The strains of "It's a Small World after All" fill the hall. The "Ode to Joy" might seem too culture-bound. The delegates crowd together, greeting one another, perhaps wondering how Poles, Hungarians, and Jews can recall the traumas (and glories?) of their past without the use of religious language, at least not deliberatively.

Peoples, Rawls argues, are the proper participants here, meeting on the anniversary of the first "original position" that chalked out plans for a liberal polity. The veil of ignorance descends once more, shrouding the participants from each other and even from themselves, as pious couples were once urged to place a bed sheet between them when making love, with just a narrow slit for passage of the necessary fluids and a minimal exchange of passion or perception.

Peoples, not states, were invited, Rawls explains. States still bear the scars of capricious warfare and the hubris of claims to sovereignty. Clausewitz's ghost is raised, to warn off any lingering statists. Peoples, we learn, are like persons: They too "see themselves as self-authenticating sources of claims, and capable of taking responsibility for their ends."[32] "Peoples (as opposed to states) have a definite moral nature."[33] Does that make peoples blameless then? Surely any moral nature has at least two sides: Peoples too can rise up on their hind legs and affirm their sovereignty. Lockean political legitimation (hence every liberal constitution) rests right there. But having a moral nature does not entail acting morally. Peoples, like persons, can commit hideous crimes, including genocide, as the Hutus did, among many others.[34]

Peoples, like states, can be self-serving. It is rare, as Thucydides was hardly the first to notice, for a state *or* people to call its wars anything but fair expressions of sacred rights and vital interests. Even more rarely do states or peoples acknowledge mistreating their own. The Soviet Union and East Germany, North Korea and Zimbabwe all called their crimes necessities, in the service of the people. Where are the Serbs or Croats, Rwandans

---

[32] Rawls, *Law of Peoples*, 34.

[33] Ibid., 34.

[34] Peoples, for Rawls, David Reidy stresses, are "corporate moral persons." Thus "outlaw states" are corporate but not moral agents! So "Liberal democratic peoples need not theorize the demands of international justice with these states in mind." For "A people is always a system of social cooperation aimed at and justified by reference to the good of its members." "Rawls on International Justice," 297. "Outlaw states are the corporate body politic analogue not to the domestic individual criminal who possesses the capacity to be reasonable but fails to perfectly realize it (and who is therefore owed justice in punishment), but rather to the sociopath who fails to possess the capacity to be reasonable to the requisite minimum degree and is thus properly quarantined and offered appropriate forms of care" (303). Yet peoples do make corporate choices. Being a moral agent is no guarantee of moral action, and action in the self-proclaimed interests of covenantors is no guarantee of justice. States may be evil, not just demented. Some sociopaths too, I fear, are evil. The facile rhetoric of illness is lawyer language at best and no diagnosis. The carnage assiduously planned and artfully concealed by sexual predators, serial killers – or genocidal states *or peoples* – does not level the perpetrators with their victims and make them somehow equally helpless and hapless. In the case of outlaw states, quarantine is often ineffective, and care sounds more like a reward than an appropriate response to a destructive and menacing regime.

or Cambodians, who confess and own the heinous acts of genocide committed by masses of their people? How few were the
Germans who admitted their complicity with Hitler – and how
numerous are the apologists who see causes for the Nazi crimes
or who blend them with a general distaste for banal humanity.

Rawls's privileging of peoples over states is romanticism.
As George Schultz once pointedly remarked, it was the break-
down of the state that loosed the warlords of Somalia and
Afghanistan.[35] Al-Qa'ida hatches its hate crimes in the pacific
spaces afforded by the civility of the states it seeks to infest and
destroy and operates overtly in the crannies and potholes of failed
states. Rawls anthropomorphizes, assigning peoples not only cultures and languages but also personalities and beliefs – but not
criminal agency! He elides the most salient fact about peoples
today – their dispersion in a thousand places and conditions –
calling his homogeneous societies a simplification for the sake
of analysis, as though analysis can thrive on stereotypes. Echoing Mazzini's wishful ethnography, he gives each people a land,
large or small, rich or poor – as if no people were ever exiled or
dispossessed by invaders.

Projecting an imaginary map of the world, Rawls casts his veil
of ignorance over the representatives of its peoples, not asking how their delegates are chosen, but presuming only that
they faithfully serve the interests of their constituents. They
now renew the contractual work of the original position, inter-
ethnically, but in ignorance of the land and resources each people
will receive and without thoughts of any linkage of a people to
its soil. History is forgotten. Finland and the Balkans, Armenia,
Uganda, and Birobidzhan are assigned by lot to the waiting virtual masses. The operation calls to mind those board games of
Diplomacy that students of international relations used to play
before computer games shifted the stress from strategy to speed.
But the object of the Rawlsian game is to show critics first that
liberal societies can live in peace with one another and then that

---

[35] George Schultz, Kissinger Lecture, Library of Congress, Spring, 2004,
excerpted in the *Wall Street Journal*, March 29, 2004.

they can live in peace with not so liberal counterparts. The claim is not that a new age has dawned, but that Rawls has not failed to look beyond the borders, geographical or historical, of a single type of state or to consider ideals and ways of life foreign to those he found self-evident in the *original* original position. The object, in short, is to prove that Rawls's theory permits "a reasonable pluralism," a world of diverse peoples stably committed to the standards they grew up with and interacting respectfully with one another.

Rawls repeatedly evinces his earnestness by challenging readers to see that the terms on offer are "what you and I, here and now" would accept as fair.[36] He situates his scheme in our actual world. But as the stipulations mount up, the horizon is increasingly bounded by what prove to be the premises of an abstract mathematical model, of facts governed by postulates. Rawls labels his schema "a realistic utopia"[37] – realistic for its workable rules, but a utopia because it preserves the primacy of rights and all receive the goods needed for the effective exercise of those rights. Utopian here means ideal. But Spinoza offers a more perspicuous definition: A system is utopian if it *presupposes* the transformation of human nature.[38] How, exactly does Rawls know that generations will grow up loyal to the values they were raised in, when history so often frustrates that hope – when even Plato, sometimes thought the arch-utopian, finds seeds of instability within his own Republic, not in its principles, of course, but in the accidents of history that permit decay?[39] How can Rawls know that *his* world is stable, if not by fiat?[40] And if stability,

---

[36] Rawls, *Law of Peoples*, e.g., 32.

[37] Cf. John Tasioulas, "From Utopia to Kazanistan."

[38] Spinoza, *Tractatus Theologico-Politicus* I 1.

[39] Plato, *Republic* VIII 545–46.

[40] The overlapping consensus is to secure the stability Rawls assumes: The adherents of diverse comprehensive doctrines support the basic practices and principles of a liberal society, albeit for diverse reasons. No one such doctrine, Rawls assumes, wins unanimity without oppression. But political liberalism does. Dismissing the worry that some might object to the practices and principles he deems liberal, Rawls stipulates that the populace of a *liberal* society would not mount such objections. Everything becomes stipulative.

satisfaction, and homogeneity come by postulate, why not world peace?

The idea of a reasonably just society of well-ordered peoples will not have an important place in a theory of international politics until such peoples exist and have learned to coordinate the actions of their governments in wider forms of political, economic and social cooperation.

Thus the limiting postulate, but from that comes utopia:

When that happens, as I believe, following Kant, it will, the society of these peoples will form a group of satisfied peoples. As I shall maintain, in view of their fundamental interests being satisfied, they will have no reason to go to war with one another. The familiar motives for war would be absent: such peoples do not seek to convert others to their religions, nor to conquer greater territory, nor to wield political power over another people.[41]

That sounds so nice. Little is said now about the coercive powers that loomed so large in Rawls's account of (even democratic) governance. Indeed, the system Rawls expects to "coordinate the actions" of a diverse array of governments is not even called a government. Yet, to Rawls's interlocutors this system raised the specter of Auschwitz.[42] Why so? Well, perhaps in part, because they remember or can read in history books how the nations stood by when Germany on the mend – a rising democratic,

---

The thought experiment hemorrhages its heuristic value: Liberal principles are those that liberal people would agree to. We know they would, because they are liberal people.

[41] *Law of Peoples*, 19. Rawls follows Sen here and a long line of messianic thinking. As I argued in *On Justice* (Chapter 5), biblical messianism avoids utopianism (in Spinoza's sense) by relying on laws and practices that promote the transformation of human relations and thus the transformation of human character. But Rawls puts the cart before the horse, presuming the transformation his utopia requires. One cannot just wave the banner of satisfaction and leave it unclear just how satisfaction is achieved – or what precisely constitutes it and insures it against the decadence and anomie that seeming satisfaction seems often to engender. World government, rather loosely described, is presumed here to be somehow sufficient to achieve and preserve world peace. But that premise demands two more posits: that such governance is possible, efficacious, and fair and that once instituted it will be and remain acceptable to those it regulates, not provoking revolution or rebellion.

[42] *Law of Peoples*, 19–20.

constitutional people – turned to Hitler as a savior and made the Jewish people the race enemy, a threat to the *Volk* and all humanity to be obliterated at all costs. The lines between a world state and world conquest have never been easy to draw since the times of Alexander or Caesar Augustus.

Can we really say that democracies do not make war? Didn't the imperial democracies of ancient Athens and modern Britain doggedly pursue hegemony? John Stuart Mill himself vehemently supported the Opium War. Can we honestly say that satisfied peoples do not make war, when Belgium raped the Congo; when our own United States made war with Mexico and Spain, not to mention the native Americans; when a burgeoning China swallowed Tibet; when Italy overran Ethiopia; and a modernizing Japan conquered Manchuria, occupied Taiwan and Korea, and threw in with the Axis? The familiar claim Rawls leans on is that democracies do not make war *against each other*. But historians readily list at least two dozen seeming exceptions. Each can be dismissed by denying that one or both of the parties was stable and long lived enough to be a real democracy – or denying that what happened was a real war. But the argument often turns on definitions – truth, once more, by postulate.[43]

To the living memory of the Holocaust, Rawls responds as if the challenge were purely to his rhetoric and deserved only a rhetorical response: He makes the mention of the Holocaust an opportunity to pay lip service to the uniqueness of the Shoah,[44] an empty gesture as one reflects on the Armenian, Serbian, Cambodian, and Rwandan genocides – as empty as the nod in the direction of the Middle Passage in Rawls's glancing tribute to

---

[43] Ibid., 8, 52–54. Cf. Matthew White, "Democracies Do Not Make War on One Another – or Do They?" White writes, "Although there is no undisputed case of two democracies at war, the evidence certainly casts doubt on the thesis. In fact, the thesis is not nearly as strong as the statement that no two countries with a McDonald's Restaurant have ever gone to war with one another. So why do you never hear distinguished international diplomats expound on the need to sell more beef patties in the world?"

[44] Rawls, *Law of Peoples*, 19.

historic travails.[45] The real problem, ill concealed by rhetoric, is
that Rawls's claims for perfectibility in politics stand too close to
the posits they are built on. As if fire and smoke might distract a
serious reader, Rawls lays in a two-page tirade against religion.
The Nazi Holocaust is made a gambit allowing him to castigate
religion as a fountainhead of bigotry: Hitler used religion in his
war against the Jews and made religious claims for the ultimacy
of his Reich. So the fault lay not in the weaknesses of the liberal regime whose carcass Hitler feasted on, nor in the German
people who elected him, hailed him, and followed his orders into
battle, nor in the league of satisfied nations that sued for peace
and stood by as Hitler gobbled other nations and led a prosperous, learned, industrial, and cultured society into the abyss of
barbarism. No, the fault lay in religion. Yet appeals to religion
were just one of Hitler's many political tools. Stalin, who killed
millions more than Hitler, was no friend of religion. He was
its bitter if pragmatic enemy. And the Cambodian self-genocide,
never brought to justice, ran its juggernaut course with no color
of religion, unless the term is defined persuasively – to make any
act of consummate brutality religious for the zeal brought to the
slaughter. But that would make Rawls's charge tautologous.

Stalin made his separate peace with Hitler, shared in dismem-
bering Poland, and was prepared to keep the peace had Hitler
not invaded Russia. Chamberlain looked anxiously away, pro-
claiming "peace in our time," in denial of the Nazi menace and
in sympathy with its seeming counterweight to Bolshevism. The
Austrians, as a people, welcomed Hitler. The French, in large
numbers, collaborated. Japan and Italy rushed to Hitler's side,
eager for spoils they did not need. Spain, a poorer and more pious
country, cagily sat out the war – and missed the reconstruction.
Rawls fulminates against religion, but the smokescreen is too
wispy to hide the flimsiness of his promises of peace, sustained
by a tissue of wishes. Rawls pictures a world rebuilt, without
war, starvation, oppression, genocide, or persecution. But this

---

[45] Rawls, *Law of Peoples*, 34.

world, conjured up at a wave of the philosopher's wand, is the work of postulates and their posited effects.

The test Rawls offers to validate his hopes is his vignette of a Muslim people, which he names Kazanistan. Strictly a "-stan" should be a country, not a people. The glitch may be an artifact of an earlier draft, set out ahead of the decision to speak of peoples and not lands. Here is what Rawls postulates about Kazanistan:

This people satisfies the criteria for decent hierarchical peoples I set forth: Kazanistan is not aggressive against other peoples and accepts and follows the Law of Peoples; it honors and respects human rights; and its basic structure contains a decent consultation hierarchy.[46]

Shades of the Woody Allen nebbish who goes hunting for the pro-peace, pro-choice wing of the Catholic Church. Might a primer in Islamic theology help here?

I have devoted fifty years now to the study of Islam, as it is, as it has been, and as its most ardent followers have wished it to be. In particular, I have tracked the philosophers, scientists, and humanists of Islam and their struggles to give definition and critical credibility to the Islamic legacy. In chronicling some of their finest works, my hope in part has been that non-Muslims will see a more open, thoughtful, tolerant face than Islamic militants, extremists, and irredentists have shown. I have also hoped that greater access to their own tradition's riches will inspire and empower committed Muslims to build on the achievements of some of the world's greatest minds and souls, contributing to the mosaic of humane and humanistic civilizations.[47] But that is not a goal to be won by wishful thinking or mere stipulations. Much work needs to be done. Rose-colored glasses do not help.

Islamic theology and legal theory have never joined in clear unison to acknowledge the legitimacy of secular authority as a framework for intercommunal, interpersonal, or international relations. The religious authorities of mainstream Islam do not

---

[46] Rawls, *Law of Peoples*, 5; cf. Mitchell Avila in "Defending A Law of Peoples."
[47] See Goodman, *Islamic Humanism* and other works of mine on Muslim thought and civilization.

promote the treatment of other religions or even secular individuals in their own societies – let alone heretics, misbelievers, or converts to other religions – with the honor and respect that are the objects of Rawls's hopeful thinking. We do not see extensive study of Buddhism, Hinduism, Confucianism, Taoism, Christianity, or Judaism among Muslim scholars today, let alone a desire to situate those traditions (and the myriad varieties of belief and practice adopted by their followers) in the same intellectual and moral world as their own.

A few committed Muslims have seen potential footings for constitutional democracy, pluralism, or even a secular state in the founding documents of Islam. The so-called Arab Spring raised Middle Eastern and North African and not just Western hopes. But it is awfully hard to say that this revolution, like so many before it, will not devour its children. It has already trimmed its sails to catch the hot winds generated by the Muslim Brotherhood, Al-Qa'ida, and the Ayatollahs. As for Rawls, this much should be said: When turning Islam into a game piece for an exercise in political speculation, one needs to remember that even broad-minded Muslim thinkers, typically those who live in liberal societies in the West, tend to envision tolerance and pluralism *within* (that is, under) Islamic hegemony. Where is the Islam that has jettisoned the dream of worldwide conversion to the faith and practices of Islam? The Islamic mainstream has hardly abandoned expansionist, triumphalist visions of jihad. The terrorists who are the spearpoint of that jihad find widespread sympathy among the Muslim masses and rivers of support from wealthy and powerful Muslims. The puritanical views and practices of Salafi Islam did not fade with the coming of the twenty-first century. They gained ground, not least among young people, by promising a refuge for Muslims shocked by the perceived excesses of the West and troubled by their own attraction/repulsion by those excesses.

Generically *jihad* means struggle. The *greater* jihad, as described in the spiritual sources of Islam, is the struggle for self-mastery. But that usage is metaphoric, like the secularized usage of the word "crusade" in the West. Construed as an obligation of Islamic law, jihad is a corollary of Islamic universality. It means battle in behalf of Islam, and the Arabic word for battle, etymologically, means killing. The world is divided between *Dar ul-Islam* and *Dar ul-Harb*, the Realm of Islam and the Realm of Warfare. Christians, Jews, and some other groups are to be tolerated in Muslim domains, although subject to special imposts and disabilities because the Qur'an (9:29–30) demands their subjugation and abasement:

Do battle with those who were given Scripture but do not believe in God and the Last Day – who do not forbid what God and his Messenger have forbidden or follow the true religion – until they are humbled and pay the tribute tax. The Jews call Uzayr (Ezra) God's son, the Christians call Christ God's son. Those are their words – just like the words of the ancient unbelievers, God slay them! They are utterly perverse.

Ideally, the mandate of war and the curses that stir it might be relegated to memories of long bygone battles and pogroms. Ideally the call to battle would be sublimated fully, jihad would be made a struggle against one's baser impulses, and holy war would lose its spiritual valence. Ideally the image of non-Muslims would be rethought, and the notion of *dhimmis*, as subject scriptural minorities, would be given its long delayed burial. These are tasks for Muslim jurists and theologians, along with the work of reconceptualizing the invidious tribute tax and radically changing the treatment of Christians and Jews in majority Muslim societies. The Qur'anic dicta that God turned Jews and Christians into apes and swine (5:60; cf. 2:65, 7:166) would be reinterpreted, and the assumption that others – Hindus, Buddhists, animists – are somehow fair game would be abandoned. For Qur'anic norms deny them even the option of the tribute tax – although there were historic exceptions to the rule, as with the so-called Sabian pagans of Harran, recognized of old by a genial fiction as People of the Book. But Qur'anic norms are not readily revised. The vision of jihad – as framed in the sources, proclaimed by living jurists, and sustained by public and private funds – has yet to approach the standards Rawls posits.

All but two minor Sharia authorities of the classic age understood jihad to be aggressive and expansionist. One of the two exceptions, a jurist named al-Thawri, softened the obligation of aggressive warfare to a recommendation. The other, the celebrated essayist al-Jahiz, followed Thawri. The Ahmadiyya sect rejects jihad, as do Bahais. But orthodox Muslims persecute the Ahmadiyya as heretics and regard Bahais as infidels and apostates. Bahais in Iran were executed on religious grounds as recently as 1998, and seven Bahai leaders were on trial for their lives in Tehran in 2010.

A word about the Bahais in Iran might be in order here before pursuing our discussion of jihad. Current Iranian policy is to keep up the pressure on Bahais – especially on their leadership but also on any brave enough to defend them – but to do so in ways thought less likely to arouse international attention. Yet since the 1979 Iranian revolution 202 Bahais have been killed for their religion, according to Amnesty International. The Iranian policy of denying Bahais employment, educational access, and positions of influence has been compared by the Anti-Defamation League to the Nazi anti-Jewish laws and campaigns. From its inception the present Iranian regime has rejected the idea of tolerating Bahaism. It denies that Bahais are adherents of a religion, calling Bahaism a political rather than a religious movement. But it continues to prosecute and persecute Bahais for apostasy and for alleged efforts to convert others to Bahaism. Although dressed up in political terms, then, the policy of persecution is clearly religiously motivated. Iran is an extreme case, of course, but it is highly questionable how tolerant an Islamic government in Egypt would be of the Copts who remain in that country, which was long ago very largely Coptic. The point is not that a pluralistic Islamic state is impossible, but that Islam itself has a long road to travel before the goal of religious equality is won.

In Sharia law jihad is a public obligation (*fard kifaya*), by which the Islamic integrity of a state is judged – although most Shi^{c}ites (except the Zaydis) suspend the prosecution of jihad until apocalyptic times. The obligation becomes personal (*fard^{c}ayn*) when a Muslim population reaches the numbers deemed necessary by the proper authorities to prosecute the war. However, there is an opening for mitigation of these rules, because the obligation is suspended should victory be deemed impossible. So one could envision a Muslim polity foreswearing jihad if it deemed world domination impracticable. But that decision would be open to rebuke and even reprisal from more zealous quarters. Indeed, militants today flood the internet with the claim that jihad is *fard ʿayn*, an individual obligation, because Islam is under threat: To neglect it is a grave sin, as grave as neglecting to aid a drowning child.

In the mainstream sources of Islamic norms, as Tyan writes,

> The duty of the *djihad* exists as long as the universal domination of Islam has not been attained. "Until the day of the resurrection," and "Until the end of the world," say the maxims. Peace with non-Muslim nations is, therefore, a provisional state of affairs only.[48]

And summing up,

> The *djihad* has principally an offensive character.... There is at the present time a thesis, of a wholly apologetic character, according to which Islam relies for its expansion exclusively upon persuasion and other peaceful means, and the *djihad* is only authorized in cases of "self-defense" and of "support owed to a defenceless ally or brother." Disregarding entirely the previous doctrine and historical tradition, as well as the texts of the Qur'an and the *sunna* on the basis of which it was formulated, but claiming, even so, to remain within the bounds of strict orthodoxy, this thesis takes into account only those early texts which state the contrary.[49]

The apologetic stance, unfortunately, is often sheer window-dressing, given the human penchant to clothe any warlike posture in defensive garb. Perhaps in time Muslim jurists and theologians will shift the ground of orthodoxy, reopening what the jurists call (in language tellingly cognate with the word *jihad*) the gates of

---

[48] E. Tyan, *djihad*, *EI*, 2.538–40; cf. Khadduri, *War and Peace in the Law of Islam*.

[49] Tyan, *EI* 2.539.

ijtihad, legal creativity, rather than follow tattered precedent. But reform is not won by apologetics, still less by *bien pensant* bystanders. It will be achieved in Islam only by the efforts (and self-mastery) of Muslim thinkers whose learning and commitment earn them recognition as authorities. Few Muslim scholars who entertain ideals of pluralistic equality live in countries with a Muslim majority, let alone command a mass following. Should committed Muslims find a way to swing open the gates of *ijtihad*, they may succeed in building freer, more open versions of Islam. But Islam has yet to find its Erasmus – or its Gandhi.

So is Kazanistan faithful to the ideals of its Muslim populace, to their historic vision and sense of mission? Does it exact the statutory Sharia penalties on the bodies of thieves, adulterers, homosexuals, and fornicators? Does its commitment to human rights and gender equity part company with the Prophet on polygamy and with widely accepted understandings of the *sunnah* as to cliterodectomy, purdah, and the veil? Are the people of Kazanistan Muslims only in faith – a strange locution in Islamic parlance? Is their Islam recognizable by other Muslims? Or is it just another fictive construct? Is Kazanistan one of those children's dioramas, like "Christmas around the World," that show, say, how Christmas is celebrated, say, in Turkey, Israel, China, and Japan?

"If all societies were required to be liberal," Rawls writes, "then the idea of political liberalism would fail to express due toleration."[50] Wouldn't that be the height of illiberality? How far, Rawls asks, can his liberal society reach out toward non-liberal societies? As with the family, he faces cross-pressures here,[51] only now writ large: If other societies violate our principles, do we interfere or let them be? If systematic oppression or neglect abroad violates human personhood or group autonomy or national sovereignty, when does the blood or suffering grow thick and slippery enough to demand action to stanch it? And by whom? The veil of ignorance only muffles that question. Nor do

---

[50] Rawls, *Law of Peoples*, 59.
[51] See ibid., 89–105.

I attempt a thoroughgoing answer here, but only say that there are human needs and rights that concerns for cultural autonomy, national sovereignty, and minimal or presumptive "decency" do not override.

The default option, de facto – not an entailment of liberalism but a pragmatic choice – is a fraught laissez-faire that may at times, selectively, find exceptions to its hands-off rule. But the pragmatic barriers to action, even domestically, rise pretty high. They mount even higher internationally. The United States did not act against slavery domestically until secession had brought war. We still do next to nothing about slavery overseas, let alone denial of schooling to girls or the use of schools to promote hatred and idealize terrorism. The liberal democracies stood silent at the Holocaust, slammed the door on Hitler's refugees, and sloughed off the Nazi genocide as an internal German matter, best left unspoken – although the slaughter of Jews began in countries Hitler had invaded. Sovereignty gave the death camps a free pass and visas, safe conducts, and new identities to many a bloodthirsty Nazi.

Rawls stipulates that "decent non-liberal peoples" would respect human rights. Their governments are open to consultation (albeit hierarchical rather than democratic). They accept dissent and answer queries about the law as interpreted by the judiciary pertinently and respectfully. "Dissenters may not be dismissed as simply incompetent or lacking in understanding."[52] That last stipulation rings oddly in traditional Islamic settings, where expertise is criterial in juridical authority (as where is it not?), and the demands of traditional learning and traditional commitment intensify wherever foundational concerns loom large.

A decent hierarchical society, like a liberal society, Rawls writes, would be "well ordered," albeit on "associationist" or corporate lines. It wins the label "decent" because it forswears aggressive aims and oppressive means,[53] secures human rights for

52 Ibid., 61.
53 Ibid., 68–69.

all its members (life, liberty, equality before the law), imposes bona fide duties on its people (as members of their groups, of course), and can justify a sincere belief by judges and other officials that the law aims for a common good. It is not a slave society. It is simply not individualist but communal – perhaps even fascist or soviet? Class or clan or caste, confession or sect, union, party, or firm, tribe or ethnicity have their spokesmen in the corridors of power, faithfully representing the interests of their group as they see them. Just how such ways comport with human rights (including equal opportunity and dissent) is not clear. Hierarchical societies, after all, are typically riven with nepotism, cronyism, special preferments, and the kind of sexism that feminists call patriarchy. Oppression may be subtler and aggression more oblique than Rawls's stipulations might readily detect; it is hard to say where discrimination yields to overt oppression. Rawls's hope is that he has found a passage between the liberal impulse to intervene when human rights are violated and the impulse to let things go – so readily seconded by the trading interests of a consumer society in cheap labor, ample natural resources, ready markets, and lax environmental, safety, child labor, tax, or regulatory standards. The barriers rise when a democratic populace is indeed averse to foreign entanglements and military losses and expenditures and is receptive to populist pleas for isolation, or pacifism, or apathy toward the alien other.

In addressing relations among peoples, Rawls invokes the fiction of the original position three times: first to found the liberal society of his choice, then to connect societies he calls liberal, and finally to relate all these to "decent," nonliberal peoples.[54] What keeps the nonliberal societies stable and their members loyal is a shared commitment to common goals or distinctive priorities that all can see pursued by the local institutions. Group

---

[54] Rawls envisions a gathering of liberal peoples to hammer out the terms of their relations. Non-liberal but "decent" peoples are summoned later but have no part in setting the rules of engagement. Their spokesmen determine only whether to sign on. The privileging of liberal values reflects Rawls's need to show how *his* thinking can accommodate societies and ideals different from his own. His answer, in effect: on terms acceptable to him.

representation, Rawls reasons, would function here on Hegel's principles to broaden a people's interests beyond the atomic individual.[55] So a state religion might wield ultimate authority in some spheres – but not in foreign relations nor domestically in ways that infringed on freedom of conscience. Will there be no special imposts and impositions on those outside the state religion then? Will its clergy bear no privileges? Will theologians and canon jurists who dispute or seek to revise its precepts not be defrocked or disempowered – forced to dissolve their marriages, as the government of Egypt did to a dissenting Muslim scholar? Will minorities be isolated from contact with coreligionists and sympathizers abroad?

Rawls waffles: A reasonable state need not be *fully* reasonable, as perfect freedom of conscience might require.[56] Law in Kazanistan, he writes, does not separate "church" from state. Only Muslims hold higher office, although (contrary to familiar Muslim norms) non-Muslims do serve in the military, even as high officers. By sustaining basic rights – corporate consultation, reforms for women, even special representation for formerly oppressed groups – and shunning mass murder, slavery and serfdom, Kazanistan merits toleration by liberal societies worldwide.

Can a society that privileges one confession and affords only corporate representation effectively guarantee even these rights? Rawls stipulates that Kazanistan can do so, *ex hypothesi*.[57] The weight of history and culture cannot destabilize an artificial model. So we have hypothetical acceptance of a hypothetical society. Kazanistan is a factitious construct. It differs from Rawls's liberal ideal but not enough to provoke deep revulsion – at least not among the hypothetical subscribers to his three hypothetical agreements.

What exactly have they agreed to tolerate? Discrimination, certainly. Principle is squeezed to make the space Rawls wants to pry open between the fully reasonable and the fully

---

55 Rawls, *Law of Peoples*, 72–73.
56 Ibid., 74.
57 Ibid., 79.

unreasonable, even if that means turning a blind eye to some abuses. Only casuistry can decide what to say or do about the lax pursuit of honor killings, dowry murders, loan sharking, child marriage, child prostitution, drug trafficking, or corporate sponsorship of terrorism. Is a society "decent" when it does not make war officially but sponsors mosques and preachers through its embassies who advocate the destruction of all non-Islamist governments, or when it privileges private or state-sponsored irregulars, paramilitary forces, and movements such as Hamas, Hizbullah, or Lashkar-e-Taiba? From Bangkok to Bangladesh, Colombia, Afghanistan, China, Japan, Ireland, Honduras, and Saudi Arabia, none of this is mere theory. But Kazanistan exists only in theory. The thought experiment remains just words.

In countenancing an established religion, Rawls, or rather his league of satisfied peoples, asks only that any decent society respect freedom of conscience enough to allow emigration. If discrimination makes that a vehicle of ethnic cleansing and religious purism, at least the means are less costly and less visible than genocidal population transfers. The not-so-silent war against the Copts in Egypt is a real-world case in point. So was the oppression and expulsion of almost every Jew from almost every predominantly Arab land and from Iran. Will the resulting uniformity strengthen the hand of bigots and entrench conformity? Will *socially* imposed univocity corrupt the clerics, as religious establishment historically tends to do? Will that in turn degrade the ethos? A fair degree of homogeneity was built into Rawls's model from the start by its stereotypic description of the society it hopes to legitimate, ignoring the diversity and the natural dynamic of change found in any society. But the invidiousness Rawls labors to tolerate hardens into norms what began as postulates of descriptive convenience, ratcheting ever tighter against the rib cage of those who might gasp for a breath of life in an open society.

American colonists were once ready to take up arms against a richer, stronger power rather than pay a few pence tax on their tea, demanding that their voices be heard. In living memory, young volunteers risked or gave their lives for the right of others – including strangers of another race – to sit in the front of a bus, or learn in integrated schools, or eat a sandwich at an integrated lunch counter. That was a moral demand of Mosaic liberalism. We humans do gasp for breath and reach for an open society and an open future. But to see the good and the implicit imperative in such hopes calls for a comprehensive doctrine.

Decent peoples, Rawls writes, do not tolerate outlaw states. They impose sanctions on those who wage aggressive wars or violate basic human rights.[58] But sanctions are often political in intent and counterproductive in impact. They are also often ineffective. Saddam lived for years with sanctions, and UN officials charged with their humane implementation were among those who sluiced unlawful kickbacks from the Oil for Food program.[59] Sanctions may also be deemed a casus belli by the nations targeted, as the rhetoric of North Korea testifies – even as the local populace continues to be oppressed, enslaved, and starved.

Rawls excludes from the universe of decent peoples those whose governments violate basic human rights.[60] But just which rights are basic is a delicate question, judged differently, perhaps, by the people of Kazanistan and their global neighbors. It is hard to answer a question like that without recourse to some comprehensive doctrine. Respect, after all, means giving room to *others'* standards. But it also looks to some idea of dignity. So does one keep quiet about forced sterilization or sex selection by abortion or infanticide? Often violations of basic rights are oblique or concealed, or denied with varying degrees of credibility. What do liberal states and "decent" peoples say or do about the burning of Coptic churches or the bombing of Jewish community centers by parties unnamed, whom a government proves unwilling to capture – and another government halfway around the world celebrates? What about free-lance terrorist groups whose

[58] Ibid., 80–81.
[59] Nile Gardiner and James Phillips, Heritage Foundation online paper, No. 1748, April 21, 2004; update on data destruction, April 9, 2005.
[60] Rawls, *Law of Peoples*, 60–61.

political branches, social agencies, propaganda, and fiscal work are tolerated, even encouraged in a "decent" society? Did the well-fed militias of Darfur who burned, killed, raped, and terrorized an ethnically and credally different population reflect on the Sudan government that claimed to know nothing of how the Janjaweed were fed and armed? Does failure to protect a defenseless population from starvation violate basic rights? What about shakedowns, drug trafficking, blood diamonds, expropriation of land and seizure of businesses and their assets, or rejection of polio vaccines or AIDS medications? Is passive, or acquiescent, or unacknowledged genocide an internal matter that a liberal society should overlook? We need to consider real-world cases, not abstract models secured by stipulation.

The lash of public opinion, Rawls hopes, will enable the Society of Peoples to build a lasting peace. That lash, it seems, is spared (selectively?) for "decent peoples." But it remains a powerful deterrent: "Even outlaw regimes are not altogether indifferent to this kind of criticism."[61] Granted, but their sensitivity does not always yield reforms. Some regimes respond with disinformation and manipulation, tightening the screws and loosening the purse strings to bribe and coopt journalists, scholars, and opinion makers; to buy jurists and legislators at home and abroad. Such methods were long practiced by the Soviets and Mao and mimicked by Saddam and Iran. Ignoring such risks, Rawls presses on: "Gradually, over time, then," he writes, "well-ordered peoples may pressure outlaw regimes to change their ways."[62] Gradually. What hope is there for those who suffer in the meantime? And when public opinion fails to notice or turns away after millions perish, as they did in Cambodia and Rwanda, Rawls holds in reserve the flaccid rod of sanctions!

Only if overt aggression by a foreign power leads to war, Rawls reasons, is armed retaliation justified. Does that mean that mass attacks such as that of September 11, 2001, or its predecessor – the truck bombing meant to bring down the Twin Towers in

[61] Ibid., 93.
[62] Ibid., 93.

1993 – are not acts of war? Just what counts as overt aggression? Rather than pin down his usage, Rawls punts, invoking another abstraction or crystallization: the image of the statesman: "There is no office of statesman, as there is of president, or chancellor, or prime minister. Rather, the statesman is an ideal, like that of the truthful or virtuous individual."[63] Rawls explains, "The ideal of the statesman is suggested by the saying: the politician looks to the next election, the statesman to the next generation."[64] That is what I call a sayism. The words resonate but have little purchase on reality. Lincoln did not look much like a statesman during much of his career. But Mao, Stalin, and even Hitler did worry little about elections, and the sacrifices they extracted from their people and others could always appeal to lofty hopes for generations yet to come. Perhaps the figurine Rawls pictures is FDR, who waited until Pearl Harbor before asking Congress to declare war. But was this statesmanship or politics, deferring to appeasement on the right, false pacifism on the left (as long as the Hitler-Stalin pact held up), and isolationism in the center? Had Japan stood clear of the Axis and had Hitler completed his conquest of Europe, would it still have been statesmanship to avoid a fight while the genocide went on?

Rawls's statesman shoulders the heavy decisions about loosing the dogs of war. Statesmanship, in the end it seems, depends on outcomes in good part – once the smoke has cleared, the dead are buried, and the wounded healed or patched up insofar as may be. Only history, it seems, can judge whether the blood and treasure, as the euphemism has it, were well spent. Such judgments rest on hindsight. But real decisions are made in the clinches, when the dangers of *any* course loom savage. Real statesmen must rely on data that are fresher and richer than historians will sift, but often spotty. Cooler judgments later on may second-guess the outcome or revise it in the interest of some political agenda, or in the light of recurrent visions of earlier battles, or in fear or a yen for others yet to come. War is a horror, not a picnic. But if there

[63] Ibid., 97.
[64] Ibid., 97.

is such a person as a statesman, it is by a sense of moral necessity heavily reliant on comprehensive doctrines that a real statesman and no paper cutout makes the hard decisions. And the measure of those decisions will be outcomes, in part of course, but also the quality and depth of those ideas.

Rawls turns in the end from war to peace and the duties of liberal societies toward "burdened" counterparts – those societies lacking the political culture to become well ordered. Acknowledging some good sense from Amartya Sen, he notes that not every burdened society is poor, nor is every well-ordered society rich. In Bengal, Ethiopia, the Sahel, and Bangladesh, Sen blames poor distribution rather than sheer penury as the chief cause of famine. Extraction industries, one might add, can prove a curse, seeming to obviate work and thrift and promoting what I call the Aladdin delusion – that vast wealth and untapped power await the feckless youth who stumbles into the right cave and scoops them up.[65] Visions of vast wealth sap the work ethic and corrupt the institutions that might have channeled capital to nourish a self-sustaining economy. Stillborn are the liberal institutions that modest but diffuse prosperity can foster. Displaced and disaffected youth are drawn to sensate pleasures. Guilt and anomie make them ready prey for extremists.

In keeping with the insights of Barbara Ward, whom he does not cite, Rawls argues that population pressure (he rejects the tendentious language of "overpopulation") is best relieved by enhanced rights and opportunities for women.[66] Here he seems to be on solid ground. Repression is not the key to economic growth, let alone to political development. There is hard evidence today, based on practical experience even in China, that Ward was correct – although Chinese authorities and many a die-hard ZPG-er resist acknowledging the fact.

---

[65] Lacking oil, diamonds, gold, uranium, or rare earth metals, the Aladdin mentality turns to opium, cocaine, or hashish as a surrogate of extractive industries, sapping the social and moral infrastructure abroad even as it undermines the local culture and economy.

[66] Rawls, *Law of Peoples*, 109; cf. Ward, *The Interplay of East and West*.

In the end, despite what he learned from Sen and absorbed from the likes of Barbara Ward, and despite what we have been learning from the successes of microcapital, as pioneered by Muhammad Yunus, and from the failures and embarrassments of some large-scale programs of international finance, which too often profit dictators, bureaucrats, and their kin rather than the poorest of the poor, when Rawls talks of responsibilities he means intergovernmental aid. Poverty, compounded by endemic and epidemic illness and exacerbated by violence and corruption, remains no small part of what developing societies confront.

Do Rawls's political liberalism and his aversion to intervention mean limiting international aid? Does food aid help, or does it undercut the efforts of local farmers and marketers? Does it help to send capital or forgive loans, or do we need to oversee the uses of aid funds and try to foster the building of just political institutions? Rawls has clearly left Garrett Hardin behind by the time he comes to speak of aid. There is no trace here of Hardin's heartless, racialist homilies about lifeboat earth. But what are the proper measure and means of aid? Should industrial nations be paying ecological reparations for past developmental sins or compensation for foregoing future depredations? I would answer in terms of the golden rule: The right measure of aid globally is just what it is locally. The best help, in Maimonidean terms, is what fosters self-sufficiency. It is not helpful to undercut local industry and agriculture. But neither is it cultural arrogance to see that aid flows to its developmental, educational, and humanitarian beneficiaries, not to numbered bank accounts that fund repression and further burden development.

Any society, Rawls proposes, except perhaps for a few "marginal cases" such as the Arctic Eskimos, has the resources to become well ordered:

The Law of Peoples assumes that every society has in its population a sufficient array of human capabilities, each in sufficient number so that the society has enough potential human resources to realize just institutions.[67]

---

[67] Rawls, *Law of Peoples*, 119.

The thesis that all cultures have the resources to better their people's lives and indeed achieve openness and justice is Rawls's most
powerful positive claim, beating back Mill's relativistic shibbo-
leth that some cultures are ill suited for institutions of the sort
that liberals find choiceworthy at home. But Rawls undercuts
this strength of his argument by casting others as more uniform
and static than they are. Diversity promotes social strength. Individual and communal differences strengthen a society, just as
differentiation is what distinguishes an organism from a clod of
earth – or a melody, as Aristotle put it, from a monotone.[68]

Rawls underrates the importance of diversity in other cultures,
mistaking a dominant strain for a convenient summation of an
unruly complexity. That painter's holiday is exacerbated by his
concessions to hierarchy. He does allow for change in nonliberal
societies, but change (too often a euphemism for that embarrass-
ing word "progress") does not always take the hoped-for path.
There are revolutions of expectation, but there are also reactions,
violent or pacific. Few observers of predominantly Islamic societies in the 1950s and '60s expected the return of militant, Salafist
pan-Islamism. More widely predicted was the gradual erosion
of religious devotion and the irrepressible rise of nationalist or
socialist movements, mitigated or powered by "modernization,"
typically assumed to mean Westernization.

Rawls's stereotypic portrayal of exotic societies forcefully
brings back the question of just what is meant by "we." Keen to
defend his claims against charges of cultural bias, he insists that
the Law of Peoples is not ethnocentric:

We must always start from where we now are.... The objectivity of that
law surely depends not on its time, place, or culture of origin, but on
whether it satisfies the criterion of reciprocity and belongs to the public
reason of the Society of liberal and decent Peoples.[69]

This, Rawls insists, it does: "It asks of other societies only what
they can reasonably grant without submitting to a position of

---

[68] Aristotle, *Politics* II 5, 1253b 31–36.
[69] Rawls, *Law of Peoples*, 121.

inferiority or domination." So reciprocity, as in the *original* original position, displaces principle, exposing the price Rawls pays for tamping down deeper commitments. Substantive notions of rights, long anchored in religious traditions and metaphysical reflections, are too parochial, too rooted in the "quest for certainty" to preserve the role that first brought liberty to the plane of law.

The law of peoples, Rawls pleads, "does not require decent societies to abandon or modify their religious institutions and adopt liberal ones."[70] Is that true? Yes and no. Rawls expects liberal societies to find nonliberal societies tolerable – insofar as they adopt the minimal liberal principles that he deems critical. He expects the negotiators who shape his imaginary world to tolerate what he finds tolerable and to draw a crisp line at what he finds intolerable. But here, as when he first spread the veil of ignorance, he shifts more normative weight to his definition of reason than a mere definition should be asked to bear. Kazanistan *has* jettisoned many Islamic values, including some deemed central by mainstream Muslim authorities. Yet some of the practices the model seems to condone may well remain morally intolerable.

Justice, Islamic or otherwise, is achieved only with much creative work, pursued by thoughtful leaders and outspoken thinkers, including theologians and philosophers. It calls for much soul searching, from China and Myanmar to Beirut and Damascus. But with all the good will in the world, Rawls's tolerance for corporatism, like his intolerance for theology in public deliberations, too readily impedes that work.

Reforms such as those that Rawls posits remain on the world's to-do list. Some of his desiderata remain contested or problematic. Learning, after all, is always a two-way street or, interculturally, a multilane interchange. Cultural arrogance lies in the assumption that traditional societies must meet the standards set by liberal, secular societies, but have nothing to impart. That is not what happened with Japan. It is hardly to be expected in future interactions of the West with China, India, Africa,

[70] Ibid., 121.

Oceania, or the peoples most widely and most deeply committed to Islam. To find and implement the principles of justice
still requires both sweat and imagination – and will bring blood
and tears. Justice is not won by formal fiats, positing its conditions and postulating first their adequacy and then their fulfillment. Should desirable transformations and accommodations be
achieved within and among the nations of the world, whether
in keeping with Rawls's pieties or with ideals more familiar in
situ or more universal, the mutual acceptance merited by the
societies that shape themselves as a result will be owing not to
any veil, fictive or pragmatic, but to the open-eyed creativity of
the leaders and thinkers of those societies and the insight and
open-mindedness of their people.

A weakness at the core of Rawls's model for the relationships
of liberal states with hierarchical, burdened, and challenged societies is the risk that well-meaning efforts toward tact and toleration can give heart to brutal regimes – and breed enmity and
cynicism among those who live in hope of their fall. The problem
is real in practice, although safely ignored in the controlled environment of an artificial model. To espouse high ideals is a great
responsibility for anyone – a fortiori for a powerful state. One
always runs the risk that someone will take one's words seriously
and strive to live by them.

Some of the students at Tiananmen Square in 1989 held copies
of *A Theory of Justice* as their friends stood unarmed before
the advancing tanks and built an effigy to the ideal of liberty.
Ultimately, it was a Lockean idea that inspired them, shining
through the pale montage of Rawls's remix. The liberty for which
they risked or lost their lives and futures was no stipulative idea.
Their cries were smothered then and still have not been heeded.
Survivors of the Tiananmen massacre still languish in prison, in
exile, or under the eye of a Communist Party that has shed much
of its former pretense and exists now mainly to sustain its own
hegemony. The sacrifices of those who spent years in solitary
confinement or reeducation are still ignored by the world's self-
proclaimed liberal democracies, all of which have economic and
diplomatic stakes in courting China's ruling elite. Taiwan has

evolved from a repressive to a liberal state, but America and the West may yet throw its land and people under the Chinese bus, with rationalizations about openness, exchange, engagement – and little overt reference to America's Chinese debt and the need for Chinese labor and environmental laxity as a means of holding down domestic wages and curbing inflation.

As the memory of Tiananmen began to fade abroad – and to suffer erasure within China – television viewers in the United States were being treated to moments of nostalgia for the Normandy landing, as well as vignettes of Allied troops marching through the Arc de Triomphe and throwing open the gates of Nazi death camps. The pride, safely focused on the past, seemed undiminished by doubts and denials of the moral soundness of the newer Allied initiatives to liberate Iraq and Afghanistan. Both pride and guilt can be overblown. America was years late in confronting Hitler's overt threats. Those years increased the war casualties and raised the civilian toll, especially in the death camps for the victims against whom the world's liberal democracies had slammed their own doors and had barred emigration even to the land of Israel.

It is at junctures like these that statesmen, Rawlsian or otherwise, have their work cut out for them. A statesman must judge what powers deserve alliance and which forces merit enmity or suspicion. A statesman must judge where sanctions will work and where stronger actions might make a difference, where diplomacy can achieve what war cannot, where allies count (and can be counted on), and where they would set a stumbling block in the path of peacemaking or (as at Yalta) betray whole nations to lives of slavery. The democratic statesman must discriminate tolerable from intolerable abuses and learn how to lead a polity rightly averse to the risk of war, so as not to emulate America's empty espousal of democratic ideals for Eastern Europe in the 1940s; for East Germany, Hungary, and Poland in the '50s; and for Czechoslovakia in the '60s – rhetoric backed up, when push came to shove, mainly by hand-wringing.

Often the critical task for the democratic statesman internationally, if critical tasks have anything to do with critical moments and statesmanship has anything to do with leadership, is to find a way to rouse a democratic polity from complacency and the self-serving, self-deceiving presumption that the blessings of democracy boil down to domestic creature comforts – and from the deeper self-deception that convinces those who enjoy such blessings that liberty will endure even at home regardless of any active effort to preserve it or speak up for it at home or overseas – let alone seek and explore, discuss, and return to its religious and metaphysical roots. For even more than they seek legitimacy, tyrants constantly test for acquiescence. Complacency is their ally, and the anomie it breeds is their fifth column. Finding a statesman whose ideals come alive not just in prideful, Periclean words offered on state occasions but in prudent, effectual action has always been the great issue for democracies. It remains so today and will remain so long into the future.

Some Concluding Thoughts

Diversity of outlooks, practices, values, and ideas is inherent in the human condition. Cultures differ. So do personal histories, circumstances, and prospects. Differences between generations may widen as trade, travel, exile, migration, and communication speed our cultural interactions. The question of this book has been how we should cope, as individuals and communities, with the dazzling diversity we confront. The answer I have proposed is rooted in the ideal of openness. Openness does not mean relativism, and skepticism is not its nutriment, although it may be a byproduct or a motive. One can respect differences without abandoning one's commitments. One needs to know oneself if one is to engage in fruitful dialogue with others. A relativism that pretends all views are equally sound or welcomes all practices as equally wholesome or apposite is not generous or practical but patronizing. A skepticism that dismisses all thoughts but what seems self-evident is just the opposite of open-minded. And neither relativism nor skepticism affords stable ground for self-cultivation.

Groups, like individuals, are nourished by what they learn from others. So societies that favor intercommunal understanding are the richer for it. They make a resource of what too often seems a difficulty. The notion that diversity spells trouble may stem in part from the illusion that societies need a common ideology and uniform practices. I do not think either sort of unity has ever existed, unless as an artifact of lazy analysis or simple stereotyping. Just consider how different idiolects can be. Ways of living and thinking are far more varied. Neuroscientists find more synaptic connections in each human brain as it actively responds to experience than there are elementary particles in the universe. So efforts to impose lockstep ideas or behaviors belong not to any history of harmony but to the black record of oppression, be its idols and ideals secular or sacred. The carnage and wreckage left by attempts to cast humanity into a single mold still clutter the world in the broad wake of the Inquisition and Europe's religious wars. They scar living memory in the aftermath of the Holocaust, the Gulag, the Cultural Revolution, and the Cambodian killing fields. Ironing out or burning away diversity is a fantasy that ends in tragedy. What social bodies need is a way of learning and profiting from differences – not denying, minimizing, trivializing, or romanticizing them. Still, an open mind is not an empty head. Not every idea stands up to scrutiny, and not every way of life is tolerable. Some ideas are vicious; some practices hack away at life itself. Yet much that passes for pluralism today invites a suspension of moral or intellectual judgment. That is misguided charity. Only critical appropriation can make receptivity effectual even in relating to the values and traditions one might call one's own. The alternative is superficiality, be it welcoming or hostile.

Much of this book discusses Rawls and his search for norms that regard diversity. I am disappointed by Rawls's attempt in *Political Liberalism* to address differences of conscience by placing a kibosh on deliberative appeals or even motives that rely on religious or other "comprehensive" doctrines. And I am unconvinced by Rawls's project to anchor world peace in hopes for liberal amity toward "decent" peoples. Too much seems to rest on wishful thinking. Posits and definitions cannot take the place or plot the course of the hard work and hard choices that international and intercultural relations demand.

I find the regime Rawls calls political liberalism illiberal and impractical. Many of us have no deeper motives or higher ideals than those that we voice religiously. Efforts to universalize such values typically take the form of metaphysics, the natural home of comprehensive doctrines. America's founding fathers were not uncomfortable with religion or with metaphysics, perhaps because in their age men of parts, as they might have put it, were expected to reflect for themselves on what made sense to them religiously or philosophically. When those founders paired the allusive "endowed by their Creator" with the openly metaphysical "inalienable rights," the philosopher standing just behind the scrim was John Locke, arguing that there are goods an individual would sooner fight for than surrender, even to escape the asperities of a Hobbesian state of nature. Prudentially, the founders' claim was that in the end oppression must prove futile. But the argument gained moral traction because many saw as God's decree the laws of nature that summon every creature jealously to guard its interests.

The language of inalienable rights secularized the biblical tropes that clothe human dignity in the metaphor of man's creation in God's image. But the normative edge held, in images – and tales, not all of them fictional – of homely self-assertion. Blunt that moral edge and rights become mere claims. Then we are back in Hobbesian nature or in Bentham's world, where natural rights are nonsense; and absolute, "imprescriptible rights," are "rhetorical nonsense – nonsense upon stilts." If it is not brute force that rules here, then it is special pleading – the world of Jarndyce and Jarndyce where real rights are irrelevant and professional advocates and their sophist coaches find nothing left in claims of right beyond the claim.

Religious and metaphysical appeals, as my Rawlsian friends imagine them, sound pretty hollow to me. They lean heavily on contested notions or defer awkwardly to scripture. They do not sound quite so coercive as Rawls makes out – or very compelling either. Doubtless there have been times where such heavy-handedness had the kind of clout that liberal societies must guard against. There are places even now where that is true – North Korea and Iran come speedily to mind. And even in the freest lands, we find that some things may not be said. Some of the views argued in this book are anathema and debarred in some quarters. Any orthodoxy is oppressive, even when fashion has done a somersault and pretends to celebrate heresy, having found new modes of enforced conformity. So it is always proper to be chary of invasions of the mind. But conformity is the enemy of exploration here, not religion per se or metaphysics as such. The stifling of religious motives or metaphysical reasoning is no part of liberation but just a new path of dogmatism. In an open society the sort of special pleading warned against by Rawls makes little headway. Those who do not share a canon or read their canon uniformly will not find much to change their minds or hearts in rival games of Bible thumping, let alone in metaphysical disquisitions. In a diverse society they will be more likely to find that sort of rhetoric off-putting, limited in appeal to the ranks of the alienated and marginalized. Alienation and social exclusion are real problems, but they are social problems, not problems to be solved or salved by silencing religious voices in the public square or metaphysics on the internet.

Appeals to the incalculable worth and inherent dignity of the human person bear the special force they claim precisely because they do invoke a comprehensive doctrine But many people have trouble voicing their authentically humane concerns in more abstract terms than the scriptures they know well. Affirmations of inherent worth and dignity do make metaphysical claims. Rawls himself, I have argued, is implicated, by his interest in rights, in liberty, in justice itself. I doubt that the normative demands he meant to speak for can be freed of metaphysics. Bare equality itself cannot be. But, even if it were so neutered, it would offer little of substance to the human project; that is, to the enhancement of human dignity and welfare. My focus here is less on the *tu quoque* than on that project and the liberty at its core. Few gains for liberty or humanity have been won without the kind of ideals that religions inspire and are inspired by. And politics does not go far in any normative direction without some orienting body of metaphysical assumptions.

There is good metaphysics and bad metaphysics, just as there is good and bad politics – or religion or statistics. Politics can drive metaphysics just as well or badly as metaphysics may drive politics. So, despite the bad taste that bad metaphysics has left in the mouths of some – indeed, precisely because we need to cleanse the palate of such bitter residues – the nexus of politics to metaphysics needs to be sustained and revitalized. I shudder at the thought of stopping up the mouths and stripping off the bumper stickers of everyone whose religion offers words and images, narratives and practices that carry a normative message with bearing on our lives together. Politics, like any other prescriptive enterprise, stultifies – just as religion or even science does – without ever new reflection on its own foundations. Part of the problem with trying to do political philosophy by posit and postulate is that it seeks to close off argument just where argument should begin.

Formalism simply does not work: The syntax of prescription can no more sustain a normative message than can the deep baritone of Sergeant Preston of the Yukon ordering some miscreant, "HALT, IN THE NAME OF THE CROWN!" The logic of judgment will not do much better, despite the good intentions of many a talented and well-intentioned philosopher. Formalism is morally arid – ultimately, sterile. Culture, as a friend writes, "is the medium in which norms have their life." Unlike a mathematical algorithm or abstraction, what lives will grow and change, suffer injuries and risks. Cultures, like any living thing, can fall ill, even contract cancer, as we have seen. If we are to be physicians of our souls, all the more must we be hygienists, dieticians, and sometimes surgeons of our cultures. Even philosophers cannot do such things by fiat.

Some, at this point, may appeal to God. I do not think that helps much, not because God has no authority or nothing to say about right living, but because not everyone will recognize authority of that kind and not everyone recognizes the same God. Many find it irritating just to hear God mentioned. Others differ over how to spell out God's expectations. We have got to start from where we live and reason from what we know, not because we are sure to find each other's starting points wholly reasonable – people differ, after all, about where to start even in mathematics – but because I see values in living that prove rather livelier than those of topic-neutral formalism. I start from the sanctity of the human person – human, because that is near to hand; sanctity, because that directs our gaze beyond utility. The sanctity of selves gestures toward God, not a line of sight that everyone is prepared to look in. But pointing toward an open-ended goal, one that is irreducible and not for sale, at least spares us from trying to derive our norms from disputed fiats or arbitrary rules.

We have considered some minimal and maximal norms: The minimal involve slavery, polygamy, cliterodectomy, human trafficking, and the like. Focusing concretely on abuses may help bring moral boundaries into focus and stake out some of the core demands of human dignity. The larger norms I have singled out from the Decalogue are voiced as God's commands, but are centered on human dignity. A communal identity vested in a shared sense of mission fleshes out these prescriptions. A concrete vision of the possibilities of personhood helps keep these norms from deliquescing into abstractions. Boldly anchored in God's command, the prescriptions of the Decalogue shelter a subtext when they make the human person their cynosure: It is in no stone or wooden icon, but in humanity itself, in each living person, that we find God's image.

Our barest obligations, signaled by the laws forbidding murder, theft, and adultery, are complemented by higher calls to moral growth – in the command to discipline our hankerings for all that someone else holds dear – and to spiritual growth, in the invitation to pursue the avenues toward transcendence that Sabbaths open up. Other biblical norms enrich those of the Decalogue. Alternative constellations of norms arise elsewhere, rivaling or complementing the Mosaic tablets or seeking kindred goals by other pathways. Moral universality does not mean universal acceptance or unison lip service. It is anchored in the respect due every being and persons in particular. What is called for most broadly are thought and action that enable flourishing. But ideas of flourishing vary, and the richness of our nature and intricacy of our relations preclude complete detail in any merely abstract scheme or uniformity in any concrete one. At the minimal edge of normativity, where obligation asks little more than the restraint of violence against another's personhood, there is room for broad consensus. Yet even here details may differ. At the higher reaches, where holiness and authenticity are sought, cultures and their rituals afford the languages, the disciplines, and the models of human virtues and attainments – weaving a fabric too fine for the coarse fingers of the state. Hence the need for secularity in government.

But secularity, I have argued, is not secularism. Nor is liberalism. Governments are not rightly neutral about those bodies that promise to promote human flourishing – be they educational, recreational, spiritual, or ethical. The threat of mind control and exploitation is real, and minds and spirits as well as bodies need protections. Parks, schools, libraries, research institutes, and universities have missions so near the minimal end of state responsibilities that their neglect is all but criminal. Withholding the nourishment that humanizes human life is a failure almost as grave as failure to protect the denizens of a country from force or fraud. So there is a mandate for state sponsorship – not direct control, since the mission of such institutions must be kept generic. But at the moral and spiritual end of the spectrum, where cultures engage most intimately with human lives, state support, I have argued, is best indirect, reflecting the free contributions of constituents to the bodies that serve their higher needs as they themselves define them.

In *The Law of Peoples*, Rawls addresses cultural diversity on an international plane. Liberal peoples, he argues, can get along with nonliberal ones, so long as those, say, hierarchical peoples are such that Rawls can call them "decent." Much latitude remains for disagreement about just what sort of regime merits that label. A society, I have argued, might meet Rawls's standards and still tolerate, perpetuate – even perpetrate – some pretty grave abuses. But beyond that there is a structural difficulty in Rawls's argument. The test he offers for his claims is an imagined Islamic society that he calls Kazanistan. When one wonders just how Muslim and just how decent Kazanistan will be, the ultimate response is that Kazanistan is a construct: It meets Rawls's standards by hypothesis. The balance it sustains between hierarchy and liberty is both necessary and sufficient to satisfy the liberal peoples of Rawls's imagined world. We know it is because Rawls posits that it is so. The argument is analytic. Its application to the real world rests on Rawls's hopes and wishes. Little more is attained by the comparably structured arguments of *A Theory of Justice* and *Political Liberalism*.

Where, then, does that leave us? Pluralism, I have argued, is a matter of ethos – of culture, tradition, and innovation. Cultures interact and grow through individual initiative, insight, and innovation; individuals gain the strength they need to contribute culturally when they find intellectual and spiritual resources to sustain them and exemplars to push off against in the traditions they encounter. It is with thoughts like that in mind, about the embeddedness of norms in a cultural matrix, that I have disputed Rawls's secularizing demands and cast a skeptical eye on his whitewashed international political vista. Political liberalism, as Rawls defines it, uses both its terms in Pickwickian senses; Rawls's league of peoples is ersatz, a figment of factitious posits, far removed from cultural, historical, or even geographical realities.

Without cultures, norms are just word pictures like those plaques pretending to represent the Ten Commandments, but stripped of operative impact. It is practice that gives life to norms, and practice is not reached in abstraction – finger pounding on a paper keyboard. Kant, we recall, with all his genius, could not derive the material, end-in-itself formulation of the categorical imperative from the formal, universal-law formulation. Rawls has done no better with his posits. Nor has Korsgaard with her excursions into the logic of self-legislation. Rawls speaks of equality, but equality does not entail caring. Rational choice, if that means keeping one's options open, does not entail kindness. Morality demands recognition of the deserts of beings in general and the special deserts of persons in particular. The claims that beings make and the ones that persons may make explicitly do not entail a way of life – but they do prescribe commitment to a certain family of lifeways.

Rawls envisions a kind of conversation that he expects will chip and buff away some of the rough edges of our differences, yielding an overlapping consensus. I am not sure we need quite the level of consensus that Rawls hopes for and at times assumes, or that it is ultimately even worthwhile. I value differences, even when I cannot make another's views or practices my own or bring that other around to my quite reasonable point of view. It is when we understand each other and recognize our differences that they matter most – when we know whether or not we are able to accept our differences and respect one another all the same. Individuals have existential commitments just as cultures have their distinctive styles and constellations of values. These are often constitutive and not readily exchanged. We should celebrate differences when we can, but we should also argue over them when opportunity and good faith permit. Imitation, at least for a philosopher, is not the sincerest form of celebration: Argument is. I am not eager to see the world come around to my way of thinking. It matters more that people go on learning from each other. I feel the same about this book: I would be content if some readers see some sense in it. But our ways of thinking grow larger and our ways of living grow more reflective and robust when we argue them out. That is where pluralism bears fruit. So, I say, let the conversation begin.

Bibliography

Abe, Masao. "Kenotic God and Dynamic Sunyata," in Cobb and Ives, 3–65.

Adams, Henry. *The Education of Henry Adams* (1918), ed. E. Samuels (Boston: Houghton Mifflin, 1973).

Allinson, Robert E. "The Golden Rule as the Core Value in Confucianism and Christianity: Ethical Similarities and Differences," *Asian Philosophy* 2 (1992) 173–85.

Alston, William. *Perceiving God* (Ithaca: Cornell University Press, 1991).

Amore, Roy C. *Two Masters, One Message* (Nashville: Abingdon, 1978).

Arens, W. *The Original Sin: Incest and its Meaning* (New York: Oxford University Press, 1986).

Aristotle, *Nicomachaean Ethics*, tr. J. A. K. Thompson (London: Penguin, 1955).

Audi, Robert and Nicholas Wolterstorff. *Religion in the Public Square* (Lanham, MD: Rowman & Littlefield, 1997).

Avila, Mitchell. "Defending A Law of Peoples: Political Liberalism and Decent Peoples," *Journal of Ethics* 11 (2007) 87–124.

Becker, C. L. *The Heavenly City of the Eighteenth Century French Philosophers* (New Haven: Yale University Press, 2003; first published, 1932).

Bellamy, Richard and Martin Hollis. "Liberal Justice: Political and Metaphysical," *Philosophical Quarterly* 45 (1995) 1–19.

Bland, Kalman. *The Artless Jew* (Princeton: Princeton University Press, 2000).

Camus, Albert. *The Rebel*, tr. Anthony Bower (New York: Knopf, 1956; Paris, 1951).

———. *The Just*, tr. J. O'Brien, in *Caligula and Three Other Plays* (New York: Knopf, 1958; Paris, 1950).

Cavanaugh, Matthew. *The Myth of Religious Violence* (Oxford: Oxford University Press, 2010).

Ching, Julia. "Response to Jeffrey Hopkins," *Buddhist-Christian Studies* 8 (1988) 131–49.

Cobb, John and Christopher Ives, eds. *The Emptying of God: A Buddhist-Jewish-Christian Conversation* (Maryknoll, NY: Orbis, 1990).

Connolly, William E. *Why I Am Not a Secularist* (Minneapolis: University of Minnesota, 1999).

Cymet, David. *History vs Apologetics: The Holocaust, the Third Reich, and the Catholic Church* (Lanham, MD: Lexington Books, 2010).

Dennett, Daniel. *Darwin's Dangerous Idea* (New York: Simon and Schuster, 1995).

Deutsch, Eliot. ed., *Culture and Modernity: East-West Philosophic Perspectives* (Honolulu: University of Hawaii Press, 1991).

Dewey, John. *The Public and its Problems* (Athens, OH: Swallow Press, 1991; first published, 1927).

Dharmarsiri, Gunapala. *A Buddhist Critique of the Christian Concept of God* (Antioch, CA: Golden Leaves, 1988).

Dikötter, Frank. *Mao's Great Famine: The History of China's Most Devastating Catastrophe* (New York: Walker, 2010).

Dombrowski, Daniel. *Rawls and Religion: The Case for Political Liberalism* (Albany: SUNY Press, 2001).

Dworkin, Ronald. *Is Democracy Possible Here?* (Princeton: Princeton University Press, 2006).

Eberle, Christopher. *Religious Convictions in Liberal Politics* (Cambridge: Cambridge University Press, 2002).

———. "Basic Human Worth and Religious Restraint," *Philosophy and Social Criticism* 35 (2009) 151–81.

Elshtain, Jean Bethke. *Public Man, Private Woman* (Princeton: Princeton University Press, 1981).

———. "There Oughta be a Law," *Emory Law Journal* 58 (2008) 71–86.

Finckenauer, James O. and Jennifer Schrook. "Human Trafficking: A Growing Criminal Market in the U.S.," International Center, National Institute of Justice.

Fletcher, George. "Talmudic Reflections on Self-Defense," in Robert Gordis, ed., *Crime, Punishment and Deterrence: An American Jewish Exploration* (Los Angeles: Wilstein Institute, 1989) 61–72.

Foot, Philippa. *Natural Goodness* (Oxford: Oxford University Press, 2001).

Fuller, Lon. *The Morality of Law* (New Haven: Yale University Press, 1964).

Galston, William A. *Liberal Pluralism: The Implications of Value Pluralism for Political Theory and Practice* (Cambridge: Cambridge University Press, 2002).

Garver, Eugene. *For the Sake of the Argument* (Chicago: University of Chicago Press, 2004).

George, Robert and Christopher Wolfe. "Natural Law and Public Reason," in *Natural Law and Public Reason* (Washington, DC: Georgetown University Press, 2000).

Goldmann, Lucien. *The Hidden God: A Study of Tragic Vision in the Pensées of Pascal and the tragedies of Racine*, tr. Philip Thody (New York: Humanities Press, 1964).

Goodin, Robert. *What's Wrong with Terrorism* (Cambridge: Polity, 2006).

Goodman, Lenn E. "Review of Franz Rosenthal, *The Herb*," *Middle East Journal* 28 (1974) 86–87.

——. *God of Abraham* (New York: Oxford University Press, 1996).

——. *Judaism, Human Rights and Human Values* (New York: Oxford University Press, 1998).

——. *In Defense of Truth: A Pluralistic Approach* (Amherst, NY: Humanity Press, 2001).

——. Mosaic Liberalism, in M. Corinaldi, M. D. Herr, R. Horwitz and Y. D. Silman, eds., *Studies in Memory of Ze'ev Falk* (Jerusalem: Mesharim, 2005) 5–24; *Judaism* 52 (2003) 21–38.

——. *Islamic Humanism* (New York: Oxford University Press, 2003).

——. *On Justice* (Oxford: Littman Library of Jewish Civilization, 2008).

——. *Love thy Neighbor as Thyself* (New York: Oxford University Press, 2008).

——. *Creation and Evolution* (New York: Routledge, 2010).

——. and D. Gregory Caramenico. *Coming to Mind: The Soul and its Body* (Chicago: University of Chicago Press, 2013).

Goodman, Nelson. *Fact, Fiction, and Forecast* (Cambridge, MA: Harvard University Press, 1955).

Greenberg, Moshe. "Some Postulates of Biblical Criminal Law," in Judah Goldin, ed., *The Jewish Expression* (New Haven: Yale University Press, 1976) 18–37.

Hall, John A. *Ernest Gellner: An Intellectual Biography* (London: Verso, 2010).

Hamburger, Philip. *Separation of Church and State* (Cambridge, MA: Harvard University Press, 2002).

Hampton, Jean. "Should Political Philosophy be Done without Metaphysics," *Ethics* 99 (1989) 791–814.

Heim, S. Mark. *Salvations: Truth and Difference in Religion* (Maryknoll, NY: Orbis, 1995).

Hick, John. "Theology and Verification," in Hick, ed., *The Existence of God* (New York: Macmillan, 1964) 253–74; first published in *Theology Today* 17 (1960).

———. Reply to C. Robert Mesle's "Humanism and Hick's Interpretation of Religion," in Harold Hewitt, *Problems in the Philosophy of Religion: Critical Studies of the Work of John Hick* (New York: St Martin's, 1991) 82–85.

Hirshman, Linda R. "Is the Original Position Inherently Male-Superior?" *Columbia Law Review* 94 (1994) 1860–81.

Hume, David. *A Treatise of Human Nature* (1739), ed. L. A. Selby-Bigge (Oxford: Oxford University Press, 1968; first edition, 1888).

———. *Enquiries Concerning Human Understanding and Concerning the Principles of Morals* (1777), ed. L. A. Selby-Bigge, rev. P. H. Nidditch (Oxford: Oxford University Press, 1982).

Ibn Daud, Abraham. *The Book of Tradition*, ed. and trans. Gerson Cohen (Philadelphia: Jewish Publication Society, 1967).

Ibn Ezra, Abraham. *Commentary on the Pentateuch*, tr. H. Norman Strickman and Arthur M. Silver (New York: Menorah, 1996).

Ibn al-Farrah al-Baghawi (fl. 1337), tr. James Robson, *Mishkat al-Masabih* (repr. Lahore: Ashraf, 1975) 2 vols.

Ibn al-Nafis (13th century). *The Theologus Autodidactus*, ed. and tr. Max Meyerhof and Joseph Schacht (Oxford: Oxford University Press, 1968).

Ignatieff, Michael. *Isaiah Berlin: A Life* (Toronto: Penguin, 2000).

Ives, Christopher, ed. *Divine Emptiness and Historical Fullness* (Valley Forge, PA: Trinity Press, 1995).

Jones, Peter. "Two Conceptions of Liberalism, Two Conceptions of Justice," *British Journal of Political Science* 25 (1995) 515–50.

Josephus, *Antiquities*, tr. H. St. J. Thackeray (Cambridge: Harvard Univeristy Press, 1998; first published, 1930).

———. *Contra Apion*, tr. John M. G. Barclay, as *Against Apion* (Leiden: Brill, 2007).

Kaplan, Mordecai, Introduction to Moses Hayyim Luzzatto, *Mesillat Yesharim* (Philadelphia: Jewish Publication Society, 1936).

Katz, Steven. *Mysticism and Religious Traditions* (New York: Oxford University Press, 1983).

Khadduri, Majid. *War and Peace in the Law of Islam* (Baltimore: Johns Hopkins University Press, 1955).

Koppelman, Andrew. "Can Rawls Condemn Female Genital Mutilation," *Review of Politics* 71 (2009) 459–82.

Küng, Hans. "God's Self-Renunciation and Buddhist Emptiness: A Christian Response to Masao Abe," in eds. Roger Corless and Paul F. Knitter, *Buddhist Emptiness and Christian Trinity* (New York: Paulist Press, 1990) 24–43; Küng's essay is rehearsed, with added footnotes, in Ives, *Divine Emptiness and Historical Fullness.* Section 4, Chapter 7, 207–23.

Lethaby, W. R. *Architecture, Mysticism, and Myth* (New York: Braziller, 1975; first ed., 1891).

Levitt, Matt. *Hamas: Politics, Charity, and Terrorism in the Service of Jihad* (New Haven: Yale University Press, 2006).

Liebermann, Debra, John Tooby, and Leda Cosmides, "Does Morality Have a Biological Basis: An Empirical Test of the Factors Governing Moral Sentiments Regarding Incest," *Proceedings of the Royal Society* B 270 (2003) 819–26.

Lloyd, G. E. R. *Demystifying Mentalities* (Cambridge: Cambridge University Press, 1990).

Luciuk, L. Y. *Not Worthy: Walter Duranty's Pulitzer Prize and the New York Times* (Kingston, Ontario: Kashtan Press, 2004).

MacIntyre, Alasdair. *After Virtue* (London: Duckworth, 1981).

Maimonides, Moses. *Dalalat al-Ha'irin* (*Guide to the Perplexed*), ed. and tr. Salomon Munk, as *Le Guide des Égarés* (Paris, 1856–66; repr. Osnabrück: Zeller, 1964) 3 vols.

———. *Teshuvot* (Responsa), ed. J. Blau (Jerusalem: Mikitze Nirdamim, 1975–86) 4 vols.

———. *The Eight Chapters* (introduction to Mishnah Avot), tr. Ibn Tibbon, ed. and tr. Joseph I. Gorfinkle (New York: Columbia University Press, 1912; repr. New York: AMS, 1966).

Masterson, Patrick. *Atheism and Alienation* (Dublin: Gill and Macmillan, 1971).

Matilal, Bimal. "Karma: A Metaphysical Hypothesis of Moral Causation in History," in T. M. P. Mahadevan and Grace Cairns, eds., *Contemporary Indian Philosophers of History* (Calcutta: World Press, 1977) 235–47.

———. "Pluralism, Relativism, and Interaction between Cultures," in Eliot Deutsch, ed., *Culture and Modernity: East-West Philosophic Perspectives* (Honolulu: University of Hawaii Press, 1991) 141–60.

May, Larry. *Genocide: A Normative Account* (Cambridge: Cambridge University Press, 2010).

McMahan, Jeff. "The Ethics of Killing in War," *Philosophia* 34 (2006) 693–733.

Mara, Gerald M. "Virtue and Pluralism: The Problem of the One and the Many," *Polity* 22 (1989) 25–48.

Miko, Francis T. "Trafficking in Women and Children: The U.S. and International Response," *Congressional Record Research Service Report* 98–649C, May 10, 2000.

Mittleman, Alan. "The Durability of Goodness," Shalem Center, Jerusalem, October 26, 2009.

Nagel, Thomas. "Rawls on Justice," in ed. Norman Daniels, *Reading Rawls: Critical Studies on Rawls'* A Theory of Justice, (New York: Basic Books, 1975) Part 1, Chapter 1, pp. 1–16; reprinted from *Philosophical Review* 82 (1973) 220–34.

Neuhaus, John Richard. *The Naked Public Square* (Grand Rapids: Eerdmans, 1984).

Nozick, Robert. "Distributive Justice," *Philosophy and Public Affairs* 3 (1973) 45–126.

———. *Anarchy State and Utopia* (New York: Basic Books, 1974).

Okin, Susan. "Justice and Gender: An Unfinished Debate," *Fordham Law Review* 72 (2004) 1537–67.

O'Neill, Onora. *Bounds of Justice* (Cambridge: Cambridge University Press, 2003).

Pangle, Thomas. *The Theological Basis of Liberal Modernity* (Chicago: University of Chicago Press, 2010).

Parekh, Bhikku. *Rethinking Multiculturalism: Cultural Diversity and Political Theory* (Cambridge: Harvard University Press, 2000).

Perry, Ralph Barton. *Our Side is Right* (Cambridge: Harvard University Press, 1942).

Philo, *Opera*, ed. and tr., F. H. Colson nd G. H. Whitaker (Cambridge: Harvard University Press, 1929–62).

Plantinga, Alvin. "Pluralism: A Defense of Religious Exclusivism," in ed. Thomas D. Senor, *The Rationality of Belief and the Plurality of Faith: Essays in Honor of William P. Alston* (Ithaca: Cornell University Press, 1995) Part 3, Chapter 8, 191–215.

Rawls, John. *A Theory of Justice* (Cambridge: Harvard University Press, 1971; revised, 1999).

———. "The Independence of Moral Theory," *Proceedings and Addresses of the American Philosophical Association* 48 (1974/75) 5–22.

———. "Justice as Fairness: Political not Metaphysical," *Philosophy and Public Affairs* 14 (1985) 223–51.

———. *Political Liberalism* (New York: Columbia University Press, 1993, 2005).

———. Interview with Bernard Prusak, *Commonweal* 125 (1998).

———. *The Law of Peoples* (Cambridge: Harvard University Press, 1999).

Reidy, David. "Rawls on International Justice: A Defense," *Political Theory* 32 (2004) 291–319.

Rescher, Nicholas. *Pluralism: Against the Demand for Consensus* (New York: Oxford University Press, 1993).

Richard, A. "International Trafficking in Women to the United States: A Contemporary Manifestation of Slavery and Organized Crime," Center for the Study of Intelligence, November, 1999.

Ricoeur, Paul. *The Relgious Significance of Atheism* (New York: Columbia University Press, 1969).

Rosenthal, Franz. *The Herb: Hashish versus Medieval Muslim Society* (Leiden: Brill, 1971).

Rothenberg, Albert. "The Process of Janusian Thinking," *Archives of General Psychiatry* 24 (1971) 195–205, reprinted in Rothenberg and Carl Hausman, eds. *The Creativity Question* (Durham: Duke University Press, 1976).

Sachedina, Abdulaziz. *Human Rights and the Conflict of Cultures* (Columbia, South Carolina: University of South Carolina Press, 1988).

_____. *The Qur'an on Religious Pluralism* (Washington: Center for Muslim-Christian Understanding, History, and International Affairs, 1999).

_____. *Islamic Roots of Democratic Pluralism* (New York: Oxford University Press, 2001).

Safrai, S. ed. *The Literature of the Sages* (Assen/Maastricht: Van Gorcum; Philadelphia: Fortress, 1987).

Sandburg, Carl, "The People, Yes," in *Complete Poems* (San Diego: Harcourt, 1970).

Schoen, Ed. "Circumcision Updated – Indicated," *Pediatrics* 92 (1993) 860–61.

_____. *On Circumcision* (Berkeley: RDR, 2005).

Segal, Ronald. *Islam's Black Slaves: The Other Black Diaspora* (London: Atlantic Books, 2002).

Sharansky, Anatoloy. *Fear no Evil*, tr. Stefani Hoffman (New York: Random House, 1988).

Siegmund, Georg. *Buddhism and Christianity: A Preface to Dialogue*, tr. Sr. Mary F. McCarthy (Birmingham: University of Alabama Press, 1980; German original, 1968).

Singer, Peter W. *Children at War* (New York: Pantheon, 2005).

Smith, Wilfred Cantwell. *The Meaning and End of Religion* (New York: Macmillan, 1964).

_____. *Faith and Belief* (Princeton: Princeton University Press, 1979; and Oxford: One World, 1998).

_____. *Towards a World Theology* (Maryknoll, NY: Orbis, 1981).

Spinoza, Baruch, *Complete Works*, tr. Samuel Shirley (Indianapolis: Hackett, 2002).

Stcherbatsky, Fedor. *The Buddhist Concept of Nirvāna* (New York: Gordon Press, 1973; first published, Leningrad: Academy of Sciences, 1927).

Steinberger, Peter J. "The Impossibility of a 'Political' Conception," *Journal of Politics* 62 (2000) 147–65.

Tasioulas, John. "From Utopia to Kazanistan: John Rawls and the Law of Peoples," *Oxford Journal of Legal Studies* 2 (2002) 367–96.

Taylor, S. J. *Stalin's Apologist: Walter Duranty, the New York Times Man in Moscow* (New York: Oxford University Press, 1990).

Thelle, Notto. *Buddhism and Christianity in Japan: From Conflict to Dialogue 1854–1899* (Honolulu: University Press of Hawaii, 1987).

Thomas, Edward. *The History of Buddhist Thought* (London: Kegan Paul, Trench and Trubner, 1933).

Tribe, Laurence. *American Constitutional Law* (New York: Foundation Press, 2000).

Tyan, E. *djihad, Encyclopedia of Islam*, 2nd edition (Leiden: Brill, 1960–2009).

Tyndale, William. tr. Pentateuch (1530), David Daniell, ed., *Tyndale's Old Testament* (New Haven: Yale University Press, 1992).

Urbach, Ephraim E. *The Sages: Their Concepts and Beliefs*, tr. Israel Abrahams (Jerusalem: Magnes Press, 1975; from the second Hebrew edition, 1973) 2 vols.

van Inwagen, Peter. *God, Knowledge and Mystery: Essays in Philosophical Theology* (Ithaca: Cornell University Press, 1995).

Vidyananda. *Tattvarthaslokavartikam* (Ahmedabad: Saraswati Pustak Bhander, 2002).

Voegelin, Eric. *Order and History* (Baton Rouge: Louisiana State University Press, 1956–1987).

Ward, Barbara. *The Interplay of East and West* (London: Allen Unwin, 1957).

Wedgwood, C. V. *The Thirty Years War* (London: Cape, 1938; reprinted, 1961, 1969, 2005, etc.).

Weiss, Helen A., Maria A. Quigley, and Richard J. Hayes. "Male Circumcision and Risk of hiv Infection in Sub-Saharan Africa: A Systematic Review and Meta-Analysis," *AIDS* 14 (2000).

Westphal, Merold. *Suspicion and Faith: The Religious Uses of Modern Atheism* (Grand Rapids: Eerdmans, 1993).

White, Matthew. "Democracies Do Not Make War on One Another – or Do They?" Internet Posting, 2000; revised, 2005.

Windschuttle, Keith. "Mao and the Maoists," *The New Criterion*, October, 2005, 31–40.

Wisdom, John. "Gods," *Proceedings of the Aristotelian Society*, 1944, reprinted in Wisdom, *Philosophy and Psychoanalysis* (Oxford: Blackwell, 1964) 149–68.

Wolff, Robert Paul. "There's Nobody Here but Us Persons," in Carol Gould and Marx Wartofsky, eds., *Women and Philosophy* (New York: Putnam, 1976) Part 3, pp. 128–44.

Wolfson, Harry. *Philo: Foundations of Religious Philosophy in Judaism, Christianity, and Islam* (Cambridge: Harvard University Press, 1962; first edition, 1947).

Wolterstorff, Nicholas. "The Role of Religion in Decision and Discussion of Political Issues," in Audi and Wolterstorff, *Religion in the Public Square.*

Yang Jisheng, *Tombstone: The Great Chinese Famine 1958–1962* (New York: Farrar, Straus and Giroux, 2008).

Zaehner, R. C. *Mysticism Sacred and Profane* (Oxford: Oxford University Press, 1961).

Index

Abe, Masao, 27–34, 40
abortion, 5, 57, 70, 88, 93–94, 157, 165, 183
Abraham, 37
abstraction, and theory, 17
Adams, John Quincy, 157
adultery, 103, 139–40, 198
Afghanistan, 9, 25, 116, 146n., 168, 182, 191
agency, 41, 99, 106, 118, 125, 168
Aladdin delusion, 186
ampliative reasoning, 74
Alcibiades, 145
alcoholism, 63
altruism, 35, 64, 149, 152
antinomianism, 23
appeasement, 1, 153, 185, 190
Arendt, Hannah, 117
Aristotle, 64; and pluralism, 20, 42; and Rawls, 148, 158–60; on community, 188; on the doable good, 103; on slavery, 118
ataraxia, 35
atheism, 11, 23, 31n., 52–53
atonement, 22
aumakuas, 142–43
automata, 159

Ayer, A. J., 40–41

Baal, 131
Babel, 33, 107
Bahais, 176
Bahya Ibn Paquda, 23
balkanize, bowdlerize, patronize, 21
Baptists, 11n., 67
Battle Hymn of the Republic, 80
Bellamy, Richard, 60
Bentham, Jeremy, 195
Bergson, Henri, 74
Bickel, Alexander, 95
bigotry, 11, 21, 41, 57, 63, 81, 172, 182
Bill of Rights, 67, 106; First Amendment, 24; Second Amendment, 70, 157
Bin Laden, Osama, 42, 113, 117, 184
biodiversity, 5, 65, 72, 83, 164
blind men and the elephant, 16
blood transfusions, 23
Borowitz, Eugene, 28, 31, 33
Brahman, 30
Branch Davidians, 74
Buddhism, 16n., 25, 27–32, 34, 39, 42–43, 78n., 89n., 103, 110, 151–52, 174; at Bamiyan, 25
Burke, Edmund, 158